PRAGUE

PRAGUE
A Guide

Lucy Abel Smith
with Jiří Kotalík

JOHN MURRAY

First published in 1991 by
John Murray (Publishers) Ltd
50 Albemarle Street, London W1X 4BD

Photoset by Rowland Phototypesetting Ltd
Bury St Edmunds, Suffolk

Printed in Great Britain by Biddles Ltd
Guildford and King's Lynn

British Library Cataloguing in Publication Data
Abel Smith, Lucy
Prague: a guide.
1. Czechoslovakia. Prague – Visitors' guides
I. Title II. Kotalik, Jiri
914.37120443

ISBN 0-7195-4779-2

DEDICATED to Helen Lowenthal for all she has done to forge friendships between the Czechs, the British and the Americans through her initiation of Central European scholarships for the Attingham Summer School and for her infectious wit, knowledge and broad vision

CONTENTS

Illustrations viii

Maps ix

Acknowledgements xii

Introduction xiii

1 The Historical Background 1
2 The Hradčany 28
3 The Malá Strana 68
4 The Staré Město and the Josefov 99
5 The Nové Město 138
6 The Prague Suburbs and Vyšehrad 169

Appendices:

The main rulers of Czechoslovakia 201
Brief biographies of major figures 203
Culture in Prague 220
Eating in Prague 221

Index 227

ILLUSTRATIONS

(*between pages 112 and 113*)

1. Charles Bridge from the Malá Strana
2. The Malá Strana from the garden of the Lubkovic Palace
3. The south transept of the Cathedral of St Vitus
4. Vladislav Hall
5. Statue of St Wenceslas
6. Diamond Monstrance in the Treasury of the Loretto Monastery
7. The Sala Terrena in the gardens of the Wallenstein Palace
8. Theological Hall of the Strahov Library, Strahov Monastery
9. Chinese Pavilion at Cibulka
10. The west towers of Our Lady before Týn
11. The façade of the Hradčany Town Hall, Loretánská
12. House sign in the Malá Strana at 'The Three Fiddles'
13. The Villa Bertranka in Smichov, Mozartova
14. Church of St Thomas, Malá Strana
15. The Nostic Theatre, Staré Mešto
16. Vyšehrad Cemetery
17. Tychon Street, 268/6, Prague 6
18. The Hanavský Pavilion from the Jubilee Exhibition, 1897
19. The main station, Wilsonovo
20. Villa Müller, Prague 6
21. Veletržní Palác (Trade Fair Palace)
22. The Church of the Sacred Heart
23. Pařížská Street
24. A Cubist street lamp

MAPS

I	Prague	x
2	Prague Castle	29
3	St Vitus' Cathedral	39
4	The Castle Area	57
5	The Malá Strana	70
6	The Staré Město and the Josefov	101
7	The Nové Město and Vyšehrad	140
8	The Prague Metro	199

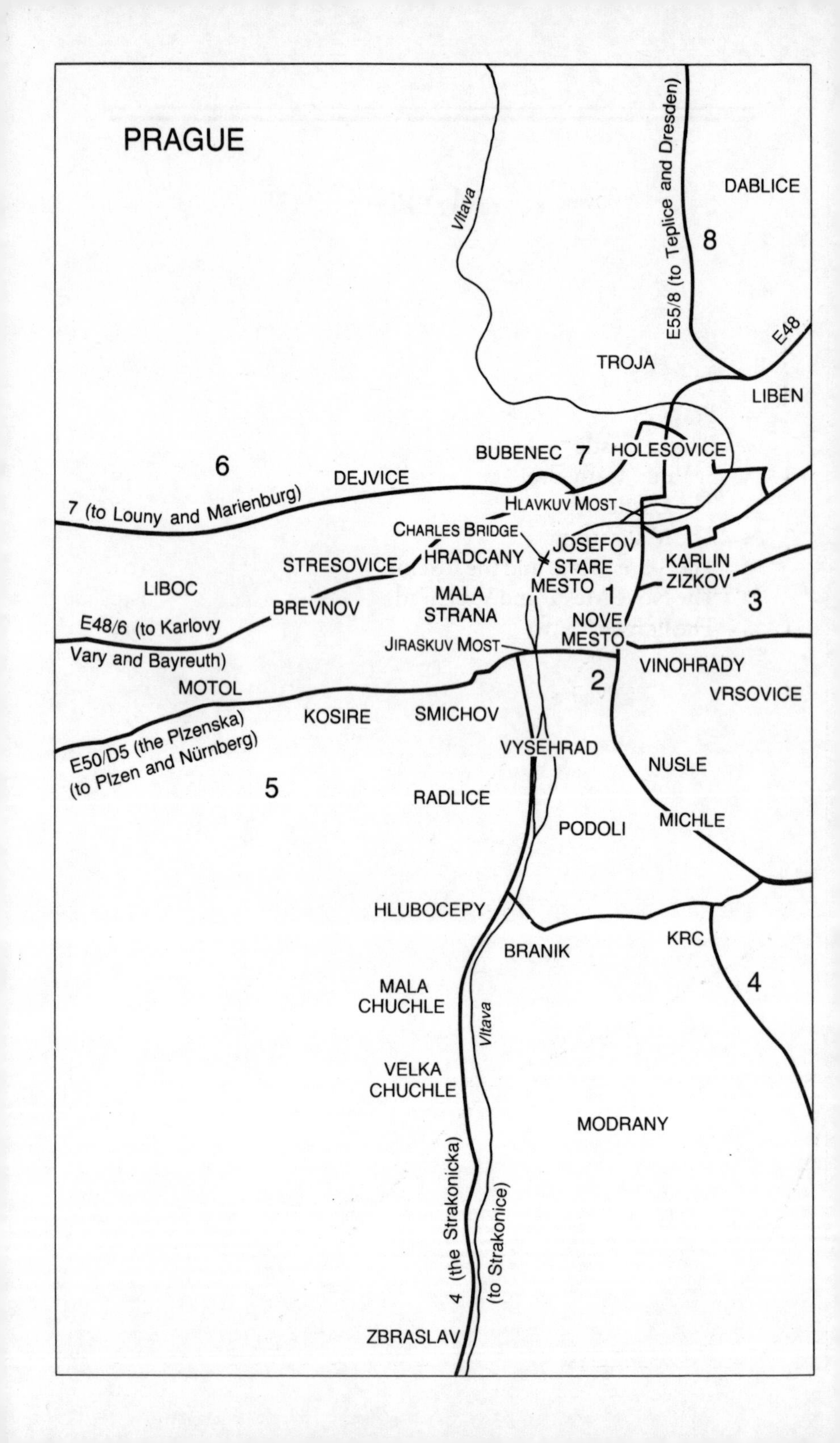

PRAGUE
Vltava
E55/8 (to Teplice and Dresden)
DABLICE
8
E48
TROJA
LIBEN
BUBENEC
7
HOLESOVICE
6
DEJVICE
7 (to Louny and Marienburg)
HLAVKUV MOST
CHARLES BRIDGE
JOSEFOV
STRESOVICE
HRADCANY
STARE
MESTO
KARLIN
ZIZKOV
LIBOC
MALA
STRANA
1
3
BREVNOV
E48/6 (to Karlovy
Vary and Bayreuth)
NOVE
MESTO
JIRASKUV MOST
VINOHRADY
2
MOTOL
VRSOVICE
KOSIRE
SMICHOV
E50/D5 (the Plzenska)
(to Plzen and Nürnberg)
VYSEHRAD
NUSLE
5
RADLICE
MICHLE
PODOLI
HLUBOCEPY
BRANIK
KRC
4
MALA
CHUCHLE
Vltava
VELKA
CHUCHLE
MODRANY
4 (the Strakonicka)
(to Strakonice)
ZBRASLAV

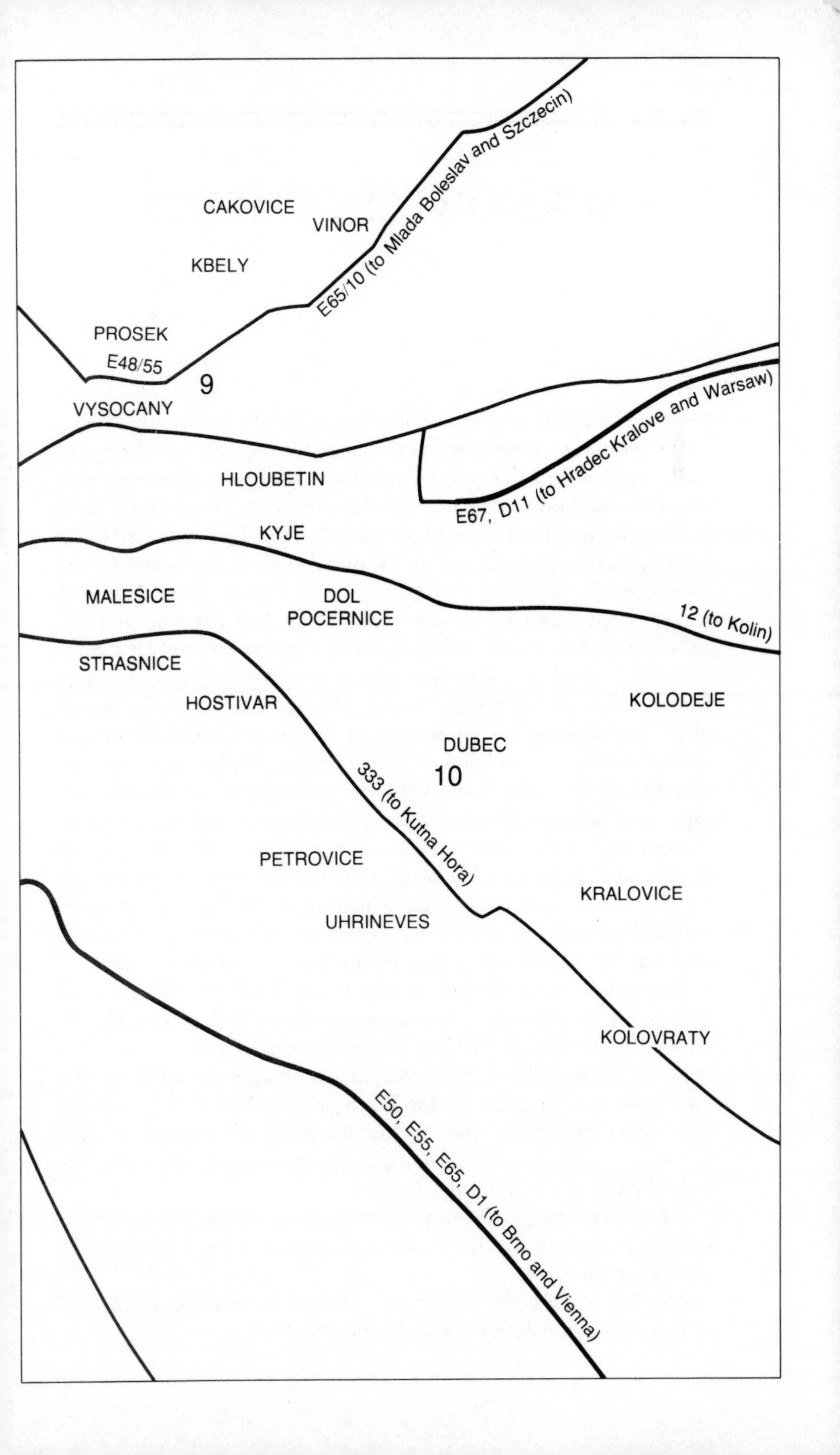
E65/10 (to Mlada Boleslav and Szczecin)
CAKOVICE
VINOR
KBELY
PROSEK
E48/55
9
VYSOCANY
HLOUBETIN
E67, D11 (to Hradec Kralove and Warsaw)
KYJE
MALESICE
DOL
POCERNICE
12 (to Kolin)
STRASNICE
HOSTIVAR
KOLODEJE
DUBEC
10
333 (to Kutna Hora)
PETROVICE
KRALOVICE
UHRINEVES
KOLOVRATY
E50, E55, E65, D1 (to Brno and Vienna)

ACKNOWLEDGEMENTS

TO WRITE any guide attempting to do justice to Prague would have been impossible without the generous help and friendship of Dr Olga Pujmanová who was unsparing with her time and knowledge and who has, from the National Gallery, facilitated the spread of art history scholarship. I am indebted to Dr Ladislav Kesner, Director of the National Gallery, for advice on the collections in St George's Gallery and to others in the National Gallery including Dr Lubomír Slavíček, Dr Eva Ziková, Dr Gabriela Šimková and staff in the education department and Dr Libuše Urešová of the Decorative Arts Museum whose husband, Emanuel Poche, wrote the matchless *Walks Through Prague*, sadly out of print. For sharing his knowledge of post-war Czechoslovakia, a special thanks to Čeněk Sovák whose courage is inspirational; I am grateful to Dr Jana Kotalíková for advice on restaurants and aspects of nineteenth-century art, her tolerance and her delicious dinners and to Dr Daniela Retková, a frequent fellow traveller in Prague and Bohemia. The weight of thanks must go to Dr Jiří Kotalík for the generosity with which he shares his wide interests and enthusiasms and for the hours he has given in the preparation of this guide. Lastly, my thanks for the patience of my husband.

The author and publishers would like to thank the following for permission to reproduce photographs: Plates 1–16: Ivan Plicka; Plates 17–24: Zdenek Helfert; Jacket: Jaroslav Kučera.

Karel Plicka (1894–1987) Arriving in Prague in 1939 on the annexation of Slovakia by the Nazis, he worked throughout the war years becoming one of the foremost photographers and historians of the city. The photographs reproduced here were first published in *Walks Through Prague*.

Zdenek Helfert (b. 1949) is a photographer for the Prague Centre for the Protection of Historical Monuments. He is a specialist in modern architecture.

Jaroslav Kučera (b. 1955) was responsible for the exhibition 'Praga – le forme della città' in Rome (1986).

INTRODUCTION

PRAGUE, capital of Czechoslovakia and perhaps the most beautiful in Europe, is more akin to London than Paris or Vienna in that it is an amalgam of small towns, five in this case, which have been untouched by the autocratic hand intent on making grand gestures. Where there is town planning, it was carried out in the Middle Ages and still holds good today, coping with 20C traffic. The castle, founded in the 9C, overlooks the five towns – the Hradčany (the castle area); the Staré Město (the Old Town); the Josefov (the Jewish Town); the Nové Město (the New Town) and the Malá Strana (the Lesser Town) – from its vantage point above the River Vltava. These were officially founded in the 13 and 14C, although there is widespread evidence that Prague was an important urban centre in the 11C. Each of these towns had its own town hall and guild system, and each retains to this day its own distinctive features and atmosphere. It is to appreciate this fully that I suggest the best way of seeing Prague is on foot, although public transport is reliable and cheap, and there are always taxis.

In this guidebook, each chapter is divided into two walks, one leading on from the next. Although it is possible to 'do' a town in one day, it might prove a marathon, especially when browsing in many of the excellent record shops, watching the Vltava flow past from Charles Bridge and finding a good *vinárna* or wine bar have equal priority. There is also one chapter devoted to the suburbs of Prague which are unlike any other capital's in the quality of their contents. In order to explore these, I would recommend the excellent *Praha* book of town maps, published by the Geodetický a kartografický podnik v Praze. Note though that many of the street names have been changed since the book's last edition.

The majority of the buildings mentioned here have two numbers for identification. Before the introduction of numbers each house was known by its house sign. Hundreds of these, mostly modelled in plaster on the façades, survive in Prague today and are of great charm. In 1784, Josef II insisted on a numbering system within each quarter, often with the town hall as No. 1. In the following year, the streets were given names. In the early days, the numbers were given on oval stone plaques. It was not long before these were changed to red plaques – the so-called *popisné* (identification) numbers. Since many houses in Prague ended up with the same numbers under this system, the *popisné* number also shows the name of the district. If you wish to look in the city archives for information on buildings in Prague, these are the numbers used. You will also find blue numbered plaques dating from 1920 – the so-called *uličné* (orientation) numbers. Every street is numbered with odd numbers on one side and even on the other, and squares are numbered in a clockwise direction. The lowest number in this group tends to be orientated on the River Vltava.

As a general rule, Czech names of places and people have been used. Wherever an English term exists (e.g. Prague, Wenceslas Square), this has been preferred.

Conservation of Ancient Monuments

The appreciation of the value of buildings in Prague was one of the effects of the 19C nationalist movement. At first, conservation in Prague was organized from Vienna under the Central Committee for the Restoration of Historical Monuments founded in 1850. In 1918 Prague had its own organization.

The first law on building conservation was passed in 1958,

and in 1971 Prague 1 and Prague 2 were designated areas of special historical interest. At the moment further laws are under discussion.

Prague, with 2,000 listed buildings, has a special problem. The vast majority of them belong to the State which has few funds for restoration.

Information on the listed buildings is available from Pražský ústav státní památkové péče, Malé náměstí 13, Prague 1. Tel: 23 68 344.

Hotels

The main tourist information is at the state travel office of Čedok at Na příkope. There are other good travel agencies including Sportturist, Rekrea, Autoturist and CKM. For private accommodation, get information from Pragotour situated at the back of the Obecní dům, U obecního dvora, near the Paris Hotel.

First-class hotels

The Intercontinental, Staré Město, nám. Curieových 5. Tel. 28 99 and 231 18 12

The Palace, Nové Město, Panská 12. Tel: 26 83 41

The Forum, Kongresová ul., Prague 4. Tel: 410 11 11

Second-class hotels which are smaller and have more local colour

The Three Ostriches, (U tří pštrosů), Malá Strana, Draž–ického nám. 12. Tel: 53 61 51

The Paris Hotel, U Obecního domu 1, Prague 1. Tel: 232 20 551

The Europa, Václavské nám. (Wenceslas Square) 25, Prague 1. Tel: 236 52 74

The Alcron, Stěpanská 40, Prague 1. Tel: 235 92 16

The Ambassador, Václavske nám. (Wenceslas Square) 5, Prague 1. Tel: 22 13 51

The Esplanade, Washingtonova 19, Prague 1. Tel: 22 25 52
The Panorama (modern and large), Milevská 7, Prague 4. Tel: 41 61 11
The Jalta, Václavské nám. (Wenceslas Square) 45, Prague 1. Tel: 26 55 41
The International, Dejvice, nám. Družby 1. Tel: 331 91 11
The Atlantik, Na poříčí 9, Prague 1. Tel: 231 85 12
The Olympik II, Karlin, U Sluncové 14, Prague 8. Tel: 83 47 41

Small hotels out of the centre
The Hvězda, Na rovni 34, Prague 6. Tel: 36 80 37 and 36 89 65
The Moravan, U Uranie 22, Prague 7. Tel: 80 29 05
The Praga, Plzeňská 29, Prague 5. Tel: 54 87 41
The Union, Jaromirova 1, Prague 2. Tel: 43 78 58

Cheap but central
Central, Rybná 8, Prague 1. Tel: 231 92 84
Hybernia, Hybernská 24, Prague 1. Tel: 22 04 31
Meteor, Hybernská 6, Prague 1. Tel: 22 92 41 and 22 42 02

Botels (floating hotels moored in the Vltava)
Admirál, Hořejší nábř., Smíchov, Prague 5. Tel: 54 74 45
Albatros, Nábř. Ludvíka Svobody, Nové Město, Prague 1. Tel: 231 36 34
Racek, Podolské nábř., Podolí, Prague 4. Tel: 72 32 41

1
THE HISTORICAL BACKGROUND

Since the end of 1989, events in eastern Europe have been fast unfolding, revealing not only a bankrupt political and economic system, but an Alladin's cave of varied peoples and culture of extraordinary wealth. That music, art and literature have held so prominent a position in people's lives in eastern and central Europe in comparison to our own in the west, may be thanks to a political system which made everyday life so drear. Culture provided a form of escape, and in some ways the only reality.

Czechoslovakia at the heart of central Europe has for long held an important place in European art and culture, making much of western Europe appear provincial. Because of its geographical and political position it was strongly influenced by developments in the west, but at the same time its intellectuals and artists have themselves made important contributions to European culture. It is remarkable that, since 1848, Czechoslovakia's important revolutions have been led by her intelligentsia.

It is to be hoped that this small guidebook will be the antidote to Chamberlain's view that it was 'terrible, fantastic, incredible . . . that we should be digging trenches and trying on gas masks here because of a quarrel in a faraway country between people of whom we know nothing . . .' There can be no one who leaves Prague without the realization that it is the home of a culture at once ancient, rich and original, and of great importance to us in the west.

That many in the west know as little of Czechoslovakia as Chamberlain did is due not to the fact that it is 'a faraway country' – Prague is west of Vienna – but perhaps to the fact that for so long it has been under the yoke of foreign powers. First under the Holy Roman Empire and the Austrian Empire of the Habsburgs, then under the German Reich, and lastly under Soviet Russia, with two brief periods of independent democracy between the World Wars and from 1945 to 1948.

Czech history is complex, one of its more confusing aspects being the country's relationship with the German peoples. At times the links were close, at times nebulous, at times oppressive. But from the 10C there had been relations with these powerful neighbours and from the 12C many Germans moved into Prague as traders.

Around 900 the Slavs in Bohemia made themselves independent of the Moravian empire, already in turmoil and to be conquered by the Magyars in 907. The reunification of Bohemia and Moravia with Slovakia would not now take place until 1918, Slovakia still being ruled by Hungary until the end of the First World War.

The unification of the Czech Slav tribes took place under the Přemyslid dukes who had already founded their impressive fortress on the headland overlooking the River Vltava in Prague by the end of the 9C. In legend, Prague Castle was the home of Princess Libuše and Prince Přemysl, founders of the Přemyslid dynasty in the 7C. But this was just a tale made up to justify a rather shaky dynasty.

In 935, as a mirror of turbulent times, Duke Wenceslas (elevated to a king in our Christmas carol) was murdered by his brother and became, as a result, the country's patron saint. He was buried in the rotunda of St Vitus (now the site of St Wenceslas' Chapel) within the castle. During periods of unrest the Přemyslids tended to turn to the German kings and Holy Roman Emperors for support and gradually, over the next 300 years, the dukes of Bohemia were raised to the principal Electorate of the Holy Roman Empire. In the middle of the 12C Duke Vladislav II (1140–97) gave aid to Emperor Frederick Barbarossa and, as a result, at the Diet of Regensburg in 1158, was granted the title of king. The Holy Roman Empire and the kingdom of Bohemia were even closer enmeshed.

In the 12C the country, comprising Bohemia and Moravia, covered about 20,000 square miles but was cut off from the west by forest and mountains. There are signs that Prague was already a prosperous, thriving city to which the large number of Romanesque remains found in Vyšehrad, the Hradčany (the castle area), much of the Old Town (Staré Město) and in the scattered monasteries and castles without its walls all bear witness.

In the 13C under Wenceslas I (1230–53) and his sister Agnes, the influence of French Gothic architecture is first felt, in the main showing the influence of the restraint of the Cistercians. Important examples still visible in Prague are the remains of the St Francis and the Salvator Chapels in the St Agnes Convent, and the Old-New Synagogue, both in the Staré Město.

At the beginning of the 14C, in 1306, the last of the Přemyslids, Wenceslas III (1305–1306), was murdered, thus throwing Bohemia into a succession crisis. The ruling Diet in Czechoslovakia was made up of three Estates comprising the nobility, the gentry and the burghers, each having equal vote in the choice of the next king. The Germans attempted to press their claim and indeed, Albert I, the German king, invaded Bohemia. He was killed the following year and Henry Count of Luxemburg was elected king of Germany. The Estates could then turn with relief not to the Germans, already felt to be too powerful and already a growing economic force in Bohemia, but to the Francophile counts of Luxemburg. Henry VII of Luxemburg was to become Holy Roman Emperor in 1312. It was his son, John, who was offered both the hand of the last of the Přemyslid princesses and the kingdom of Bohemia by the Diet in 1310. Thanks to John's expansionist policies, Bohemia and Moravia became the centre of a kingdom embracing Silesia, Brandenburg, Upper and Lower Lusatia and parts of the Duchy of Luxemburg.

Trade and the economy flourished, as did the arts. John of

Luxemburg was killed at the Battle of Crécy in 1346, fighting with his brother-in-law, the king of France, against the English. His son Václav, or Charles IV (1346–78), succeeded to the throne of Bohemia and continued his father's policies. He was elected Holy Roman Emperor in 1355 and under him, Bohemia came to the forefront of European artistic and intellectual development in the later Middle Ages.

Prague was now both capital of Bohemia and of the Empire. In its new role and backed by the vast wealth of the silver mines of Kutná Hora and Silesia, Prague was the most important intellectual and artistic capital north of the Alps. Its Golden Age had arrived. In 1348, Charles founded the university or Carolinum – the first in Central Europe – and here he encouraged intellectual pursuits in literature and theology. It was he, brought up in the French court and building on his father's initiatives, who encouraged the most beautiful flowering of late Gothic art – the International Gothic – with its mix of Italian and French influences showing itself in architecture, sculpture, painting and manuscript illumination. His patronage attracted artists from all over Europe – hence the name 'International Gothic' – but he also encouraged native Czech craftsmen. This courtly art provided an exquisite backdrop to his civilized court, which was aped by most of Europe.

Prague, during his reign, saw the development of the Nové Město or New Town, where his father's architect Matthieu d'Arras laid out a farsighted plan that would be envied by today's urban developers. Work was also started on the Charles Bridge. The E end of St Vitus' Cathedral arose under the skilful hands of Peter Parler and his workshop, its rich sculptural decoration setting a new style. The lavish decoration of Karlštejn Castle and St Wenceslas' Chapel, with their glittering hard stones and paintings by the hand of Master Theodoric was again innovative.

Charles attained some success in creating a centralized monarchy. He issued an imperial Golden Bull which regulated the position of the Czech kingdom within the Holy Roman Empire. He also ironed out the problems of succession to the

Bohemian throne by ensuring, through the Diet, that the Luxemburgs would inherit the crown. He was also successful in introducing some legal reforms which limited the power of the Czech nobility, but when he attempted, through the Maiestas Carolina, to codify customary laws usually administered by the nobility, the Diet opposed him.

Charles's son Wenceslas IV (1378–1419) was not a man of his father's stature. At the beginning of his reign he left the castle to take up residence in the Old Town. In 1394 he was taken prisoner by his cousin and some rebellious nobles and in 1400 was deposed as king of Germany by the Electors because of his inactivity. On the artistic side, the Prague workshops produced the exquisite 'soft style' in painting, while sculptural decoration became yet more elaborate.

It was during Wenceslas IV's reign that the teaching of Jan Hus (1369–1415) was starting to cause ferment against the doctrine and power of the Catholic Church, thus foreshadowing the Protestant Reformation. Hus and his followers were influenced by the teachings of John Wycliff (d.1384), whose writings and ideas became accessible through cultural links, both when Czech students arrived at Oxford University, and as result of the marriage of Richard II of England to Anne of Bohemia, daughter of Charles IV in 1382.

Hus had been building on religious ideas already current at Charles University during the reign of Charles IV, ideas such as preaching in the vernacular and encouraging a Czech translation of the Bible. He was burned at the stake as a heretic in 1415 by order of the Council of Constance, but by this time his beliefs were already widely disseminated in Bohemia, where questions of nationalism and social unrest were also coming to the fore.

From a quest for reform within the Church, the Hussite movement became a revolt against the king as he sought to quell their activities and return to the status quo. It then developed into a revolution, plunging Bohemia into a civil war from 1419 until the extreme wing of the Hussites, the Táborites, were defeated in 1434. The trigger for the revolt, the so-called First Defenestration of Prague, took place from a window in the New Town Hall of Prague. The New Town was a stronghold of the Hussites, but Wenceslas had nominated anti-Hussite burghers to run the town. It was thirteen of these unfortunates who were thrown out of the windows by an angry Hussite mob demanding the release from prison of those accused of heresy.

During this period the visual arts suffered, especially in Prague, although the Hussites produced much fine theological literature. After the death of Wenceslas IV, his brother Sigismund of Luxemburg (1419–37) had himself crowned king. It was hoped that he would reconcile the Hussites to the Church, but he failed and managed to alienate the Czechs who rose in revolt and banished him from Prague. He returned to the throne at the end of the war and reigned for only a few months, before his death in 1437. His son-in-law and successor, Albrecht Duke of Austria, did not last long either and between 1439 and 1452 the Bohemian throne lay empty, although claimed by Albrecht's son, Ladislav Posthumus.

In fact, his guardian, George Poděbrady, was elected regent from 1452 and became king in 1458 after Ladislav's death. He was a man of broad vision and tried unsuccessfully to mediate between the Catholics and the reformers. He himself was a supporter of the moderate wing of the Hussites, the Utraquists. They believed in the layman's right to take both the bread and the wine at communion (*utraque*, each) an idea that was anathema to Catholics. This became one of the fundamental sticking points of any agreement between the two sides. George Poděbrady was renounced and attacked by Emperor Frederick III and deposed by the Pope, who meanwhile had been encouraging George's son-in-law, Matthias Corvinus, king of Hungary, to grab the throne. George died in 1471 and the succession was once more an open question.

The Diet then chose the Catholic Ladislav (Vladislav) Jagiello, son of Casimir IV of Poland, to succeed in the hope that by their choice of a foreigner they could heal their war-torn kingdom. Corvinus continued to press his claims to the Bohemian throne, but on his death Vladislav was elected to the throne of Hungary as well and thereafter took less interest in Bohemia.

Now the Estates were in control, with the upper nobility taking the lion's share at the expense of the other Estates. Bohemia had become an aristocratic oligarchy where the nobility ruled the countryside and curbed the privileges of the towns and the gentry.

During Vladislav's reign there was a further burst of activity in the arts. Vladislav decided to quit the Old Town and restore the throne to its former glory in the castle. A move no doubt meant to impress the Diet. Glimpses of the Italian Renaissance are now seen in the arts although as yet only in detailing copied from pattern books. The decoration of the window surrounds of the castle in 1493 are an example, attributed to craftsmen from Hungary and to Benedikt Ried. However, Ried and his contemporaries, Matěj Rejsek and Hans Spiess were rather more at home and certainly more inventive when creating their extraordinarily wonderful vaulting systems and vigorous naturalistic carvings, both unique to Bohemia. The prime examples of these in Prague can be seen in Vladislav Hall (1493–1502), a glory no doubt created to impress the Estates and still one of the most impressive interiors in central Europe.

In 1494 the Habsburgs persuaded Vladislav to agree, if he did not have children, to a Habsburg succession. Vladislav subsequently produced a son and a daughter, so the noose had to be tightened by Emperor Maximilian I by the proposal of a double marriage in 1506 of his grand-daughter Mary (sister of the future Charles V) to Vladislav's son Ludvík, and his grandson Ferdinand (who succeeded Charles V as Emperor), to Vladislav's daughter, Anne. Vladislav died in 1516 and was succeeded by his son Ludvík II who, in turn, died from wounds received fighting the Turks at the Battle of Móhacs in 1526.

The Habsburg Ferdinand now claimed the Bohemian throne through his wife, Anne. The Estates elected him king but insisted that Ferdinand should respect their traditional liberties, including the right of freedom of worship for all. The majority of the Czech people were Utraquist but other, more extreme forms of Protestantism were now widespread. Lutheranism, for example, was popular in the German-speaking areas, while the Anabaptists had a strong following in Moravia, and Calvinism was also rapidly being disseminated. These differences in the Protestant ranks were of great advantage to the Catholic party and Ferdinand was able to exploit them, leaving the Catholics with somewhat more power than the Protestants.

Ferdinand decided not to interfere with the nobility but instead to concentrate on curbing the power of the Third Estate, the burghers. Flooding it with his own nominees gave him a lever to ensure that the Estates would formally recognize his hereditary rights over Bohemia and acknowledge his son, Maximilian, as heir to the throne of Bohemia. From now on the Czech Diet ceased to elect kings and, with the exception of the initial years of the Thirty Years' War, instead accepted what they were given, with the result that the Habsburgs ruled Bohemia uninterrupted until 1918.

In the 1530s, the classical forms of the Italian Renaissance were found increasingly in Bohemia. They were used with a greater understanding of their function and no longer merely as a two-dimensional pattern. In fact, this flourishing of Renaissance style was taking place all over northern Europe. The gardens of the Hradčany (where tulips were grown for the first time in Europe) were an early venture in this new style. Prague's most beautiful example of the influence of the Italian Renaissance is the exquisite Belvedere in the castle gardens, whose elegant classical arcade of 1538–44 owes more to Brunelleschi's architecture of 14C Florence than to any building of the Italian High Renaissance of contemporary Rome.

The influence of Italy brought innovation not only in form but also in function. A new type of building was now introduced in Prague thanks to the brilliant patronage of one man, the governor, Ferdinand of Tyrol. He created a *maison de plaisaunce* just outside the capital. Its unusual star shape gave it the name Hvězda. Its interior is decorated in the crispest stucco with classical motifs. Such new forms must have been quite startling to a medieval town like Prague and in effect presented a new way of living.

Ferdinand I's son, Maximilian II (1564–76) attempted a religious balancing act by trying to persuade the Pope to recognize communion in both kinds to please the Utraquists while, at the same time, encouraging the Jesuits to come to Prague and spread their gospel. He also expelled the weaker sects such as the Anabaptists (the Bohemian Brethren). The nobles presented Maximilian with the 'Bohemian Confession', a religious compromise which would allow the peaceful co-existence of Catholics and Protestants. Maximilian gave it his verbal approval, but would not make it legally binding. He is said to have died a Protestant.

At his death in 1576, about two-thirds of the population were Protestant. He was succeeded by Rudolf II (1576–1611), one of the last of the conciliators. Rudolf needed the support of the Bohemian Estates against rebellion by his brother Matthias to whom he was forced to cede large tracts of territory in 1608. To this end, in 1609, Rudolf was forced to issue the Letter of Majesty, a decree granting freedom of conscience to all his Bohemian subjects and guaranteeing a body known as the Defensors to safeguard it.

Although a weak king and emperor, he was one of the greatest art patrons in Europe. Once more Prague became the centre of art and culture as Rudolf chose Prague rather than Vienna as capital of the Holy Roman Empire. The proximity of the Empire's old enemy the Turks to Vienna was no doubt an element in this choice.

In comparison to the other arts, little building was carried out during this period and much has been destroyed, although within the castle, Rudolf's art gallery and the adjoining rooms must have been magnificent. These now make up the Spanish Hall. Rudolf encouraged not only the decorative arts, but also painting, philosophy, music, astrology and, in common with many of his contemporaries, the study of the occult. A number of Italian and northern Mannerist artists made their way to Prague, many of their families remaining for some generations. One such family, the Miseroni, was to provide the foundations for Bohemia's now-celebrated glass industry. An element of Rudolf's patronage of the arts must have been a desire to emulate the Golden Age of Charles IV.

Rudolf did not succeed in holding out against his brother Matthias and in 1611 he was forced to abdicate the throne of Bohemia. He died in ignominy in 1612 when Matthias became Holy Roman Emperor.

The Emperor Matthias (1612–19) was childless and the Austrian Habsburgs had agreed that Ferdinand of Styria should succeed to the Empire on his death. This did not go down well with the Estates as they rightly suspected that Ferdinand was totally unsympathetic to Protestantism. But the Protestants could not agree on an alternative successor and put forward as candidates both the Elector of Saxony and the Elector of the Palatine. A compromise was reached in 1617 when Ferdinand of Styria was accepted as king of Bohemia on condition that he agree to the Letter of Majesty.

This marked the end of a rare moment of religious freedom and indeed the power of the Estates. As in so many cases of serious long-term disagreements, a relatively minor event was now to cause full-scale war. There was a tussle over the building of two Protestant churches on royal land which Ferdinand claimed belonged to the Roman Catholic Church. Count Thurn, a prominent German Protestant, declared that the Letter of Majesty was being infringed and, with a group of angry Protestants in May 1618, marched to Hradčany where two of Ferdinand's Catholic deputies and their secretary were thrown out of a window on to a dung heap. This was the second and famous Defenestration of Prague which led to the Thirty Years' War.

The Bohemians proclaimed their loyalty to Ferdinand and blamed the Jesuits for having misled him. They then called on the Estates in other Habsburg lands to help defend religious and political freedom. Alas, they did not speak with one voice, as class and religious factions fought each other. The Emperor Matthias died suddenly in March 1619 and there was a rush for the throne of Bohemia. Ferdinand succeeded as king but the Protestants, led by Count Thurn, fought his succession. With the Machiavellian powers of Christian of Anhalt behind him, the Protestant Frederick, Elector Palatine, was propelled in the direction of the Bohemian throne. He had married Elizabeth Stuart (sister of the future Charles I of England and later famed as the Winter Queen). The general Diet of all the crown lands of Bohemia pledged their assistance, deposed Ferdinand and elected Frederick to the throne, in the hope that England would send military aid.

Meanwhile the seven Electors of the Holy Roman Empire, of whom three were bishops, declared for Catholic Ferdinand and the Catholic League led by Count von Tilly, 'the monk in armour', was mounted against Frederick. Poor Frederick therefore, had already been deposed by the Electors when, in October 1619, he and Elizabeth arrived in Prague and set out on a round of parties.

Frederick's soldiers proved ill-equipped, unpaid, and ill-led by Christian of Anhalt and Count Thurn who quarrelled amongst themselves. In November 1620, the Imperial army and Frederick's Czech army met on a hill on the outskirts of Prague in what became known as the Battle of the White Mountain. It was more of a rout than a battle and Frederick barely had time to leave Prague. The outcome was a disaster for the Protestant cause and for an independent Bohemia. In June 1621, the victorious Ferdinand had 27 of the Protestant leaders executed and gave about half the land of Bohemia belonging to Czech noblemen to his German Imperial supporters. In the same year all Protestant churchmen were exiled and in 1627, Ferdinand gave his subjects the choice between Catholicism or exile. The elective monarchy was ended and Bohemia and Moravia were declared hereditary lands of the Habsburgs. Serfdom was extended and the Estates continued in name only.

During the Thirty Years' War Prague, in the main, festered

in apathy. The Church and Habsburg supporters did begin to build churches, monasteries and palaces in a tentative Baroque, the finest early example of which must be the Valdštejn (Wallenstein) Palace. Here the Baroque still retains some of the earlier Mannerist elements. The garden too, is a magnificent survival in spite of the removal by the invading Swedes in 1648 of the Vredeman de Vries bronzes which now festoon the Castle of Drottningholm. But the Baroque building boom really began after peace was declared in 1648 at the end of the Thirty Years' War.

Foreign architects and craftsmen, in the main Italians, monopolized the building industry until the end of the century when Germans, Austrians and native Czechs took over. It was the Italians who made the greatest impact, introducing first the severe designs of early Roman Baroque and later the exuberant late Baroque of Bernini, Borromini and Guarini. The vigorous sculptural form of this architecture made a significant impact in Prague's medieval streets.

Gardens too, in 17C France, Holland and Italy were becoming increasingly important as an extension of architecture. This trend was copied in Prague and examples may be seen in the gardens of the Malá Strana.

But if foreign influence was strong, so was the originality of these designs planted on Bohemian soil. By the end of the century an array of great palaces and churches was being built in the city, many decorated with fine limestone stucco, plaster and scagliola as a substitute for decorations in marble which was scarce in Bohemia.

However one 18C English traveller, Lady Mary Wortley Montague was blind to all this. Writing in November 1716, she is worse than dismissive about the Bohemian countryside and its villages, and then continues on the subject of Prague: 'This town was once the royal seat of the Bohemian kings and is still the capital of the Kingdom. There are some remains of its former splendour, being one of the largest towns in Germany but, for the most part, old built and thinly inhabited, which makes the houses very cheap, and those people of quality, who cannot easily bear the expense of Vienna, choose to reside here where they have assemblies, music and all other diversions (those of a court excepted), at very moderate rates.' She finishes this belittling description by decrying the provincialism of the women's dress.

At about this time Kryštof Dientzenhofer, who originated from Bavaria, was hard at work on some of the most important Baroque buildings in Prague, including St Nicholas' Church in the Malá Strana, the Loretto Monastery, St Catherine's and the great Břevnov Monastery. His son Kilián Ignác began his first independent commission in 1717 by building the Villa Amerika or Michna Summer House. The young Dientzenhofer created his great Baroque buildings by gathering round him important sculptors, painters, cabinet-makers and metal-workers to create works of art to his designs, thus giving art and architecture in Prague by the mid-18c an extraordinary unity. This was yet another Golden Age when Prague saw the work of sculptors of the quality of M. B. Braun and F. M. Brokof, and painters like Karel Škréta and Petr Brandl.

Between the end of the Thirty Years' War in 1648 and the accession to the throne of Maria Theresa in 1740, Bohemia was firmly part of the Habsburg Empire. The literate classes were taught and spoke only German and every aspect of life from literature to the civil service was germanized. The king and emperor was an absentee based in Vienna and Charles VI (1711–40) relied solely on Austrian advisors.

Maria Theresa, his daughter, succeeded to the throne of Bohemia and Hungary in October 1740, but by December the Duke of Bavaria claimed the Habsburg inheritance and Frederick II of Prussia had seized Silesia. The Habsburg monarchy was already looking insecure. In 1741 Prague was invaded by a joint French and Bavarian army which caused some damage. Prussia laid siege to the city in 1744 and Silesia was officially lost to the Bohemian kingdom in 1745. When peace came in 1748, Maria Theresa instigated wide-ranging reforms and centralized the government, introducing for the first time a tax of 'God-pleasing equality'. Realizing that wealth would only come to Bohemia with the growth of industry and exports, she turned her attention to the education of the future workforce, the improvement of the lot of the peasantry, and the reform of the Church.

Her organizational ability was mirrored by the tidy neo-Classical façade which the Viennese architect Pacassi now applied to the castle. The one piece of blind intolerance she showed was in her expulsion of the Jews from Prague in 1748. However, many Jewish families were important in trade and industry, so their expulsion was actually detrimental to her industry and trade policies. The Jews were expelled on the pretext of being in league with the Prussians, an understandable fear in view of the fact that, in 1757, the Prussians invaded Bohemia again. The Battle of Prague followed, with the Prussians leaving some cannonballs well embedded in various buildings.

Josef, Maria Theresa's son, became her co-regent in 1765 and emperor from 1780. After a journey he made in 1771 through famine-stricken Bohemia, he realized more had to be done. He continued with his mother's reforming zeal but went farther, abolishing serfdom and bringing in a Patent of Toleration which included religious toleration for the Jews. Most notorious of all, he carried out the Dissolution of the Monasteries, at least the dissolution of those deemed not to be doing a useful job. In Bohemia, the clergy owned one-seventh of the land as well as huge endowments which many felt was wealth not being used to best advantage. The Jesuits had already been suppressed by Pope Clement XIV in 1773 and, as they had had three foundations in Prague, the effect of further dissolution must have changed the face of the city.

By the time Josef II died in 1790, Prague was still largely a medieval and Baroque city. The economic situation during the second half of the 18C did not allow much scope for growth in the arts. The Empire's finances were in a poor way and were not helped by further war with France. The Church, once a major patron, had of course ceased to play this part. New building in Prague in the neo-Classical style was, apart from the work of Pacassi, relatively rare.

Theatre in Prague was one art form which did flourish during the 18c. The theatre has a long history in Bohemia. In the late medieval period, plays in the Czech language had been performed. Then, under the Jesuits in the second half of the 16c, the theatre bloomed again as they spread their message by using theatre in the vernacular. In the first half of the 18c there was a theatre devoted to Italian opera and German plays under the patronage of Count Franz Sporck who, in 1701, set up his theatre in Hybernská. From the 1730s there was a regular Italian season of opera in Prague. It was only at the end of the century that German operas replaced the Italian. In 1783 the German National Theatre, later the Estates Theatre, opened under Count Francis Nostic. Here, in 1787, Mozart gave the première of his *Don Giovanni* and he followed this in 1791 with the first performance of *La Clemenza di Tito* for the coronation of Josef's brother Leopold II.

Prague was also a centre for orchestral and sacred music. One of the first native composers was Father Bohuslav Černohorský (1684–1742) and Franz (1709–86) and Georg (1722–71) Benda were the earliest Czech orchestral composers. Franz Xavier Brixi (1732–71) composed church music and became a celebrated choirmaster of St Vitus', and the Churches of St James and St Francis of the Cross retained a strong tradition of church choral music. The former still continues today. Under Josef II, state funding was not very forthcoming and, with the closing of the monasteries, there came a certain air of puritanism and austerity. Aristocratic patronage ceased, but in 1803 a symphony orchestra was founded in Prague and a conservatory was established in 1811.

It is interesting and typical of Bohemia that the arts and language should play a vital part in the development of the country and of Prague from this period until 1918. Independence from the Habsburg Empire achieved by force of arms would have been fruitless, as the events of 1848 were to prove later. The seeds of nationalism lay in the rebirth of the Czech language – a language well-nigh dead by this date and only used by the peasantry.

Czech was revived by academics writing dictionaries or translating classic literature from abroad. Among the initiators in the revival was Josef Dobrovský (1753–1829), an ex-Jesuit priest who realized that his Latin training in the seminary and the monopoly held by the German language in the Empire meant that he did not know his native tongue. He set about learning it using an old Slavic grammar written in Latin. Though he wrote his pioneering history of the Bohemian language in German, interest was nevertheless stimulated. Josef Jungmann (1773–1847) carried the work farther by translating Milton, Pope and Goethe amongst others into Czech, and by compiling a Czech dictionary. Thanks to his efforts the authorities permitted the teaching of Czech in secondary schools, although the language of instruction was German.

Alongside the revival of the Czech language went the revival of Czech culture. Contemporaries of Dobrovský and Jungmann began to collect folk-songs and historical documents, and a whole series of patriotic societies was instituted. Among the most important was the Society for the Study of Bohemian Culture which was founded under the patronage of a group of Czech noblemen, including Prince Karl Egon von Fürstenburg, Count Ernst Wallenstein, Count F. J. Kinský and Count Sternberg. There followed in 1779, the Society of the Patriotic Friends of the Arts which laid the foundations for the National Gallery, and in 1781 the Society for Bohemian Industry appeared. From these seeds, nationalism arose.

In 1848 the International Slav Congress convened in Prague under the Czech historian, František Palacký (1798–1876), to put forward the idea of the union of all the Bohemian lands under a representative constitution. The idea floundered. The June Uprising of 1848 followed when, as in so much of Europe, barricades went up in the streets of Prague against the agents of the Empire. The barricades were manned by students from Charles University and the Polytechnique, and by workers. The battle lasted for six disastrous days and was orchestrated from the students' base in the Clementinum. The movement was brutally put down by Prince Windischgrätz whose cannon, apart from destroying lives, also damaged much of the sculpture on Charles Bridge.

Heavy as the cost was, the uprising put students at the forefront of political consciousness in the city and marked the beginning of the rise of the working class. In December, Emperor Ferdinand abdicated and his nephew Franz Josef, aged 18, refusing any new constitution, succeeded to the throne. A further conspiracy in Prague to set up a Slavic commonwealth was planned but betrayed, and the city was in a state of siege until 1853. The rise of nationalism now turned from being a culturally based movement to a political one, though the forces of reaction were to prevail until 1918.

If neither democracy nor independence were to be realized yet, Czechoslovakia was becoming increasingly important industrially. The abolition of serfdom had meant that workers were released from the land to the factories and many of the early entrepreneurs were the landed aristocracy. In 1845, thanks to the energies of Count Chotek, the railway came to Prague and Prague's suburbs expanded with workers' housing estates and factories. A harbour was built too on the Vltava, connecting the capital with Europe. The developments in Prague were far from unique and were mirrored in Bohemia and Moravia. By 1914, Czechoslovakia was producing 70 per cent of the entire industrial output of the Austro-Hungarian Empire.

Much of this wealth was behind the series of national institutions, academic bodies and museums which, towards the end of the 19C burgeoned throughout Prague. One patriotic individual was the industrialist V. Lanna who financed the establishment of the Decorative Arts Museum to encourage improved industrial design. But until the last decades of the century, opportunities for training in the arts were limited. The Academy of Fine Arts founded in 1799, taught only painting, while the guild system maintained its control over other branches of the arts. The Prague Polytechnique, founded in 1717 and brought up to date in 1806 under Kristian Josef Willenberg, an industrialist and engineer, had a department of architecture under Professor J. Fischer, the General Director of Building for Bohemia and Moravia. A School for the Applied Arts was set up in 1885 but it was nothing more than a grammar school for craftsmen. The Academy started to teach architecture, but sculpture was still omitted from the curriculum. The work of sculptors such as Josef and Emanuel Max in the middle years of the 19C appears rather lifeless and two-dimensional, something which may be explained by the fact that they had been trained as painters.

As a consequence of the lack of opportunities in the arts, many artists went to Vienna. One such was the architect Josef Hlávka who, in 1859, became head of the Prague Polytechnique. Lured away from Prague he ended up winning the architectural commission to design the Ring in Vienna. Having made a vast fortune there, he returned to Prague and founded the Academy of Sciences, encouraged colleges for musicians and gave financial support to the National Museum, all between the years 1880 and 1907.

The architecture of Prague in the latter part of the 19C followed patterns laid down in other capitals in its use of a wide range of Revivalist styles based on historic example as, increasingly, students were sent to the Decorative Arts Museum for study. Many of these buildings would have been at home in Vienna, and in a period when so much new thought was coming out of those very institutions believed to be so vital for the future Czech state, the buildings themselves were far from innovative in the architectural sense, with the detailing alone betraying their Bohemian origin.

Not all the new building programmes in Prague in the 1880s were desirable. In this period the Josefov or Jewish Town was largely demolished and the area around St Agnes Convent was only saved thanks to the efforts of a group of intellectuals, the Friends of Old Prague.

Gradually, in the closing years of the century, Czech art in many forms became more innovative. The Academy of Fine Arts became the State Academy in 1896 and now included a department of sculpture, and in 1910 a School of Graphic Design was set up in Prague. The architect Jan Kotěra (1871–1923), pupil of Otto Wagner in Vienna, became head of the School of Applied Art in 1888. In 1910 he founded a studio of architecture in the Academy of Fine Arts and in 1911 invited one of the most outstanding architects in central Europe, the Yugoslav Jože Plečnik (1872–1957), to take up the chair of architecture at the School of Decorative Arts. The International Exhibition – the Žemská Jubilejnt Mstava – of 1891 became the showcase of the new art in Prague.

In the second half of the 19C painting flourished, reaching its apogee in the work done for the National Theatre, built by subscription in the 1880s. This became a veritable gallery for young artists such as M. Aleš and V. Hynais.

Earlier the bland sculptures of the Max brothers had replaced some of those damaged on the Charles Bridge in 1848, but it was not until the last twenty years of the 19C that a wave of new sculpture, with the work of J. V. Myslbek at its head, presaged the arrival of Art Nouveau. An exhibition of the works of Rodin in Prague in 1902, including *The Kiss* and *Balzac*, had a great influence on an entire generation of Czech sculptors.

The other showpiece of contemporary art in Prague and vessel of nationalism, was the new nave of St Vitus' Cathedral, begun in the 1340s as the dynastic church of the Luxemburgs and completed from the 1860s under J. Kranner and J. Mocker, the Czech Viollet-le-Duc. The last of the stone reliefs on the w façade were only put in place in 1952. The cathedral displays not only the continuation of a great tradition of craftsmanship in the Gothic style, but includes many examples of Art Nouveau in the contributions made by Alfons Mucha (1860–1939) and František Bílek (1872–1941) among others.

Music flourished around this time too, and the second half of the 19C was the great age of Czech Romantic music. Smetana (1824–84) and Dvořák (1841–1904) were the leading figures in this movement. Even today, the great Prague Music Festival begins with a procession from Smetana's grave at Vyšehrad and opens with his magnificent *Ma Vlast* (My Country), composed in the late 1870s, performed in the Smetana Hall.

So it was that much was achieved in the second half of the 19C in spite of the fact that, since the creation in 1867 of the Austro-Hungarian Empire, the Habsburgs had concentrated all their energies on Hungary, forcing Czechoslovakia to take a back seat.

From the last decade of the 19C, there was a vast pool of young architectural talent waiting to be commissioned by an equally vast array of private clients who ranged from the lower-middle class to the aristocracy. The results of this first period of Czech Modernism create much of the architectural interest of the Prague suburbs as found in the garden suburbs, the Baba estate or the Ministry of Science in Prague 2.

From the beginning of the 20C, the State too became an important patron. New schools were built and civic centres, industrial offices, banks and insurance houses sprang up all over Prague. The main station in Prague and the Representatives' House (Obecní dům) must now rank amongst the finest examples remaining of a robust Art Nouveau style which was the first in the new art movements to break with historicism. The decorative arts were once more important in Prague architecture and it is interesting to note that even under the recent Communist regime, 5 per cent of the budget of any new building had to be spent on decoration.

In the years leading up to the First World War, Prague produced some of the most exciting and original buildings under the influence of the Tvrdošíjní or Graphic Artists' Group (1911–14), which included architects and designers like Gočár (1880–1945), Novotný (1880–1959), Hofman (1884–1964), and Chochol (1880–1956). They formulated a mix of Primitivism, in their use of simple materials and shapes that harked back to 14 and 15C Bohemian vaulting, to which they added Cubism, echoing the work of the Cubist painters E. Filla and J.

Čapek (1887–1945) and the sculpture of O. Gutfreund (1889–1929). This outstanding architecture is unique to Prague. When the group was first formed, it was greatly influenced by the work of Jože Plečnik. Plečnik used much imagination in his range of materials and in his ability to distil significant historical forms and reuse them with impact in 20C Prague, as is seen in the work he did for Masaryk in the castle in the 1920s.

The assassination of Archduke Franz Ferdinand, heir to the throne of the Austro-Hungarian Empire, in Sarajevo in 1914, was catalytic to the start of the First World War. At its end, the Austro-Hungarian Empire was dismantled. In October 1918, Bohemia and Moravia were free to go their own way and joined with Slovakia, previously part of Hungary. In 1919 Ruthenia (later annexed by Russia) was added. The Treaty of Versailles coming into force in 1920 recognized the new boundaries, and the democratic republic of Czechoslovakia was born.

Pre-war Czech culture had already veered towards the west, but Pan-Slavic interests now made it look north to the Russian empire. Between the wars, Czechoslovakia walked the tightrope between the rising German nation (Czechoslovakia was still home to many Germans not only in Sudetenland but in her cities) and the Soviet Union, but yet kept her independence until 1939.

The philosopher and humanist, Tomáš Garrigue Masaryk (1850–1937) was the first president of the Czech nation. He had spent the war years in exile in the United States and with the help of President Wilson had conceived the idea of a Czech and Slovak democratic state. He became, as his ideas still are, an important moral force in the country. Karel Kramář was the first prime minister, with Eduard Beneš in the Foreign Office.

This new country found itself once more at the centre of the various streams of European art. Two giants of early 20C Czechoslovakia, the writer Franz Kafka and the composer Leoš Janáček died in 1924 and 1928 respectively. However both men were little recognized in their own country, Kafka's *Trial* and *The Castle* being published after his death, and

Janaček only achieving celebration near the end of his life when the première of his first opera *Jenůfa* was given in 1904. The next generation of artists and writers were looking for new ways to express the novelty of their situation. As a result they largely eschewed the work of the pre-war years, although some members of the old Graphic Artists' Group joined the newly formed Devětsil Group (1920–31) which became the ideological centre of Czech avant-garde.

The most progressive writers, painters, architects, photographers, composers, theatre managers, critics, and journalists in the country were attracted to the group. They looked for inspiration to the plethora of similar avant-garde movements throughout Europe in the 1920s, such as Dada, Surrealism, late Cubism, Constructivism, Poetism, Bauhaus, and Futurism. The main spokesman for the group was Karel Teige (1900–51) who led the group progressively towards the Soviet Communist artistic model with its disregard for the aesthetic values of art in favour of art as ideology. In his writings Teige articulated and developed his concept of *ars una* – a total art form embracing every aspect of life. When the Communists took power in 1948, in spite of its sympathetic leanings, the new regime took no interest in the past members of Devětsil and indeed its protagonists became the first victims of the purges. As a result, much of what they produced has been lost, although it is certain that, as interest grows, more of their work will come to light in private collections.

The theories of Devětsil are best seen in the Constructivist architecture which is found all over Prague, but especially in the Nové Město and the state housing of the 1920s and 1930s. The Devětsil architects, including Chochol, Krejčar, Frágner, Honzík, Linhart and Obrtel, attempted to abandon all decorative details while using new technology, materials, and building techniques – form was to follow function. Teige went to such extremes in his belief that architecture was purely economics, technique and sociology, that even Le Corbusier protested that aesthetic theory had to be respected.

The most celebrated painters of the Devětsil group were

Jundrich Štyrský, Josef Šíma and Toyen who could hardly follow the theories of Teige for, if these were taken to their ultimate conclusion, such a non-functional art as painting would cease to exist. These three artists in the 1930s formed the nucleus in Prague of an important group of Surrealists. Other members of the group were the elusive composer Mirslav Ponc, and the photographer Funcke who was much influenced by the American, Man Ray. The Devětsil synthesis of Constructivism and Poetism may also be found in the work of the Liberated Theatre, established in Prague in 1926. This combined the influences of circus, music-hall, and cabaret with the Theatre of the Absurd, all played against stage-settings which were functional and anti-illusionary.

Surrealism followed the break-up of Devětsil. Prague formed close links with Paris and became the third most important centre for Surrealism in Europe. In 1932 there was an international exhibition held in Prague where several foreign artists including Arp, Dalí, Ernst, Giacometti, Miró, and Tanguy exhibited alongside the Czechs, Filla, Hoffmeister, Janousek, Makovsky, Šíma, Štyrský, Toyen, and others. Linked as the Czech Surrealists were to the Communist Party, the group was dissolved in 1942 during the Nazi occupation of Czechoslovakia.

On the eve of Munich, in September 1938, Czechoslovakia appeared to have full guarantees from the European powers of its national integrity. But within six months the Nazis had dismembered the Czech state after invading in October 1938 on the pretext of liberating the Sudeten Germans. By the following March, Prague had capitulated, having been betrayed by her allies France and Britain: both these nations, in spite of pleas for help, were unable and unwilling to come to her aid. In the first months of occupation, Prague became the centre for anti-Nazi demonstrations. Public figures were taken hostage and the universities were closed, many students being shot or sent to concentration camps. Obergruppenführer Reinhard Heydrich was appointed Reich Protector and instituted a reign of terror. All over Prague bronze hands held up in blessing mounted on plaques commemorate the places where Czechs fell during the occupation. The lists of Jews killed in concentration camps makes numbing reading.

In October 1941 a special commando of parachutists, both Czechs and Slovaks from the Czechoslovak Army in Great Britain, was parachuted into Czechoslovakia and, after some months in hiding, in May the following year they assassinated Heydrich. A state of emergency ensued with many arrests and executions, and to avenge Heydrich's assassination the mining village of Lidice was razed to the ground and most of its occupants killed or sent to camps. The villagers had had nothing to do with the assassination. Seven of the parachutists hiding in the Orthodox Church of St Charles Borromeo in the Nové Město were betrayed. They died there fighting and the scars of battle still remain around the windows of the crypt.

Meanwhile President Beneš had set up the Czech government in exile in London, and while such destruction was continuing under the Nazi occupation, London was proving a valuable source of information and resistance. Anti-Nazi support also came from the Communists in their headquarters in Moscow under the leadership of Klement Gottwald. The Czech Communist Party, although always a small minority, had been growing since the 1920s and was given strong support from Moscow. Although discouraged by the Western Allies, Beneš went to Moscow in 1943 to sign a pact of friendship with Moscow, something that was later to prove difficult to shake off.

As the German army retreated, in April 1944 the Soviet army reached the Czech border and annexed sub-Carpathian Ruthenia. Prague was declared an open city and excitement rose as the American and Russian troops moved near. (It was not until recently that the authorities were prepared to admit that the Americans had reached the outskirts of Prague and were forced to turn back on Russian orders to their high command.) The Prague Uprising began on 5 May and lasted for three days against a heavily armed and desperate German army. The day was saved by General Vlasov – a man of

Russian origin but fighting for the Germans – changing sides and helping the Czechs, and the Prague garrison capitulated.

From 1945 the expulsion of the Germans living in Czechoslovak Sudetenland began, although many by this time had already left of their own accord. Prague, before the war, had a German population of 50,616. By 1946 their numbers had decreased to under 5,000. It was not until 1953 that citizenship was granted to persons of German nationality again. The Czechs' first democratically elected president since 1948, President Havel, has apologized to the German nation for these expulsions.

After the war the State renewed its democratic and parliamentary traditions, with Slovakia, Bohemia and Moravia each having their own parliament with a federal parliament above both. But already in these post-war years Russia was becoming a powerful ally, and the Czech Communist Party held a strong position in the new parliament with 40 per cent of the vote. This was a state of affairs encouraged both by disgust for the west since Munich, and in line with the leftist swing in Europe after the years of war. Soon the Communists began preparing their power base by building up armed militias to guard factories and installations. Surreptitiously, Communist army officers were put in positions of power in the War Ministry and in February 1948, Communist border guards marched into Prague and, with the assistance of the militia, occupied vital posts. Under the threat of civil war, President Beneš dissolved parliament and the Communists took power under the leadership of Klement Gottwald.

Forming a coalition with the National Front and the National Socialists, they held 87 per cent of the vote. Arrests of anti-Communists began and within the first three years, 178 people had been executed. Others, including many of those who had already suffered in German concentration camps, were tortured, imprisoned and later sent to the uranium mines where thousands died. Wives and children of the victims lost their jobs and their right to higher education. In 1954, the monasteries and convents were closed and the monks and nuns imprisoned or forced to find other work. Only a certain number of nuns were allowed to carry on to fill the shortage of nurses and people to look after the elderly.

Under Khrushchev in the 1950s there had been moves to release political prisoners but nothing was done, and only in 1960 was there a general amnesty for political prisoners many of whom, though highly skilled, were forced to take work as stokers or night guards. Apart from a brief remission in 1968, this remained their position until 1989.

After 1948, in each district of Prague, committees were set up to reallocate living space and many of the houses were divided into smaller units, but little was done to improve amenities and none of the rents was reinvested in the buildings themselves. Only comparatively recently are historic buildings being refurbished which explains why so much of Prague is under scaffolding today.

People shake their heads when being questioned about art and culture in the 1950s under Stalinist Russia. A few examples of the architecture of Socialist Realism – the so-called SO-RE-LA – remain, but it is much discredited. But at Expo '58 the Czechs won acclaim from the international community for their design and throughout the early 1960s there was a flourishing activity in the arts especially in film and literature. Writers come to the fore such as Jaroslav Seifert, winner of the Nobel Prize for literature, Milan Kundera, and Bohumil Hrabal. In 1964 it was leading members of the Writers' Union who started to protest against the government. Once more it was the intellectuals of Czechoslovakia who sowed the seeds of change.

In 1968, the Prague Spring came, an uprising against the government, like so many before and since led by the intelligentsia and students. President Novotný was replaced by General Svoboda, and Dubček became general secretary of the Communist Party. Here was 'Socialism with a human face' although the Communist Party still dominated everything including the economy, the army, the secret police, and the media. Everyone's hopes for a more lenient regime were raised, only to be dashed by the invasion by Warsaw Pact troops led by Russia on 21 August 1968.

Prague had gone too far in its liberalizing policies and her allies were rattled. About a hundred people were killed when the troops entered Prague. In January 1969 one young student, Jan Palach, burned himself to death beneath the saint's statue in Wenceslas Square in protest. This is commemorated now by a large circle of candles and is a most moving sight.

From 1977, many of those who had signed the Charter 77 for human rights suffered persecution. During the 1980s there were several demonstrations against the Communist government, many of which were put down with brutality, including that in January 1989 to commemorate the death of Jan Palach. Demonstrations continued until November 1989 when President Gustav Husák was overthrown. The playwright and former political prisoner Václav Havel replaced him, and the 'Velvet Revolution' began.

Havel is now president of a democratic Czechoslovakia. No one, least of all the Czechs, think the transition to democracy and capitalism is going to be easy. They are also aware that the artistic heritage they have so far preserved is now threatened by aspects of capitalism and tourism – fast-food chains with their detritus and the look-alike shops of other European capitals, plus the sheer number of tourists who are now making their way to Prague could, if not carefully monitored, quickly destroy the uniqueness of this lovely city. The Czechs have time to learn from our mistakes, and our appreciation of this great capital of European civilization can help provide money to preserve its wonders and encourage it in the field of modern art, where interesting work is being produced especially in the graphic arts, glass, jewellery and ceramics.

2
THE HRADČANY

The Castle of Prague

The Matthias Gate – the Na Baště Garden – the Spanish Hall – the Treasury of St Vitus – the Prague Art Gallery (Rudolf II Gallery) – the Royal Gardens – the Pavilion of Queen Anne – St Vitus' Cathedral – the Royal Palace – St George's Gallery of Bohemian Art – the Museum of Bohemian History

A visit to Prague must start with the castle. It is here that so much of Bohemia's power, history, spirituality, and creativity is expressed. The castle dominates the city and one of the best views of its imposing mass is from the opposite bank of the River Vltava in the Old Town (Staré Město) either by day, or floodlit by night. From afar the appearance is one, not of a medieval fortress, but of an elegant, welcoming 18C palace, created when Maria Theresa commissioned her architect Nicolo Pacassi to regulate the conglomeration of medieval and Renaissance buildings that had accrued since the 9C. He achieved this between 1753 and 1775, using a rather dull text-book style neo-Classicism. Yet beneath the exterior lies a wealth of fascinating art and history.

As befits a building of such national importance, there are numerous myths concerning the castle's foundation. However, according to the archaeology of the site, there was a defensive building and a small Church of Our Lady here from the 9C, founded by the Christian Prince Bořivoj. Strategically set on the headland above the River Vltava, the castle commanded the trade routes between Vienna and Kiev, a perfect site therefore for communication and defence.

From the 12C until 1918, the castle was the official seat of

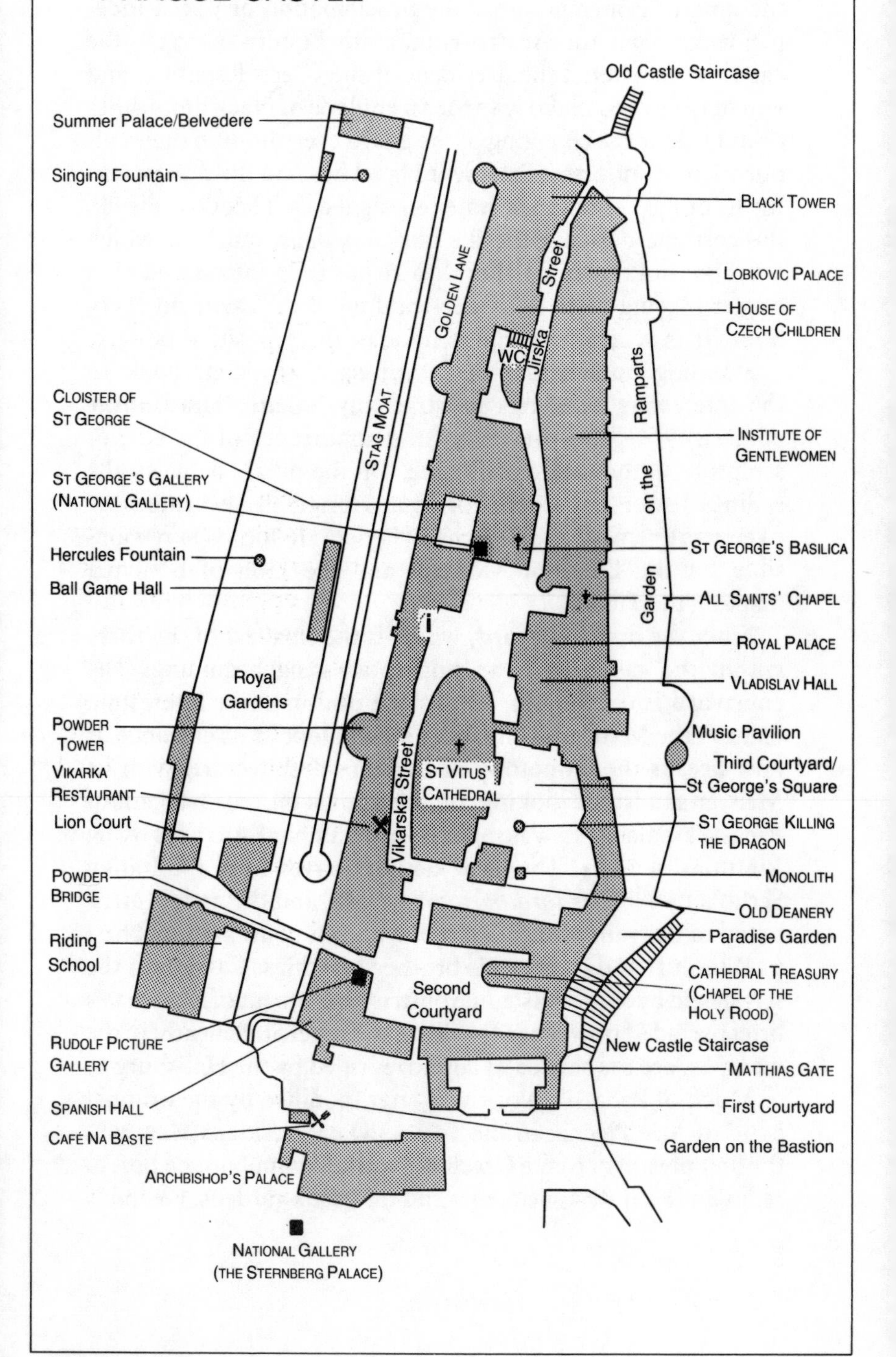
PRAGUE CASTLE
Old Castle Staircase
Summer Palace/Belvedere
Singing Fountain
BLACK TOWER
GOLDEN LANE
Jirska Street
LOBKOVIC PALACE
HOUSE OF CZECH CHILDREN
WC
STAG MOAT
Ramparts on the Garden
CLOISTER OF ST GEORGE
INSTITUTE OF GENTLEWOMEN
ST GEORGE'S GALLERY (NATIONAL GALLERY)
Hercules Fountain
ST GEORGE'S BASILICA
Ball Game Hall
ALL SAINTS' CHAPEL
i
ROYAL PALACE
Royal Gardens
VLADISLAV HALL
POWDER TOWER
Music Pavilion
Vikarska Street
ST VITUS' CATHEDRAL
Third Courtyard/ St George's Square
VIKARKA RESTAURANT
Lion Court
ST GEORGE KILLING THE DRAGON
POWDER BRIDGE
MONOLITH
OLD DEANERY
Riding School
Paradise Garden
Second Courtyard
CATHEDRAL TREASURY (CHAPEL OF THE HOLY ROOD)
RUDOLF PICTURE GALLERY
New Castle Staircase
MATTHIAS GATE
SPANISH HALL
First Courtyard
CAFÉ NA BASTE
Garden on the Bastion
ARCHBISHOP'S PALACE
NATIONAL GALLERY (THE STERNBERG PALACE)

the king of Bohemia. Since the proclamation of Czech independence from the Austro-Hungarian Empire in 1918, the castle has sheltered the president of the Czech Republic, and you may have to make way for an enfilade of black limousines or indeed for the changing of the guard every hour in their colourful new uniforms. President Havel has had the dreary uniforms of the Communist state redesigned by Theodore Pištěk, the costume designer for the film *Amadeus*, much of which was shot in Prague. Further theatre has been introduced by a bugler playing from an upper window of the castle on every hour. It is worth arriving at midday for a positive fanfare.

Standing outside the castle railings with your back to the interesting buildings in Hradčany Square (Hradčanské náměstí) you get a preview of the importance of the role of sculpture in the fabric of Prague. On the pillars between the railings tower 20C copies of Titans originally executed between 1767 and 1770 by Ignác Platzer. He too, was responsible for the Eagle of Moravia and the Lion of Bohemia flanking the Titans.

Enter the first courtyard, which is the smallest of the three within the castle. It is an unprepossessing beginning. The courtyard is on the site of a ravine and its most interesting feature, the Matthias Gate, once stood alone at its entrance. It now breaks the monotony of Pacassi's architecture, with its Meissen sandstone looking sombre against the cream façade of Pacassi's palace. It was built as a triumphal arch for King Matthias in 1614. The basic design derives from the Italian Serlio's *Libro Extraordinario* of *c.*1550, and the arch is attributed to Giovanni Maria Filippi, who was court architect first to Rudolf II and then to his brother Matthias. Carved on the scroll held by some masculine putti is a statement of Matthias's brief period of power as Holy Roman Emperor. Beneath, in the metopes, are the shields of countries ruled by the Habsburgs.

Much of Pacassi's work was later modified by the original hand of Jože Plečnik in the 1920s, when President Masaryk, the first president of the Czech Republic, commissioned him to redesign the State apartments and the castle gardens. Plečnik's modifications within the castle included the paving of this courtyard (later removed) and the monumental flagpoles on either side of the Matthias Gate. In 1926 he was made Castle Architect. Nine years later Masaryk resigned and Plečnik left too, amidst attacks on his designs by the conservation group the Friends of Old Prague.

Walk through the Matthias Gate and this great castle becomes increasingly fascinating. Under the arch, look to your left at Plečnik's dramatic staircase rising through three floors, severe with its hypostyle of stumpy Doric columns (1927–31), later known as the Plečnik Room. This contrasts strangely with the late Rococo interior of Pacassi to the right.

Touring the second courtyard purely visually for a moment, ahead to the right, lies the Chapel of the Holy Rood, now displaying the treasure of St Vitus' Cathedral. This little building appears to be of the 19C but that is an illusion as the Chapel was planned by Pacassi and built by Anselmo Lurago between 1756 and 1760. On the left is a fountain with a lion, the symbol of Bohemia, by Vincenc Makovský and Jaroslav Frágner, a work of the mid-1960s. Frágner was the author, too, of the present paving. Continuing anti-clockwise round the courtyard, to your left is a charming Baroque fountain, the work of Francesco de Tore and Hieronym Kohl of 1686, and a well which, like many in Prague, has its original wrought-iron canopy. Continuing our survey, past the entrance into the third courtyard, on the left is the site of the Renaissance stables of Rudolf II, now the art gallery of the castle. Next comes the passage and gate of 1603 by the Mannerist Giovanni Antonio Brocca. This is the route to the Royal Gardens. On the left-hand side of this passage is the façade of the Spanish Hall. Before going any farther, I suggest you go through the opening to the left of the Spanish Hall to catch a glimpse of the small garden called Na Baště, 'on the Bastion', with its grand oval staircase leading to the entrance of the Spanish Hall and its neo-Classical pavilion by Plečnik's follower, Rottmayer.

The Spanish Hall and the Rudolf Picture Gallery are now used for state receptions. Many of the greatest artists in Prague worked on these important interiors, including the Fleming Adrian Vredeman de Vries at the beginning of the 17C. But these rooms were much altered between 1865 and 1868 in a neo-Rococo style that was intended to blend with the 18C Rococo designs of Pacassi for the proposed coronation of Emperor Franz Josef I. In the end the emperor refused the crown of Bohemia deeming it too dangerous to accept it and upset the Hungarians. The interiors are not open to the public but there is coffee to be had in the pavilion.

Returning to the second courtyard, start by visiting the Chapel of the Holy Rood. There are excellent plans on the wall as you enter, describing its transformation from some early kitchens. The present interior dates from 1852 when it was used by Emperor Ferdinand the Gracious, the last king of Bohemia who abdicated in 1848 in favour of his nephew but who lived on in the castle until his death, in 1875. In the entrance, at the ticket office, there is enough of value and variety to give a taste of what must be one of the richest cathedral treasuries in central Europe. The core of the collection dates from the reign of Charles IV but there are objects from the 10 to the 19C. The cases display a mainly 19C head reliquary of the grandmother of King Wenceslas, Ludmila; the 10C sword of St Stephen wrought by Ulfberth and a 13C mitre set with seed pearls.

Moving into the chapel itself, look first at the interior decoration. The ceiling frescos depicting the Old and New Testaments are by Vilém Kandler, the paintings on glass by Jan Zachariáš Quast and the statue of St John Nepomuk is by Emanuel Max. All these artists were the height of fashion in the middle years of the 19C. The angels on the altar by Ignác Platzer and the Crucifixion by F. X. Balko are well worth looking at. The glory of the chapel, however, rests in the contents of the display cases. Note the series of great processional crosses of rock crystal and silver gilt, many studded with precious stones, baroque pearls and antique cameos, some with ingenious settings. Many pieces of both 14 and 17C metalwork display a distinctive spiky naturalism which is paralleled elsewhere in stone and wood. Exquisite, too, is the 14C rock crystal flagon, possibly French, and the superb 13C cross decorated with the finest filigree work. Here and in the adjoining passageway is some of the wealth and drama of the Counter-Reformation Church where magnificent rings, crucifixes and resplendent vestments played such a part in the ceremonial.

Leaving the chapel, go left across the square, to the Rudolf Gallery. The Italian, Giovanni Gargiolli, may have been the author of its noble portals. Inside, the collections here are not nearly as fine as those you will find in St George's or the National Gallery. But they are worth looking at in that they give an understanding of royal taste in the 16 and 17C, and indeed their founder, Rudolf II, is considered to be one of the greatest European patrons of the arts (see p. 9). His collections in Bohemia and those of succeeding Habsburgs are now mere shadows of their former glory. Much was taken to Vienna, the capital of the Habsburg Empire. The Swedes helped themselves in 1648 and Josef II held a number of spectacularly philistine art auctions at the end of the 18C. The first room of the gallery contains the work of some of those artists favoured by Rudolf II, whose outstanding patronage gave rise to Prague's remarkable circle of Mannerist painters, sculptors, and goldsmiths, known as the School of Prague. As Holy Roman Emperor, Rudolf II was the most important crowned head in Europe; as king of Bohemia he made his capital, Prague, a Mecca for the cream of northern artists, scholars, and philosophers.

Rudolf, who was born in 1552, and succeeded to the throne in 1576, has been described as one of the most ineffectual though one of the most cultured Habsburg rulers. He cuts an enigmatic and sympathetic figure: a recluse who would go around his palace incognito dressed as a groom; a man who had his future foretold by Nostradamus; who employed the English occultists, Dee and Kelley; who dabbled in magic and yet was one of the greatest patrons of the Renaissance in Europe. He prized the great masters of the high Renaissance, and collected around himself artists of the calibre of Hans von Aachen, Giuseppe Archimboldo, Josef Heintz and Roelant Savery. He was advised in the arts by the century's greatest antiquaries, Jacopo Strada and his son, Ottavio. As pointed out by the collector and historian van Mander writing in 1604, 'Whoever so desires nowadays has only to go to Prague to the greatest art patron in the world at the present time; there he may see at the Imperial residence a remarkable number of outstanding and precious, curious, unusual, and priceless works.' Alas, this is no longer true of what is left of Rudolf's collections.

In the entrance to the gallery is a copy of Adrian de Vries's bust of Rudolf with his distinctive profile. Here too is Hans von Aachen's portrait of this maecenas, with his fleshy Habsburg lips. He is magnificently dressed in damask decorated with peacock feathers, and wears the Order of the Golden Fleece. Note also here the works of Bartholomeus Spranger and Cornelius van Haarlem, both important Mannerists. On the left is Adrian de Vries's Adoration of Christ. Continue through the succeeding rooms to the montage with a description of Rudolf's collections. The masterpieces he once owned by Leonardo, Correggio, Veronese, Rubens, Holbein, Breughel, Dürer, and Titian are now scattered among the world's major art galleries. He had a particular love for the work of Dürer and Breughel, two artists much admired by his grandfather, Maximilian I also. Rudolf's gallery of Dürers was legendary. It is well known that he organized the transportation of Dürer's Rosenkranzfest (a painting full of Habsburg symbolism, including the portraits of Maximilian I and Pope Julius II) across the Alps from Venice, with four bearers to hold it upright. This great canvas is one of the few of Rudolf's collection to remain in Prague.

Rudolf's reign saw a growing interest in decorative arts of great refinement and opulence, as found in the work in gold and jewels of the Jamnitzers or the designs of the Vredeman de Vries family, the *pietra dura* panels of the Castrucci or the glass and cameos of the Miseroni family (see p. 121).

The third and fourth rooms were adapted in 1965 by F. Cubr and house paintings from the collection founded by the Emperor Ferdinand III. Some of these came from the Duke of Buckingham's important collection, bought at auction in 1648 by the archduke Leopold Vilém, brother of the emperor. Among these are the St Paul by d'Arpino, The Sacrifice in the Temple and The Building of the Temple of Solomon both by F. Bassano, J. Bassano's Noah's Ark, Tintoretto's Flagellation of Christ and an Adoration by Veronese. In the fifth room are canvases from the Czech high Baroque, including works by Jan Kupecký, Petr Brandl and Jan Rudolf Bys, though these painters are best represented in the St George's Gallery. A reassessment of the work of these artists is long overdue among western art historians, and many will find these paintings a revelation and a delight.

One of the great joys of looking at anything in Prague is that as yet there are few distracting labels in English, we are all forced to make our own discoveries and everywhere this is rewarded.

On leaving the gallery, turn right through the passage and on to the Powder Bridge from where there is a wonderful view of the 15c fortifications built by the architect Benedikt Ried of Piesting and of the towering cathedral. The bridge once connected the castle to a complex of pleasure gardens, now largely vanished. To your left, standing above the steep valley of the Brusnice River is the Riding School erected in 1694–5 by Jean-Baptiste Mathey. Since the Second World War, this has only been used for storage. The terrace by Otto Rottmayer stands on the site where Fux's opera, *Constanza e Fortezza* was performed to celebrate the coronation of Emperor Charles VI in 1723. Rottmayer played an important role in Czech architecture between 1918 and 1939. Sunday is the only day when the Royal Gardens are open. To visit them continue to the main road and immediately turn to your right through the gates. The gardens are the earliest example of Italian design in Bohemia and were laid out in 1534 by Giovanni Spazio for Ferdinand I. They were enlarged and altered by Jan Vredeman de Vries in 1563 and, following the vagaries of fashion, were transformed into French Baroque style in 1730. Until April 1990 the gardens were closed to the public as indeed they had been since the 50s when the tiny summerhouse through the gates on the right became the residence of President Husák. Both the gardens and the castle are said to be undermined with escape tunnels built during the years of Communism. If this is true, they illustrate the edginess of the Communist regime. The gardens are now a mixture of municipal bedding and 19C specimen trees, all somewhat disfigured by eye-level lollipop lighting.

The garden buildings nevertheless merit attention. On the right-hand path is the magnificent Ball Game Hall with its exquisite, though much restored sgraffiato decoration depicting allegories of the Sciences, Virtues and Elements. This was designed by Bonifac Wohlmut and Ulrico Aostalli in 1567–9. At the E end of the gardens is one of the most harmoniously and perfectly proportioned buildings in Prague. This Summer Palace of Queen Anne or Belvedere, commissioned by Ferdinand I as a gift to his queen, was built by G. Spazio and J. Maria de Pambio between 1538 and 1552 to a design by Paolo della Stella. It was given a hull-shaped upper floor by Bonifac Wohlmut between 1557 and 1563. Its arcade, with a light elegance reminiscent of Raphael, was revolutionary in Gothic Prague. Such classical purity was unknown north of the Alps. It has been suggested that this was the first time a summer pavilion had been adapted from a Greek temple. In the centre of the formal gardens laid out in the 1930s is the Singing Fountain by F. Terzio, cast in 1564–8. In the corner, passing through the wonderful 18C grille, lies the Lion Court, the first zoological garden in Prague, designed for Rudolf II. Refreshments are now served here.

Return to the castle and its second courtyard, then walk through into the final and greatest courtyard, past the limestone blocks of the Romanesque White Tower. Immediately ahead is the W end of St Vitus' Cathedral. This great Gothic building is now a gallery of Czech art of the 14 and 20C.

Most of the building of the cathedral took place during two periods of intense patriotism in Bohemia. The first of these began under Charles IV. It was he who, in 1344, the year in which Prague became an archbishopric, laid the foundation stone on the site of a Romanesque basilica, the remains of which may be seen in the crypt. His architect was a Frenchman from Avignon, Matthieu d'Arras, who worked in the then fashionable high Gothic style. Matthieu was also responsible for drawing up a plan of the New Town (see p. 138) but he died in 1352 before completing more than four chapels in the cathedral choir. Charles IV summoned Peter Parler to Prague from Swabia and in his hands, St Vitus' became the most important architectural commission in Bohemia. From now on Prague was to develop an exciting and original form of late Gothic architecture and it increasingly became the mainspring of the courtly 'International Gothic'. Parler's hallmarks lay in decoration: vaulting and sculpture poured from his workshops. Decorative vaulting had been used to effect in England, but in Parler's imaginative hands, first the crazy vault and then the net vault, reached their full potential. Parler completed the arcades and constructed the elevation of the choir with a net vault in 1371–6, finalizing the complicated support system in 1385. The nave was begun in 1392 and the great crossing tower four years later, but they were never finished as the start of the Hussite Wars in 1421 put a stop to most artistic activity in the capital (see p. 6). Parler died in 1399, but his sons John and Wenceslas carried on in Prague, Vienna and Milan. Such art patronage does not come cheap. During the 14C, Prague was the largest city north of the Alps and the king had the sole right to the silver from the mines of Bohemia and Silesia which John of Bohemia had acquired in 1331. Prague, after all, was now the capital of the Holy Roman Empire.

To match the city's importance Charles was determined to make St Vitus' the pivotal church of his kingdom and of the Luxemburg dynasty. In the E end is a shrine to the four patron saints of Bohemia, St Wenceslas, St Adalbert, St Sigismund and St Vitus. The latter's relics rest on the main altar. The decoration of the elevation of the E end is symbolic. At arcade level, lie the tombs of past Bohemian kings. Farther into the light at gallery level are sculptures of those who helped build the cathedral: Charles IV, his mother, his third and fourth wives and his son, the two architects including the self-portrait of Peter Parler, the master masons and three archbishops. This is a collection of strange bedfellows, but is an interesting reflection of the high esteem in which artists were held at the time. Some of the representations are thought to be actual portraits. If so, Parler's is the first self-portrait known in medieval art. Amidst the blaze of light in the clerestory, are the idealized sculpted heads of the patron saints. These were completed by 1385, the year of consecration.

In the reign of Charles's son, Wenceslas IV, the cathedral became the centre of liturgical reform under the preachers Konrad Waldhauser and John Milíč. Hymns were sung in the vernacular, ecclesiastical corruption and the worship of images were renounced. Indeed some of these reforms were later put forward by the Hussites but with the Hussite Wars, this great period of cathedral building came to an end.

Then it was not until 1861 that the Union for the Completion of the Cathedral started its work, carried along on a wave of Romantic nationalism. The work was supervised first by Josef Kranner, then from 1871–99 by Josef Mocker, the Bohemian Viollet-le-Duc. The cathedral was finally completed under the eye of Kamil Hilbert in 1929, in time to commemorate the death of St Wenceslas one thousand years earlier.

Outside, facing the W door it is difficult to remember that this is the most modern part of the cathedral, created at the same time as Prague's Functionalist architecture. Ruskin's credo 'decoration is the better part of architecture' has clearly been put into practice here. Begun in 1892 and inspired by the completion of Cologne Cathedral in 1880, the decoration was by a number of eminent artists and sculptors. Note the portraits of the builders by Vojtěch Sucharda and the tympana by Karel Dvořák. The superb bronze doors realized by O. Španiel after designs of V. H. Brunner depict the legend of St Wences-

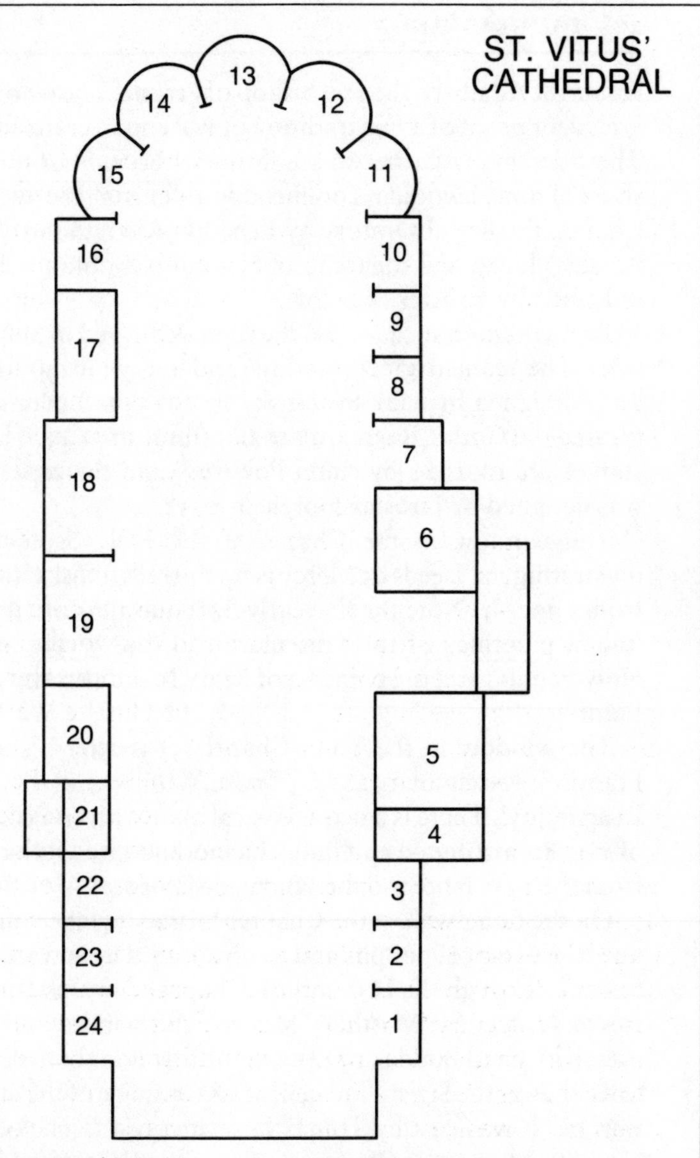

1. Chapel of St Ludmila
2. Chapel of the Holy Sepulchre
3. Thun Chapel
4. Chapter Library
5. Hazemburk Chapel
6. Wenceslas Chapel
7. St Andrew's Chapel
8. Chapel of the Holy Rood
9. Royal Oratory
10. Chapel of St Mary Magdalene/ Wallenstein Chapel
11. Chapel of St John Nepomuk/ Vlasim Chapel
12. Chapel of the Holy Relics/ Sternberg Chapel
13. Chapel of Our Lady/Imperial Chapel
14. Chapel of St John the Baptist/ Arnosts' Chapel
15. Archbishop's Chapel/Pernstejn Chapel
16. St Anna's Chapel/Nostic Chapel
17. Old Sacristy
18. Chapel of St Sigismund
19. Screen by Wohlmut
20. New Sacristy and staircase
21. Neo-Gothic staircase
22. New Archbishop's Chapel
23. Schwarzenberg Chapel
24. Chapel of the Bartons of Dobenin

las and St Adalbert, the 10C bishop of Prague. The whole effect is evident proof of a fine tradition of Bohemian craftsmanship. There are many glories to see in the cathedral but if you are short of time, I would recommend four 'musts': the Wenceslas Chapel, the Royal Oratory by Benedikt Ried, the window by Alfons Mucha and the tomb of St John Nepomuk. These are indicated by an asterisk below.

Begin at the first chapel on the right dedicated to St Ludmila (1).† The stained glass window and the wall mosaic were both designed by Max Švabinský in 1933–6. Emanuel Max created the Gothic Revival altar and statue in 1845. The other statues are of 1921 by Karel Pokorný, and the superb grille was designed by Jaroslav Horejc in 1938.

The window in the Chapel of the Holy Sepulchre (2) illustrating the Deeds of Mercy is by Karel Svolinský and dates from 1932–3. Note the fine early Baroque altar of 1674, two Italian paintings of the Presentation of the Virgin and The Holy Family, and the painting of Mary Magdalene by Aurelio Lomi.

The window in the Thun Chapel (3) is after a sketch by František Kysela of 1928–9, 'Those Who Sow in Tears shall Reap in Joy'. There is a neo-Classical altar with an Ecce Homo of *c.*1580 attributed to Giulio Licino and late Gothic reliefs from the 15C. Note too the sanctuary lamps.

On the outer wall of the Chapter Library (4) there are some fine Renaissance epitaphs and tombstones. The entrance to the tower is through the Hazemburk Chapel (5) which contains a fresco (1631) by Matthias Mayer. The window is from a sketch by Cyril Bouda (1934). On the first floor of the crossing tower hangs the Sigismund bell, at 18 tons, one of the largest in Europe. It was cast by Tomáš Jaroš in 1549. The clock is by Hans Bechler (1597). Before continuing to the S transept, look at the fine Crucifixion sculpted by F. Bílek.

Go into the S transept with its rose window of the Last Judgement by Max Švabinský, 1935–8, the Emblem of Prague

† See map on p. 39.

City in metalwork by Karel Štipl, 1946, a statue of Christ by Čeněk Vosmík, a fine memorial of 1921 dedicated to those who fell in the Great War by K. Pokorný, and the statue of St Wenceslas by Karel Dvořák, 1922. On the piers of the crossing is a fine Madonna dating from the early 16C, and a series of gilded wooden sculptures of patron saints by František Preiss, 1699. In the E wall is a neo-Gothic door of 1925 decorated with mosaic after a cartoon by J. Šimák. This leads to the Wenceslas Chapel.

We are now in the 14C part of the cathedral, the Wenceslas Chapel* (6), designed and built by Peter Parler on the foundations of the S apse of the Romanesque rotunda. Dedicated to St John the Evangelist and St Wenceslas in 1367, the latter's remains were reburied here, near the site where his murderous brother had lain them in the 10C. This was the most sacred part of the cathedral and also of the castle itself. Unfortunately it is not possible to enter the chapel. The decoration is lavish as befits a bejewelled reliquary writ large. The lower part of the walls are faced with 1345 semi-precious stones of Bohemian origin, such as cornelians, amethysts, chalcedonies, jaspers, chrysoprases and agates set in gilded plaster. The chapel played an important part in the coronation ceremony. Each new king presented himself here with his various dignitaries for a robing ceremony before proceeding to the High Altar. The crown of St Wenceslas and the sacred coronation oils were carried to the High Altar from here too.

The wall paintings under the cornice are *c.*1370. A second series of paintings followed in *c.*1470 to commemorate the coronation of King Vladislav. The upper part was not painted until 1509 by the workshop of the Master of Leitmeritz for Vladislav's son, King Ludvík. The Master of Leitmeritz was the most important artist working in Bohemia in the late Gothic period. The central altar and the tomb of the patron saint was arranged by Kamil Hilbert between 1912 and 1913, when the chapel was restored. The delicate stained glass of the windows is the work of S. Libenský and J. Brychtová and dates from 1968. Note the limestone statue of St Wenceslas on the cornice. This is the work of Henry Parler of 1373. The emblem of the Parlers, a runic square, can be seen carved in the base. The statue was painted by Oswald, court painter to Charles IV. In the corner, by the entrance, is a Renaissance bronze candlestick, the work of Hans Vischer of Nuremberg, 1532. In the SE corner lies a ciborium in the form of a Gothic steeple, perhaps even a model of that planned for St Vitus'. This is an example of outstanding metalwork from Peter Parler's workshop. Note the small painting of St Wenceslas by the Monogrammist I. W., 1543.

Near the window lies the entrance to the Crown Chamber on the first floor. This has been locked with seven locks since 1867 and contains the coronation jewels from the 14C. The royal crown of Bohemia, or the crown of St Wenceslas, was the gift of the saint and was entrusted to the king for his lifetime. It was re-made for Charles IV by his court goldsmith in 1346. On three further occasions later that century more jewels were added, and so it remains today. The sword of St Wenceslas dates from the beginning of the 14C, but the sceptre dates from the reign of Rudolf II. The Crown Jewels were last seen by the public in 1978, during an exhibition dedicated to Charles IV.

Return to the chancel via the original Gothic portal with its pinewood doors and note the 13C bronze knocker in the form of a lion's head. Against the wall of the chancel is the tombstone of the Lobkovic family (1590). On the opposite pier is the monument to General Field Marshal Šlik, who was chancellor of Bohemia in 1723. This is an important monument, the fruit of co-operation between the great Baroque architect F. M. Kaňka, and M. B. Braun, the greatest sculptor of Bohemian Baroque.

Continuing round towards the E end you come to a series of chapels. Although they still retain fine Rococo grilles, these have been over-enthusiastically revamped in neo-Gothic style between 1870 and 1890. The man behind the remodelling was the architect Josef Mocker and the work was carried out by official artists such as Čermák, František Sequens and Antonín Lhota.

In St Andrew's Chapel (7) or the chapel of the Martinic family, note the marble altar made in Rome by T. Achterman, *c.*1870. The epitaph in stone of Jan Popel of Lobkovic dates from 1582.

The Chapel of the Holy Rood (8) contains fragments of 14C frescos; an icon from 1400, and a Lombardian sculpted Corpus Christi from the 16C. Among the paintings of the 18C is a St John Nepomuk by Augusto Masucci. This dates from 1729 and was presented to the cathedral by Pope Benedict XIII. From here we descend to the crypt and find ourselves surrounded by the 11C remains of the Romanesque basilica. The royal crypt was laid out by the architect Kamil Roškot in 1928–35.

The Royal Oratory* (9) by Benedikt Ried is an extraordinary example of late Gothic art in Bohemia. Its stone balcony was carved by Hans Spiess of Frankfurt in 1493 for Vladislav Jagiello, son of the king of Poland who became king of Bohemia in 1471, and then king of Hungary in 1490. He died in 1516 after having transformed much of the castle (see p. 6). The letter 'W' for Wladislaw can be seen in many of the oratory's decorations. The sculpted figures of mineworkers with their lamps are the work of M. B. Braun from 1721–5 and are a salient reminder that without the silver mines of Jihlava and Kutná Hora royal patronage of the arts would not have been possible.

In the Chapel of St Mary Magdalene (10) of the Wallenstein family, note the early Baroque altar with its modern statue by J. V. Čermák. Against the walls lie the two Gothic tombstones of the builders of the cathedral, Matthieu d'Arras and Peter Parler. Opposite, forming part of the choir screen, is a fascinating relief portraying the devastation of the cathedral by the Calvinists in 1620, an act of desecration encouraged by Frederick of Bohemia. It is the work of the court joiner Kaspar Bechteler (1623). One of the masterpieces in the cathedral is the silver tomb of St John Nepomuk*. The central section was made in Vienna in 1733–6 after a sketch by the celebrated architect Fischer von Erlach. He worked in collaboration with the sculptor Antonio Corradini and the goldsmith Jan Josef Würth. The vases were modelled by J. A. Quitainer, and the angels spilling around the baldachin are by I. F. Platzer, 1771. Here are fine reminders of the tenacity of the Baroque style.

The altar of the Chapel of St John Nepomuk (11) and oratory of the Vlašim family, which encases the relics of St Adalbert, is after a sketch of Kamil Hilbert. The four silver busts of the patron saints of Bohemia date from 1699 and are by František Preiss. The painting of the 'Passauer' Madonna dates from 1601 and the funeral monument of Bishop Jan Očko of Vlašim and the fragmentary frescos are from 1370. The beautiful sculpted Gothic Madonna is of *c.*1500. On the left wall is the magnificent bronze monument of Ludmila Thurn, 1558. The grille, like that in all the other chapels, is of 1731.

On the altar of the Chapel of the Holy Relics (12), the Saxon Chapel or Sternberg family chapel, is a collection of reliquaries from the 14–18C and against the wall are the tombstones of the Přemyslid dukes Otakar I and Otakar II from the Parler workshops. The one of Otakar I is superb and is said to be from the hand of the master himself. The siting of these tombs dates to about 1376–7. On the pillar is a cannon ball from the Prussian bombardment of Prague in 1757.

The Chapel of Our Lady (13) or Imperial Chapel was founded by Charles IV but the altar is of a much later date, to a design by Josef Mocker, 1903. On the transverse beam hangs a Calvary of 1621 by Daniel Altman von Eydenburk. The frescos depict scenes of the Life of St Mary and the Presentation of the Remains of St Vitus to the cathedral.

The Chapel of St John the Baptist (14) or Chapel of the Arnošts was founded by Archbishop Arnošt of Pardubice. The original chapel collapsed and was rebuilt in 1863–4. The terracotta figures in the arcade niches are by two pioneers of Czech modern sculpture, Václav Levý and J. V. Myslbek. The 'Jerusalem' candlestick is a fine example of Romanesque metal-casting. According to chronicles it was won as war booty by Czech warriors in Milan in 1158. The stem is of later date (1641). Note also the Death of St Joseph by Francisco Trevisano, 1656.

The Renaissance family epitaph from 1582 in the Archbishop's Chapel (15) or Pernštejn family chapel was designed by Jan Vredeman de Vries, one of the most important of the northern Mannerists working at the court of Rudolf II. Opposite the chapel is a monumental bronze sculpture dating from 1895 of Cardinal Friedrich Joseph Schwarzenberg by J. V. Myslbek. Schwarzenberg was bishop of Salzburg and archbishop of Prague, yet managed to combine this holy status with being a member of the House of Parliament and of the Reichsstaat. Around the choir is a wooden bas-relief depicting the flight in 1620 of Frederick of the Palatinate to Warsaw after his defeat at the Battle of the White Mountain. It was carved by Kaspar Bechteler in 1623.

In the altar of St Anna's Chapel (16) or chapel of the Nostic family, note the early Gothic panel from 1266, originally from Trier Cathedral but given to St Vitus' by the Nostic family. The sculpted Madonna dates from the 16c and a fresco of the life of St Anna is by Jan Sweers.

In the wall of the aisle in the Old Sacristy (17), formerly St Michael's Chapel, is a good example of a high Baroque confessional (1730). J. K. Liška's St Maurice, The Baptism of Christ by Petr Brandl and J. J. Hering's Visitation are all fine examples of Czech Baroque painting. In the interior is Parler's original vaulting with two pendant keystones, the remaining furnishings dating from 1730, and an array of portraits of the archbishops of Prague.

The frescos in the Chapel of St Sigismund (18) or chapel of the Černín family portray scenes from the Life of St Sigismund, and are Augsburg work from the late 16c. He was the patron saint of the Luxemburg family. Note too The Assumption by D. Alexius of *c.*1600. The fine main altar is glorious in red lacquer, silver and gold and is by the architect F. M. Kaňka and the sculptor F. I. Weiss. Note too the balustrade, (1735). The walls of the chapel are studded with tomb slabs, mainly of the 16 and 17c.

From the 14C to the nearly modern, there is a perceptible drop in the floor level. Standing at the E end, gaze upwards at the conception of space created by Peter Parler with his fine net vault of 1367. In the chancel, the windows are after a cartoon by Max Švabinský, 1946–8. The High Altar is neo-Gothic, 1868–72, by J. Kranner, decorated with enamels by František Sequens and reliefs by Ludvík Šimek. The pulpit is early Baroque by K. Bechteler (1618). The Royal Mausoleum is prominent in front of the High Altar. On the tomb are medallions with busts of Charles IV and his four wives, Wenceslas IV, Ladislav Posthumus and George Poděbrady. Reclining are the figures of Ferdinand I, his wife Anne of Hungary and his son, Maximilian II. These are the work of the Netherlandish sculptor Alexander Collin, 1566–89. The monument still retains its fine Renaissance grille by G. Schmidthammer, finished in 1591.

In the N transept is part of the choir screen designed by Bonifac Wohlmut (19), 1557–61. Originally this enclosed the medieval interior of the cathedral but it was transferred to its present location in 1924. Note the mixture of the early Baroque doors of the choir chapel dating from 1639, with the central modern part of 1929. The organ dates to 1757.

The New Sacristy (20) contains copies of the busts from the triforium. The wooden altar is by František Bílek, one of the finest Czech sculptors, and the wooden statue of Christ carved in 1899 has been in the cathedral since 1929. The neo-Gothic spiral staircase (21) leads to the Treasure Chamber. There is more than a hint of Art Nouveau in its decoration.

The New Archbishop's Chapel (22) has, since 1909, been the burial chapel of the archbishops of Prague. The window* is the work of Alfons Mucha in 1931. Its subject is a celebration of the Lives of SS Cyril and Method. There are similarities between a stained glass window and a poster and Mucha was a master of both. Don't fail also to see the Assumption of the Virgin by Bartholomeus Spranger, 1593.

In the Schwarzenberg Chapel (23) the stained glass by Karel Svolinský illustrates the family tree of the Schwarzenbergs. Set in the altar is an attractive late Gothic panel from southern Bohemia depicting The Last Judgement.

In the chapel of the Bartoňs of Dobenín (24) the window and wall mosaics by F. Kysela, 1931–5 show the Eight Blessings. The Gothic arch is a north Italian work from *c.*1400. The bronze grille is by Karel Štipl, 1937. Here too is the Reliquary of St Anežka by Karel Stádník, 1989.

As you leave the cathedral you pass on your left the former Old Deanery, rebuilt in 1662. This conceals the remains of the Romanesque Bishop's Palace. In the corner is a statue of St Wenceslas of 1662 attributed to Jan Jiří Bendl.

This third and largest courtyard, St George's Square, is in a uniform neo-Classical style by Pacassi. On the far side of the square, the most attractive aspect of this façade is the fine wrought-iron balcony with figures of torchbearers from the workshop of Ignác Platzer. The presidential offices nestle behind this and a balcony provides a fine platform from which the public can be addressed. Here, as in Wenceslas Square, is an important public meeting place. Although the courtyard has an undoubted 18C feel to it, there is much that is modern, by Jože Plečnik. His is the monolith of granite, in memory of the victims of World War I and the tenth anniversary of the Republic in 1928. Comparisons with Lutyens come to mind. There is also an equestrian bronze statue of St George, for which Plečnik designed the base. The original St George is an outstanding example of bronze casting in the 'International Gothic' style. It foreshadows the work of Donatello or Verrocchio, but is decorated with minute details of nature so beloved by the 'International Gothic'. It was cast by Georg and Martin of Cluj (Klausenburg) in 1373. The statue in the courtyard is a copy: the original is in St George's Gallery.

Now stand and view the S transept portal of the cathedral, or Golden Portal, which was formerly the main entrance from the Royal Palace. How glorious it must have been when its mosaic, created in 1371 by Venetians using Bohemian glass, was newly installed. At the time it would have been the only glittering example of this technique north of the Alps. Alas, it is difficult to see it now, due to poor restoration at the beginning of this century, but it does depict Charles IV and Elizabeth of Pomerania with Czech patron saints. Beneath the mosaic the porch (Hostium Magnum) has beautiful triangular vaulting by Peter Parler of *c.*1366–7 above the door. The door itself is by Jan Sokol and the modern mosaic is after a cartoon by Karel Svolinský. The fine decorative grille in front of the doorway is by Jaroslav Horejc of 1954. Look up at the Great Tower which was built by the sons of Peter Parler in 1396–1406, with a Renaissance gallery by B. Wohlmut, 1560–2. The dome dates from the same time as the courtyard façades, that is from 1770, but the fine clock and golden grille are from the Rudolfian period.

Continue to your right to see, in the corner, the covered gate to the Promenade Garden by J. Plečnik, 1927–34. The bulls supporting the baldaquin are thought to be a reference to the peasant background of Queen Libuše's husband and co-ruler, the first Přemysl. It may not be an accident that it has echoes of Knossos. Alice Masaryk, with whom Plečnik worked on much of the castle, was fond of reflecting that Slovakia was the Greece of the Slav nation. Note here how the architect plays with the idea of form being independent of material, the canopy being of bronze.

Behind the Baroque Eagle Fountain carved to a design by Francesco Caratti in 1664, lies the entrance to the Royal Palace. The palace is made up of many layers of Bohemian royal history. At foundation level is the Romanesque palace built by Duke Soběslav (1125–40); then comes the Gothic building with its Přemysl arcades of the 13C; next follows the palace of Charles IV, and finally the magnificent rooms created between 1477 and 1511 under Vladislav Jagiello.

Enter the palace, walk from the antechamber with its remains of a Romanesque tower, then turn left to the Green Chamber bedecked with the emblems of the associate judges of the courts. On the ceiling is a Baroque fresco, The Judgement of Solomon which originally came from the Burgrave's House. There follows the so-called Vladislav Bedroom with late

Gothic vaulting by Hans Spiess of 1486, and beyond, the room used to house the archives of the land rolls. Return to the antechamber and enter the Vladislav Hall, on the site of the hall of Charles IV, surely one of the most exciting spaces created in 16c northern Europe. Here, it is easy to imagine the coronations, banquets and knightly tournaments taking place. During the time of Rudolf II and later it was used like some grand art market, the stall-holders setting up their wares in the window embrasures. Since 1934 the elections of the presidents of Czechoslovakia have taken place here. The most recent celebration was in December 1989, when Václav Havel was elected president. A High Mass followed in the cathedral. The most remarkable feature of the Hall is the ribbed vaulting by Benedikt Ried which unites walls and ceiling in one single undulating movement. Yet there is no heaviness here: the ribs are pure decoration and do not even follow their expected course; they end abruptly as if there is no final solution. Ried created this work of architectural bravado between 1493 and 1502. English fan vaulting is the only comparable style and that is dreary copy book by comparison.

Leave the Hall, turn right and pass to the Louis Wing, built by Ried in 1502–9, a mixture of Renaissance and Gothic. Originally the living quarters, its use changed after the great fire of 1541 which destroyed so much of the castle area and some of the Malá Strana (see p. 69). Thereafter it became the offices of the Czech Chancellery and the Imperial Court Council. Even more important however, it was from the eastern window here that Jaroslav Martinic and William Slavata, both fanatical Catholics and Habsburg supporters, were defenestrated by members of the Bohemian Protestant Estates in 1618 (see p. 10).

From the antechamber of the Czech Chancellery a spiral staircase leads to the early 16c hall of the Court Chancellery which contains original furniture of the time of Rudolf II. On the walls are copies of portraits of the Habsburgs from Rudolf II to Maria Theresa. On 19 June 1621, the death sentence was passed here on 27 members of the Bohemian nobility and gentry who had led the revolt against Ferdinand II. The inlaid door was designed by Jan Vredeman de Vries, *c.*1600.

Return once more to the Vladislav Hall, walk to the end and turn right to visit the Observation Terrace. This, together with the spiral staircase, was designed by Otto Rottmayer in 1951. Through the portal by Giovanni Gargiolli of Florence, 1598, we pass into the choir of the All Saints' Chapel, formerly the seat of an independent Chapter. It was built by Peter Parler between 1370 and 1387, but was rebuilt after the great fire by Ulrico Aostalli in 1579–87. The High Altar was designed by Petr Prachner in the middle of the 18C and carries a painting by Václav Vavřinec Reiner. Also note the tomb in the N of the chapel of St Procopius the patron saint of the Slavs, by F. I. Weiss, 1739. On the walls hang a series of paintings by Christian Dittman, 1669, and several works from the important Rudolfine court circle, including a triptych by Hans von Aachen. The organ is a rare example of the Gothic Revival style from the beginning of the 18C.

Return for the last time to the Hall and enter the Diet, with its throne of 1836. This room, originally from the 15C, was revaulted between 1559 and 1563 by Bonifac Wohlmut, in sympathy with the Vladislav Hall. There is a fine neo-Gothic tiled stove from 1836, but one of the most impressive things in the room are the fine frames surrounding the Habsburg portraits. Leading off the Diet is the room of the New Land rolls built in the 16C and decorated with the painted emblems of the clerks of the land rolls. The room contains original furniture from the 16 and 17C. On the staircase, Ried's hand can be seen again in the rib vaulting of *c.*1500. Note too the typical rhomboidal treatment of the ceiling, almost Art Deco in feel, but again a Bohemian invention. The door on the right (note its fine handle) leads back into St George's Square.

Enter St George's Square and walk towards the arch into Vikářská Street. On your right glance at the windows of the palace of 1493. These are the earliest examples of the Italian Renaissance in Bohemia, with their delicate arabesques and acanthus leaves. It has been suggested the windows were executed by craftsmen from the Buda workshop of Matthias Corvinus, inspired by the Palazzo Ducale in Urbino. Note too the cenotaph of St John Nepomuk by I. F. Platzer of 1763. Nepomuk was the favourite Bohemian saint of the Counter-Reformation – a Catholic alternative to Jan Hus. Nepomuk was martyred by being thrown off Charles Bridge under the orders of Wenceslas IV. The story goes that Wenceslas wished to prove his queen was guilty of adultery and Nepomuk, as the queen's confessor, denied that she was. But the real reason for his death was that, as archbishop of Prague, he challenged the power of the monarchy and won. It is the story of Thomas à Becket all over again.

Leaving the Royal Palace you can see, next to the Cloister of St George, the New Deanery, built in a rather bleak neo-Gothic by Josef Mocker in 1879. St George's, founded in 973, was the first convent in Bohemia for Benedictine nuns. Its founder, Duke Boleslav II made his sister Mlada the first abbess. The buildings were transformed rather successfully into a gallery for Bohemian art by František Cubr and Josef Pilar, in the 1960s. This St George's Gallery should not be missed, particularly as the international importance of Czech art is at last being recognized. Here are represented the 'International Gothic' style of Charles IV's court – a style that even influenced artists in that bastion of the Renaissance, Florence; the Mannerist art of the 16 and early 17C; and Czech Baroque, whose artists vied with those farther west in their range of subject matter and technique. Give yourself time to look around. If you begin to flag, there is an excellent café to revive you.

The ground floor of the gallery is given over to Gothic and 'International Gothic' art. Emotion contrasting with courtly elegance is one of the keys to Bohemian Gothic. The gallery contains a fine series of carved 'Beautiful Madonnas' mainly from the 14 and 15C, which illustrate well the so-called 'soft style' – elegant swaying Virgins, regarding their wriggling children with a gentle smile. These provide a poignant contrast to the series of moving Pietàs and Crucifixions. Such extremes, responding to the influence of Christian mysticism are part of 'International Gothic'. There are contrasts too of Gothic fantasy and naturalism in the bronze St George, the original of the copy in St George's Square. This integration of man with nature is further seen in the wood carvings of Master I. P. whose nationality is unknown but who arrived in Bohemia about 1520. His major extant work is in the Týn Church in Old Town Square, but there is a small gallery of his carvings at the bottom of the stairs.

Also on the ground floor are some fine examples of Bohemian panel painting on limewood. Under the Luxemburgs, in the 14C, panel painting was among the most important developments in European art. The quality of Bohemian work, up until the Hussite Wars, is superb and much has survived. Among the outstanding work in the gallery must be the series of panels of the Passion painted for the Cistercian monastery of Vyšší Brod in 1350–5. Different hands have obviously been involved in this great polyptych. All show an understanding of space but also a negation of it, and the exquisite colours and naturalistic detail make one think of the Italian Duccio.

The panels (1360–5) of Master Theodoric, painter to the court, are in a different vein. His massive figures appear to explode out over the frames. It is worth noticing the use of the frame as an important part of the composition, as with the later Madonna from St Vitus', *c.*1396. Note too the treatment of the decorated background created with stamped gesso under the gilding, akin to the work of goldsmiths. These panels came from the Chapel of the Holy Cross in Karlštejn Castle. A delightful parallel to the sculpted 'Beautiful Madonnas' is the Madonna of Třeboň painted around 1380, and exhibited here.

Upstairs, in the first passage, are works by the artists who set the style for Rudolf's court. Note the bronze by Adrian de Vries. This is in fact a copy of the one stolen by the Swedes in 1648 and now gracing the gardens at Drottningholm Castle. The original was dated 1545 and was one of the series Vredeman de Vries created for the great garden of Wallenstein (see p. 94). The elongated figures of Bartholomeus Spranger are well illustrated in his Resurrection, while the more etherial work of Hans von Aachen may be appreciated in his Annunciation of 1613. Note the more classicizing forms of Josef Heintz, the curious nature studies of Joris Hoefnagel, 1575–82, and the wild, romantic landscapes of Roelant Savery. Rudolf had a great love for the Alps and sent Savery there to paint them. Karel Škréta belongs to the early Baroque. His is a very rich use of paint seen both in his portraits and his religious paintings. See his portrait of the Miseroni family of 1653. The Miseroni were called to Prague to set up a workshop for crystal carving and gem cutting, and they laid the foundations for the Bohemian cut-glass industry. One of the most charming portraits in the gallery must be that by K. Škréta of Marie Maximilián of Sternberg in pastoral costume. There are some small displays of fine examples of 18C glass and other decorative arts but those who are particularly interested in this field should go to the Decorative Arts Museum (p. 120).

Other painters represented here include Michal Leopold Willmann who was doubtless influenced by Rubens. His work contrasts with the refined still-life painting of Jan Rudolf Bys, a more classical artist in the French manner, especially when he is painting historical scenes. Note the works of two great masters of Prague Baroque, the sculptor, M. B. Braun and the painter Petr Brandl. Note also the 1709 portrait of the miniaturist Karl Bruni by Jan Kupecký. Observe his glasses, his mussel shells for mixing the paint, the fine pencil which he appears to use on a copper base, but most of all note his 'bohemian' air. There is an attractive painting of Orpheus by V. V. Reiner and some noteworthy works by Kern, especially his St John on Patmos. There is a series of delicate cabinet miniatures by Norbert Grund at the end of the gallery which should not be missed.

Leaving the gallery you move out of the convent and into the Church of St George next door, founded in 921. The early Baroque façade is misleading. It was actually put up about 1670 after a sketch by Francesco Caratti. At its side is the Chapel of St John Nepomuk (1718–22) by Filip Spannbrücker. The interior of the church suffered from the dead hand of the restorer between 1897 and 1907, but it represents one of the most monumental examples of the Romanesque in Bohemia. One of the earliest buildings in the castle, it was rebuilt after the fire in 1142. On the walls fragments of paintings of *c.*1200 can still be made out. St Ludmila's Chapel at the bottom of the steps at the side of the chancel contains a tombstone of 1380. Here is also some good plasterwork. The double curving staircase leads up to the chancel where a fine Baroque grille hides the tombs of the Přemyslid princes, founders of the church and convent. In the crypt on the right stands a statue of St Bridget, a naturalistic allegory of Vanity carved in 1726 by an Italian, Spinetti in atonement for an act of violence he had committed. In the St John Nepomuk Chapel are paintings and frescos by V. V. Reiner from about 1730.

Leaving the church and looking across the road you will see to your right the Renaissance portal of the Royal Palace, the All Saints' Chapel and the Institute of Gentlewomen. This latter was a secular convent which always had a lady of the Habsburg family as abbess. Originally the Renaissance palace of the Rosemberg family, it was redesigned by Anselmo Lurago between 1753 and 1755.

Turn left down Jiřská Street (St George's Street) passing on your left the early Renaissance S door of St George's and its Romanesque chancel. Then turn to the left and enter a different world, a curious survival, the famous Golden Lane. Contrary to popular opinion this row of picturesque houses huddled against the castle wall did not house the alchemists of Rudolf's court, but the craftsmen of the castle. More recently, its romantic atmosphere has attracted several artists and intellectuals including Franz Kafka and the poet Jaroslav Seifert. Now it contains some good bookshops and some shops that are tourist traps. At the end of the street is the entrance to the Daliborka, a defensive tower of the 15C, once used as a prison.

Return to St George's Street where, on the left is the former Burgrave's House, built 1555–6 by Giovanni Ventura. In the

1960s it was modified to make the House of Czech Children for the Pioneers. Opposite at No. 36 is the Lobkovic Palace, formerly the palace of the Pernštejn family, which was built in the second half of the 16C and restored in 1651–8 by Carlo Lurago. It is now the Museum of Bohemian History and is well worth a visit. The interiors are rich in stucco and fresco decoration by Domenico Galli and Fabian Harovník, and are full of interesting furniture, glass, ceramics and historical maps.

The street is closed by the Black Tower, part of the castle's fortification system dating from the first half of the 12C. The tower was lowered by one floor after the fire in 1538. The bastion in front of the tower offers a wonderful panorama of Prague.

To the S of the tower is the entrance to the southern Castle Gardens, adapted in the 1920s by Plečnik and connected with a complex of palace gardens in the Malá Strana. These important gardens are sprinkled with small buildings by Plečnik including a neo-Classical pavilion (1925–6) with statues by I. Platzer. In the adjoining Garden on the Ramparts stand two obelisks marking the place where the victims of the Defenestration fell in 1618. The gardens descend thereafter in a series of terraces and pavilions by Plečnik. From here too, the New Castle Staircase descends. It was conceived in 1674 as a grand stairway bedecked with statues, part of the idea of a *via sacra* or Holy Way leading to St Vitus' Cathedral. Alas, this was never completed. A single solitary statue of St Filippo Neri by M. J. Brokof, has stood here on its own since 1715. If you have time, it is worth climbing on to the observation terrace on the site of the tiny Chapel of Holy Mary of Einsiedel which was part of the Theatine Monastery below. From here you can see the Old Town, the New Town and the district of Vyšehrad stretched out along the other side of the Vltava River.

Return through the castle courtyards into the Hradčany quarter.

The Castle Area

The Sternberg Palace (National Gallery) – the Museum of Arms and Armour – St John Nepomuk – the Nový Svět (New World) – the Černín Palace – the Loretto – the Strahov Monastery – Petřín Hill

Leaving the castle behind you, turn left down the hill and look out once more over Prague, over the Malá Strana or Lesser Town founded in 1257 (see p. 68) and up to the right where the great Monastery of Strahov (see p. 64) stands on its own. To the left is a scaled-down replica of the Eiffel Tower and farther up the hill is the small church of St Lawrence. Built among the woods are some attractive private houses and a 19C hospital beneath which is the elegant mass of the Lobkovic Palace, now the German Embassy. It has a fine roof with a viewing platform. Directly beneath the castle walls are the low, picturesque red roofs of the Italian quarter, where the masons and architects, artists and sculptors lodged when they first arrived from Italy to work for the kings of Bohemia. Beyond this and seemingly in open countryside, is the American Pavilion housed in what was formerly a 16C wine press belonging to the Schönborn Palace. The surrounding terracing is all that remains of Prague's vineyards.

Turning back towards Hradčany Square once more, note in passing the statue of St Wenceslas by Č. Vosmík, 1906. Its base dates from the 18C and came originally from Charles Bridge.

Standing with your back to the castle, Hradčany Square stretching ahead is surrounded with grand palaces and houses. Beginning on your right (16/56) is the magnificent Archbishop's Palace, still in use. You can only see the splendid tapestries inside by appointment. Eight houses were demolished before building on the palace began by Aostalli in 1562–4. Additions were made in 1600 including a new chapel. Its present appearance is due to the work of Jean-Baptiste Mathey from Dijon. He arrived with Archbishop Wallenstein, after having been trained in Rome and worked on the palace in

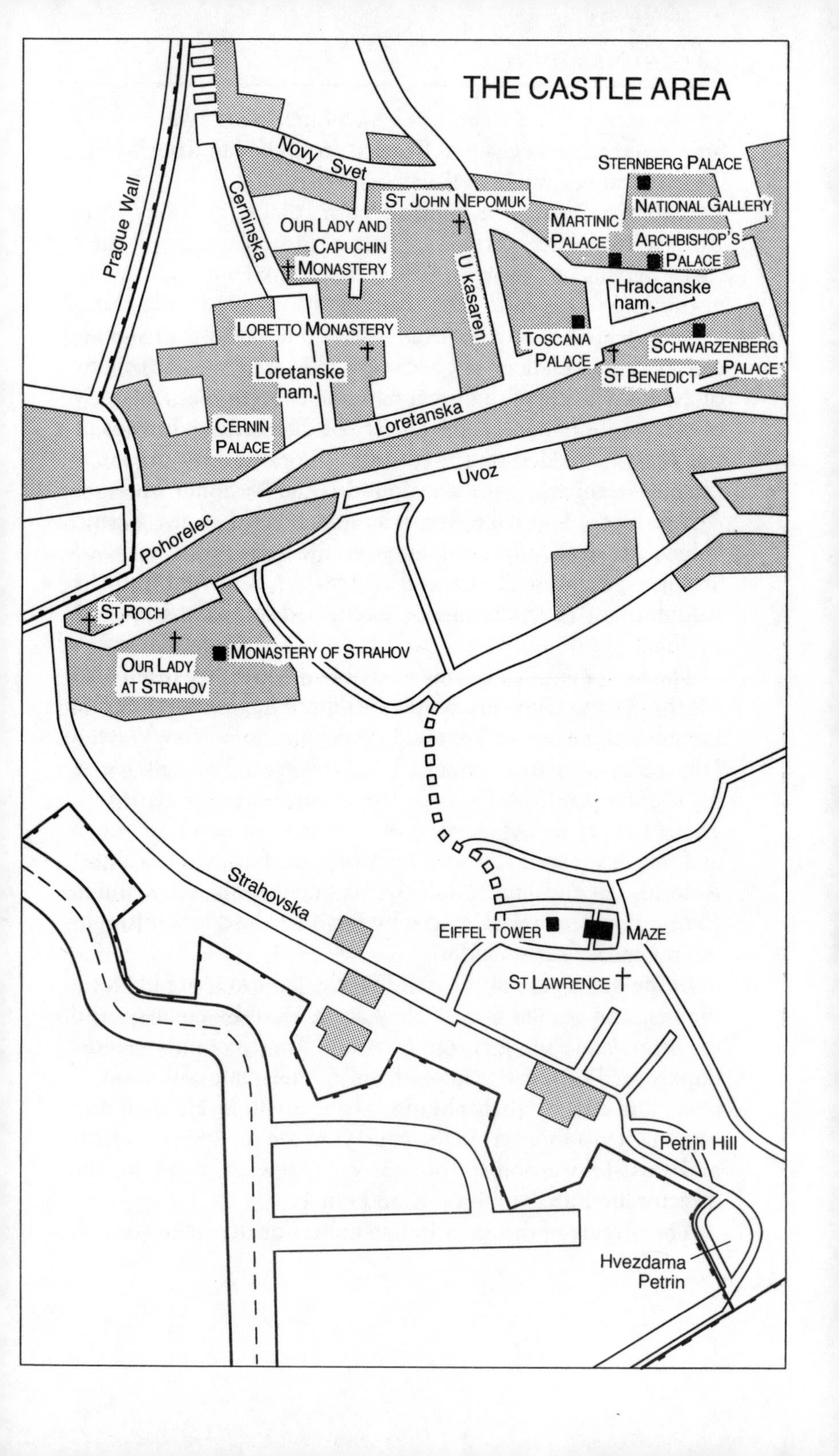
THE CASTLE AREA
Novy Svet
Prague Wall
Cerninska
St John Nepomuk
Our Lady and Capuchin Monastery
U kasaren
Sternberg Palace
National Gallery
Martinic Palace
Archbishop's Palace
Hradcanske nam.
Loretto Monastery
Loretanske nam.
Toscana Palace
Schwarzenberg Palace
St Benedict
Cernin Palace
Loretanska
Uvoz
Pohorelec
St Roch
Our Lady at Strahov
Monastery of Strahov
Strahovska
Eiffel Tower
Maze
St Lawrence
Petrin Hill
Hvezdama Petrin

1676. Between 1764 and 1765 two outer wings were added and the façade was given its Rococo scrolls by Jan Josef Wirch. This is a rare example of Rococo in Prague.

Opposite stands the sombre Salm Palace (1/186), dating from 1810. The Sternbergs had a project to build their castle here using the architect Carlo Fontana, but this came to nothing. In the end, their palace (1697–1708) was built slightly behind that of the archbishop and is now the magnificent National Gallery of Czechoslovakia (15/57). The origins of the foundation of this great national collection lie in a body of private individuals – the Society of the Patriotic Friends of the Arts – founded in 1779, under the protection of Count Caspar Sternberg, who also founded the National Museum (see p. 149). The collection was first housed in the Černín Palace at Hradčany, and later in the Clam-Martinic and Sternberg Palaces. At the end of the 19C it moved into the Rudolfinum. The paintings were returned here in 1950 purely by chance.

The Sternberg Palace was probably designed by Domenico Martinelli and Giovanni Battista Alliprandi, pupil of the great Fischer von Erlach of Vienna. It was built for Václav Vojtěch Sternberg, who also commissioned the great Troja Palace as his country house (see p. 194). The palace was only made into an art gallery in 1950 and some of the original plasterwork and frescos remain in the interior, the frescos by August Aldorandini and Jan Rudolf Bys. Inside there is also a China Pavilion by Pisani with stucco by Frisoni. The doors throughout the palace are splendid.

In the main part of the building the paintings are hung on the first and second floors. They are divided by country, and the schools are hung chronologically. They include the most important European schools from a fine small collection of icons and early Italian painting, to the 18C in Holland and Italy. Downstairs, across the courtyard are the Impressionists and post-Impressionists bought en masse in 1906 by the director after an exhibition from France.

The origins of the early Italian collection are interesting. It was formed as early as 1805 by the Marchese Tommaso degli Obizzi whose taste in 'primitives' was ahead of his time. The collection was inherited via the Duke of Modena by the Austrian line of the Este family, ending up with Archduke Franz Ferdinand who transferred the collection to his castle at Konopiště. The collection is rich, including works by Pietro Lorenzetti, Daddi, Monaco, Nardo di Cione and Vivarini. Do not miss the fine but small collection of icons in this gallery too.

The collection of the later Italian school includes work by Lorenzo Lotto Sebastiano del Piombo, Tintoretto, Sebastiano Ricci, Tiepolo and Canaletto. Netherlandish painters were favoured in Prague too and several of their works are to be found in the collection. There is Geertgen's Adoration of the Magi (mentioned in the original inventory of Prague Castle), Jan Mabuse's St Luke Painting the Virgin (once the centrepiece of an altar in St Vitus') and Peter Paul Rubens' The Martyrdom of St Thomas and St Augustus, commissioned for St Thomas' Church in Prague (see p. 92) in 1637–8. There is also a beautiful work by Pieter Bruegel the Elder, The Haymakers, as well as work by Frans Hals, Jan van Goyen, and Rembrandt van Rijn.

The German School is also well represented. There is a fine grisaille by Hans Holbein the Elder, works by Lucas Cranach the Elder and, most important of all, Albrecht Dürer's The Madonna of the Rose Garlands painted in 1506 for the church of the German colony in Venice. It is the first group portrait in German art, portraying the Virgin crowning Maximilian I and the Christ Child crowning Pope Julius II. This picture was once in Rudolf II's collection. It was sold at auction for a derisory sum by Josef II in 1782 and from 1792 until 1934, when it was bought by the State, it was in the Strahov Monastery.

The Spanish School is represented by a fine El Greco and a portrait by Goya of Don Miguel de Lardizabal.

The collection of 19 and 20C European art includes works by the major Impressionists and post-Impressionists, the

Cubists including Picasso, and the Expressionists with sculpture by Bourdelle, Maillol and Rodin.

Returning to Hradčany Square you can see one of the few original gaslamps depicting a heavily draped Allegory of Prague. These lamps were manufactured by the Komárov Ironworks in 1867 to a design by A. Linsbauer. Gas lighting was installed between 1865 and 1868 and electricity arrived in 1890. However, it was not until the 1960s that most of the gaslamps in Prague were converted to electricity. The city authorities must be congratulated on re-using all the gaslamps, thus giving the centre of Prague such charm.

On the far side of the square, with distinctive sgraffiato decoration, much romanticized in the 19C, when the walls of the building were crenellated, is the Museum of Arms and Armour (2/135). Originally started for the Lobkovic family in 1545 by Agostino Galli, it eventually came into the hands of the Schwarzenberg family. In 1871, Josef Schulz restored it and created the present fantasy. The Nazis took it over during the Second World War and made it into a museum of the German Army. It has some fine Renaissance ceilings on the second floor although these are under lock and key and cannot be seen unless the keyholder happens to be in the museum that day. This interesting museum is only open from May to September, and an alternative site for the collection is being discussed.

Crossing the square once more, the Marian column in the centre of the square is by Brokof, 1724–8. From the National Gallery to the end of the square, the remaining houses belonged to the 'close' of the Archbishop's Palace and they feature a variety of façades. Number 10/62 is on the site of the home of Peter Parler. Farther on, the Martinic Palace (8/67) on the corner of the square, with its interesting sgraffiato decoration probably much restored, dates from 1580. It is now the office of the chief architect of the city of Prague. Walk through into the courtyard to find remains of the late 16C designs of the Labours of Hercules. No. 11/68 with its late Baroque façade originally belonged to the bishop of Prague, and No. 6/65 was the house of Alfons Mucha whose stained-glass window is so prominent in the cathedral. His designs for Czech stamps may be enjoyed in the Stamp Museum (see p. 157). Mucha's son is a well-known writer who lives here now, and the house contains a collection of the artist's work but is not open to the public.

At the end of the square (5/182) rises the Toscana Palace, previously the Thun-Hohenstein Palace, built between 1669 and 1691, after Mathey. The statues on the pediment are by J. Brokof. St Michael can be seen vigorously dragon-killing on the corner. He was the patron saint of Michael Thun, who commissioned the building and the St Michael is the work of Ottaviano Mosto, *c.*1693. The colours used on the façade of the palace are said to be the same as those originally used. At No. 4/183 were the cloisters and church of the Czech Barnabite Order, founded in 1626. More recently, this was made into a luxury hotel for the top brass of the Communist world. Fidel Castro and Nikita Khrushchev were among its guests. While Khrushchev was in power the Barnabite Committee debated here in the 50s the so-called 'crimes' against the Communist Party. This committee was finally disbanded in 1969.

Leave the square by the Loretánská. On your left you will pass the old Town Hall of the Hradčany (1/173) with its remnants of sgraffiato and fresco. Notice the keystone above the door bearing the symbol of Prague. Just to the right of the door is the measure (a *braccia*) for yarn. Continue up past a very Roman Baroque palace (4/181) on the other side, the Martinic Palace, attributed to Carlo Fontana, 1702–5. It now houses the Prague Castle guard. It is also mentioned as the hospital in the novel *The Good Soldier Svejk* by Jaroslav Hašek. Here is yet another robust gaslamp. At the No Entry sign, turn right into U kasáren and peer through the basement windows into the old stables of the adjoining palace. At the bottom of the hill, on your left is the beautiful Church of St John Nepomuk by K. I. Dientzenhofer. The church was built for the adjacent Ursuline convent which has an attractive courtyard to the right of the church. The ceiling frescos are by

V. V. Reiner. Opening hours are erratic, but the church is open for Mass on Saturdays at 20.00 or ask at the Archbishop's Palace.

Bearing left off the U kasáren will take you into one of the most enchanting corners of Prague, the Nový Svět or New World. It is a district of small houses set amidst winding lanes, quite cut off from the world. It is now most fashionable but once housed the poor. Tycho de Brahe the astronomer to Rudolf II, lived at No. 1/76. On your left is a gateway to the gardens of the Capucian Order. The great wall at the end is all that remains of the Baroque fortifications of Prague. Turn left when you reach the fortifications and you will find yourself at the back of the Černín Palace (5/101). To explain the grandeur of this palace it is worth knowing that Count Humprecht Černín was an important ambassador in Rome, Venice and Istanbul. On his return to Prague, he wanted to build a superb house and went, naturally, to Bernini. The great Italian architect, however, was too busy on his abortive façade for the Louvre. The architect chosen in the end was Francesco Caratti and the interior was designed by F. M. Kaňka with paintings by V. V. Reiner on the staircase. You will now be passing the garden wall on your right. Inside, the garden was restored in the 1920s as was much of the interior of the palace, but a great deal was left unfinished. Already at the end of the 18C the palace was in the hands of the military and became the Ministry of Foreign Affairs. It was reconstructed by P. Janák between 1928 and 1932. During the war it became the seat of the Nazi occupiers, including the infamous Nazis Heydrich and Frank. It was from a window in this palace that Jan Masaryk, son of the first president of Czechoslovakia and ex-ambassador to London, fell to his death. There is still much speculation as to what happened but at least nowadays people can speculate out loud.

Facing the Černín Palace, look to your right across to the small buildings (1602) that once belonged to the Capuchins. This was a favourite Order of Rudolf II and the abbot was his second confessor. You will see cannonballs embedded like raisins in the walls: these came from the Prussian bombardment of 1757. The cloisters were, for a time, the offices of the secret police under the Communists.

In the pavement to the left of the Černín Palace is a circle. This marks the site of the Chapel of St Matthew built by Kaňka but only in existence until the 1790s. There must have been an interesting contrast in scale between palace and church. Behind you is the great Loretto Church of the Nativity (7/100). The façade, 1720–2, is patently by K. I. Dientzenhofer, with sculpture by J. B. Kohl-Severa. The bells here are famous; the clarion, 'We Greet Thee a Thousand Times' which is rung at midday was created by the clockmaker, P. Naumann in 1694. Note the figures of 1722 by Quitainer on the terrace in front of the façade. Entering the monastery, the ticket office is on the left and is one of the few places in Prague where good guide books can be bought. Go through into the cloisters. Here there is discomfort in both the scale and style of the architecture. In the centre of the cloister sits the Santa Casa, the House of Mary, designed before the monastery in 1626–31 by Giovanni Domenico Orsi and A. Allio. It looks foreign, like some late Roman altar. Originally covered in fresco, the Scenes from the Life of the Virgin in stucco were added in 1664. The patroness was a devout Spaniard, Benigna Kateřina of Lobkovic, who also donated the diamonds on a monstrance in the Treasury (see p. 64). The dark interior of this little shrine is dedicated to the Lobkovic family whose name is emblazoned on the red lacquer screen. There is a fine early 18C altar frontal and some arm reliquaries on the altar. The overall feeling is sombre despite the contrast provided by the dancing putti on the cornice. The statues of saints in their niches show the influence of Michelangelo.

Flanking the House of Mary, on either side, are statues of the Ascension of the Virgin and the Resurrection of Christ of 1739 and 1740. The cloisters surrounding this were begun in 1661 although not finished until 1740 by K. I. Dientzenhofer. Continue round the cloister, noting the chapels in the corners, especially the N chapel, with an altar dedicated to St Francis

Seraphin with a painting by Brandl and sculptures by M. V. Jäckel of 1718. The Church of the Nativity (1734–5) is behind the Santa Casa and is by J. G. Aichbauer, half-brother of K. I. Dientzenhofer. This has a marvellous rich interior, well-restored. The ceiling frescos in the chancel are by V. V. Reiner and the carvings of 1636–7 are by M. Schönherr.

Opposite the entrance are the stairs to the magnificent treasury. I would suggest going just before closing time and with luck you will be by yourself in front of the superb Diamond Monstrance of 1698 designed by Fischer von Erlach. It was made by two Viennese silversmiths. The diamonds are said to have come from the court dress that Countess Lobkovic is wearing in her portrait outside in the upper passage of the cloister. But descriptions do no justice to a design in which the vision of St John on Patmos can rarely have been so imaginatively conceived. Note also the fine Lobkovic Monstrance decorated with coral, a symbol of the Passion, made in Prague in 1673; the Wallenstein Monstrance (1721), with its chalice; the Ring Monstrance and the Big Pearl Monstrance, dripping with baroque pearls.

On leaving the Loretto, continue up the hill leaving the Černín Palace on your right. To your left stretches the Pohořelec, an area which was destroyed by fire in the 15C. The name Pohořelec means 'burnt wasteland'. Platzer was the author of the statue of St John Nepomuk in the centre of this impressively wide street. There is a hospital and church to your left and the Swedish Embassy just to the left of that, with the finest view in Prague. The house was built in the 1930s by Eliška Junkova, a celebrated female racing driver with a love of Bugatti motorcars. The neo-Renaissance house directly ahead is currently owned by the army. During the summer concerts are given in the courtyard. The most attractive Rococo palace in the Pohořelec area is the Kučera Palace of 1775–80.

On your left are dark, steep steps up through the wall into one of the greatest centres of culture in Bohemia – the Strahov Monastery and library. Since the monks were thrown out of Prague in 1954, the cloisters of the monastery have been given over to a display of Czech illuminated manuscripts, printing techniques and modern literature. It is well worth visiting and contains facsimiles of many fine and interesting manuscripts, but be prepared for the fact that it is geared to schools and is therefore rather didactic. Now, as a remarkable result of the 'Velvet Revolution', the monks are returning to this great Premonstratensian monastery, founded in 1140 by Vladislav II. Thankfully, they are planning to keep the series of remarkable libraries open to the public. What you see now has been rebuilt several times, although the medieval foundations still exist. Above the entrance is a carving of St Norbert with angels. The buildings in the courtyard are late Baroque, but on your right you will see some remains of the Romanesque building. The bronze lion in the courtyard is by B. Kafka. The main entrance hall of the monastery was frescoed by Siard Nosecký, who was a member of the Order.

Upstairs, walk past the monks' cells, until you come to a massive door. Here is pure delight. First comes the Theological Library (1671–9), by Orsi and again decorated by Nosecký, the in-house painter, between 1723 and 1727. The most ancient manuscript in the library dates from the 9C and some of the bookcases are magnificent examples of 18C Bohemian cabinet-making. It is, however, the whole – the books, their bindings, the shelving, stucco and paint – which together make up one of the most atmospheric interiors in Prague. This library can still be used by the specialist public. The bookcases now to the left are magnificent examples of 18C Bohemian cabinet-making. Next, you come to the Philosophical Library, evidently later in date (1782–4). The ceiling fresco of 1794 by the Viennese painter Franz Anton Maulpertsch, depicting the History of Mankind, is one of the painter's last works and not one of his best. The beautiful furnishings are by Jan Lahofer. This room and its collections have a strange history. It started life as a monastic barn. Under Josef II, all the libraries throughout Bohemia, with one or two exceptions, were closed, along with the monasteries, and the books were brought here, where the abbot, Václav Mayer, was a close friend of Josef's. The emperor, who loathed Bohemian, by bringing the books here, unwittingly set up a monument to the language. One is left wondering if he would enjoy seeing his profile by Palliardi on the library façade. The abbot was a clever man.

Coming out of the libraries and walking through the courtyard towards the gate at the other end, you will see on your left the façade of the Church of St Mary. It dates from the mid-18C and is decorated with sculpture by J. A. Quitainer. The interior, in which Mozart once played, is in lavish Baroque of 1601–27, and has been newly restored. The church however still retains its original Romanesque basilica form. I. J. Palliardi was the stuccoist, and Ignác Raab the Jesuit painter worked here. There are also frescos by Josef Kramolín and Neunherze depicting the Life of St Norbert, the founder of the Order who is buried here. Bohemian late Gothic forms are included in this Baroque fantasy and there are some good 18C confessionals.

On your right as you go towards the gate, is a curiosity. The Church of St Roch, now an exhibition space, was a votive church founded by Rudolf II in thanks for the ending of the plague. It was given a central plan by its Italian builders, with side chapels dating from 1603–12 dedicated to SS Salvator, Roch and Anthony. 'Gothic survival' may be one way to describe its architecture, an almost unique form of Baroque, found also in England at the end of the 17C.

Go out of the gate, turn left and follow the road up to Petřín Hill, now a public park. The word 'petřín' comes from the medieval Latin for 'stone', and it was from this land that much of Prague derived its building materials. In the 19C under Governor Chotek, several private gardens in the area were bought by the city and merged. The present gardens were created by J. Braul around 1836. At the top of the hill (which can also be reached by funicular), are the remains of the Hunger Wall, built by Charles IV to give work to the starving. From afar, the two most striking buildings in the park are the Observatory and the replica Eiffel Tower. This latter was built by The Club of Czech Tourists who had seen the Eiffel Tower at the International Exhibition in Paris in 1889. They then raised the money to build a replica tower one-third the size in 1891. Many years ago there was a restaurant here as well as a viewing platform, but nowadays it is a sad skeleton. There once was a plan to remove it and replace it with a television transmitting tower.

Walk a little farther and you come to the Church of St Lawrence which has Romanesque foundations. Nearby are two more chapels, one a copy of the Chapel of the Holy Sepulchre (1845) by Johann Ferdinand Schorr and the other, to the left of the church, containing a Calvary. This chapel marks the ultimate halt in a *via sacra* of 14 chapels which was to wind its way down the hill to the Malá Strana. The next building has a funfair quality. It is a Hall of Mirrors built in 1891, the last room of which contains a panorama of the battle against the Swedish troops in 1648. Every Saturday in the summer months there is open-air theatre in the gardens.

Walk past the Observatory which is open for public star-gazing from 19.00 to 22.00 each evening. It was adapted from a 19C house in 1927–8. There is an extensive rose garden, separate from the Observatory, laid out in the 1930s. To the right, in the distance, rise the student flats of Charles University. Following the path, continue down to the charming sunken alpinum of 1800 and arrive at a further part of the Hunger Wall.

There are two restaurants on the hill. One called Nebozízek is for tourists, but fear not, if you arrive after 21.30 you will find a seat and locals eating. Immediately beneath the restaurant is the funicular railway, built in 1891 and with trains running every 10 minutes, from 06.00 to midnight. From here is a view of the new, box-like suburbs of N, S and N-W Prague.

3
THE MALÁ STRANA

The Malá Strana or Lesser Town spreads beneath the castle to the banks of the River Vltava. The gardens of its palaces abutting the castle hill merge with those of the castle. Always an area of wealth and style, this is one of the most pleasant areas in Prague in which to live. There is a great sense of space and elegance amidst the beautiful gardens, churches and palaces. In the fifties it was very run-down and it was possible to buy the glory of a house with a painted ceiling and good stucco if you were prepared to do without the luxury of heating and hot water. The so-called Lesser Town was founded in 1257 by King Otakar II on the site of an ancient market and some scattered villages. For the period, a remarkable sense of town planning is shown here with the main square, the Malostranské náměstí or Lesser Town Square in the centre and, running from it to the castle, the wide Nerudova Street, and Mostecká, leading to Charles Bridge and Letenská. Under Charles IV, around 1360, the town was enlarged and surrounded by a new wall, known as the Hunger Wall (see p. 66). In 1419 the town suffered greatly because of the Hussite Wars, with many of the churches being destroyed and their contents damaged or the churches merely being left incomplete. In 1541 a fire consumed most of the town and much of the castle. The conflagration began in the lower half of the square at the point where the houses are set back a little from the pavement.

The aftermath of the Battle of the White Mountain in 1620, saw a building boom in Prague and the surrounding country under the Habsburgs and their Catholic allies. The buildings of this period – palaces, churches and monasteries – were in the Baroque style akin to that found in Bavaria, Turin and Rome. The Baroque had already made an appearance in Prague before 1620 and it was used by both Protestants and Catholics. But its lavish, dramatic style proved the perfect vehicle of the Counter-Reformation in the battle against the heresy of Protestantism and the power of the Estates. This must surely be one of the most beautiful forms of propaganda. Both Stalin and Hitler should have taken note of the aesthetics.

What was astonishing in Prague at this time was the exceptional quality of all the arts, not merely architecture and painting, but the work of the stuccoists, woodcarvers, furniture-makers and glassworkers. That such high quality was possible was due in part to experienced craftsmen being imported from other Habsburg lands but even more important was the nucleus of craftsmen already based in the Italian quarter, from the period of Rudolf II. The Italian quarter is to be found in the Malá Strana, its lovely pantiled roofs spreading under the castle walls.

The Malá Strana

The Italian quarter – the Lobkovic Palace – the Schönborn Palace – the Church of St Nicholas – the Town Hall – the Vrtba Gardens – the Church of Sta Maria della Vittoria – the Michna Palace – the Kinský Summer Palace

If you have taken the previous walk around the Hradčany leave the Strahov Monastery by Úvoz Street, the road originally connecting the Hradčany with the Malá Strana and marking the boundary between the two districts. If you are starting from Lesser Town Square, follow Nerudova Street uphill until you reach its continuation at Úvoz.

Standing in Úvoz Street, to your right is a fine panorama of Prague and the Petřín Hill (see p. 66). On either side of the street are attractive houses and among the more important is

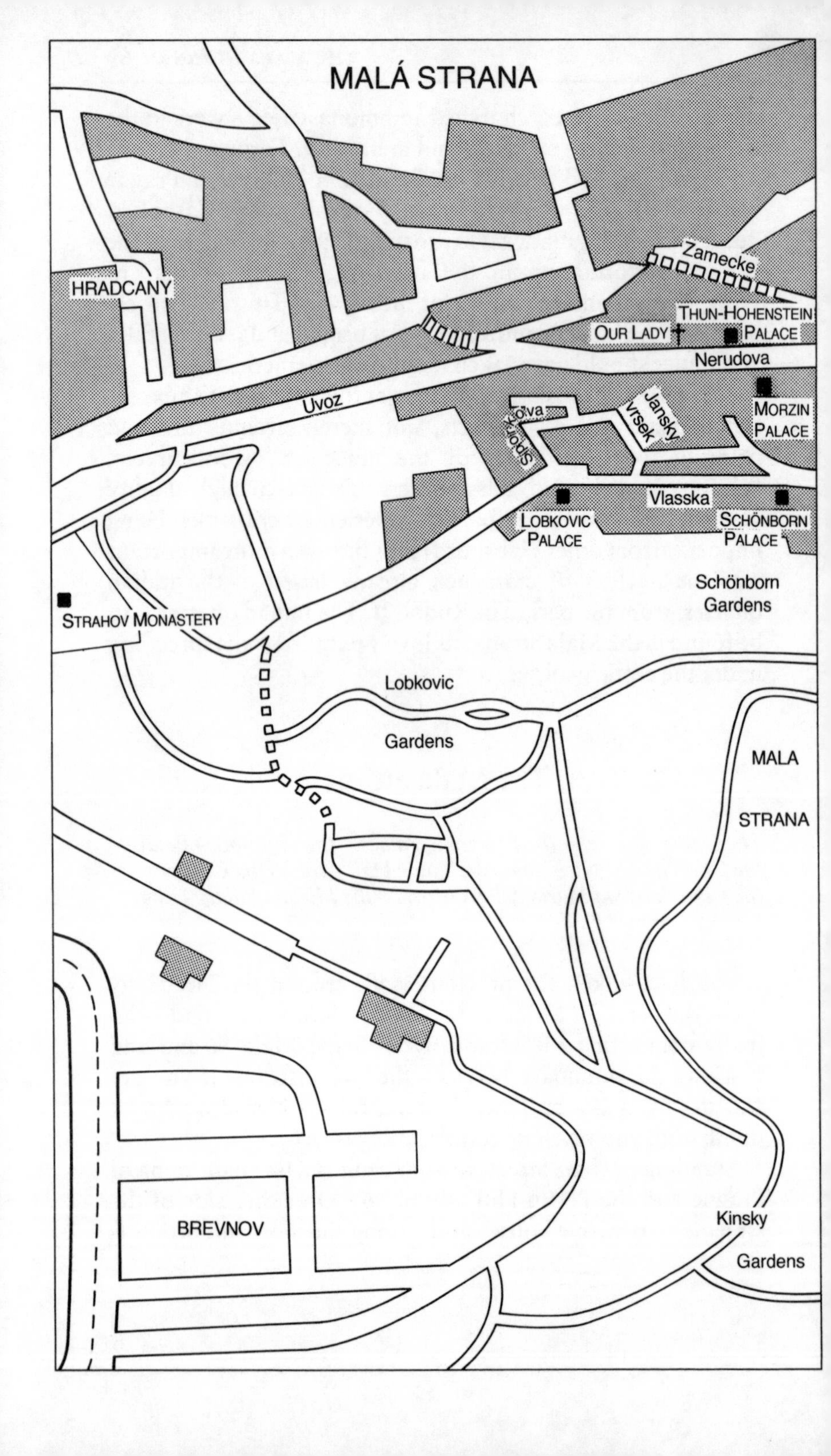

MALÁ STRANA
HRADCANY
Zamecke
THUN-HOHENSTEIN PALACE
OUR LADY
Nerudova
Uvoz
MORZIN PALACE
Jansky vrsek
Sporkova
Vlasska
LOBKOVIC PALACE
SCHÖNBORN PALACE
Schönborn Gardens
STRAHOV MONASTERY
Lobkovic Gardens
MALA STRANA
BREVNOV
Kinsky Gardens

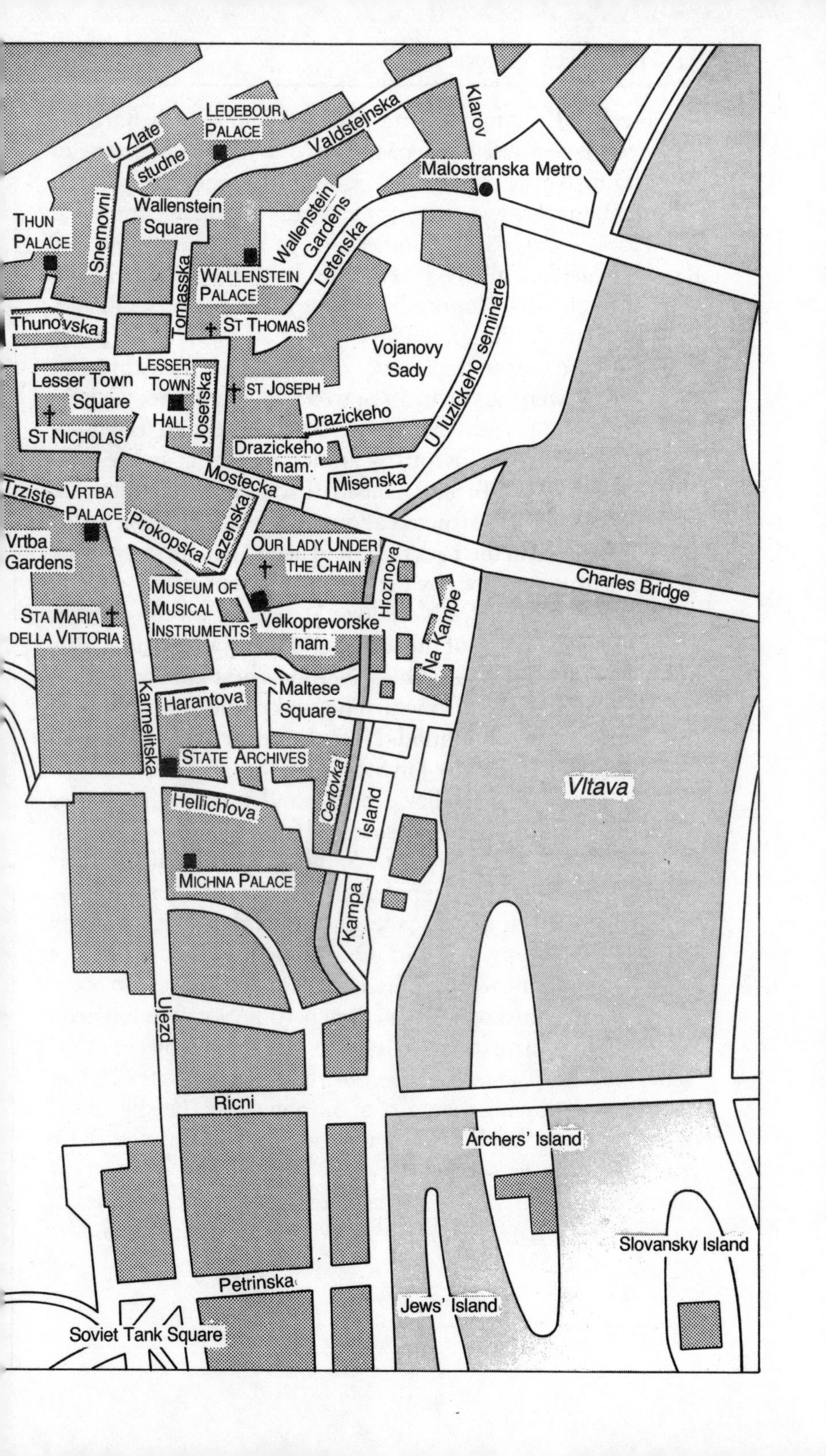

Ledebour Palace
U Zlate studne
Valdstejnska
Klarov
Malostranska Metro
Snemovni
Wallenstein Square
Thun Palace
Wallenstein Gardens
Letenska
Wallenstein Palace
Tomasska
Thunovska
St Thomas
Vojanovy Sady
U luzickeho seminare
Lesser Town Square
Lesser Town Hall
Josefska
St Joseph
St Nicholas
Drazickeho
Drazickeho nam.
Mostecka
Misenska
Trziste
Vrtba Palace
Prokopska
Lazenska
Vrtba Gardens
Our Lady Under the Chain
Hroznova
Na Kampe
Charles Bridge
Museum of Musical Instruments
Sta Maria della Vittoria
Velkoprevorske nam.
Karmelitska
Harantova
Maltese Square
State Archives
Certovka
Island
Vltava
Hellichova
Michna Palace
Kampa
Ujezd
Ricni
Archers' Island
Slovansky Island
Petrinska
Jews' Island
Soviet Tank Square

the so-called Columna Cellata (24/160), a tiny, early Baroque house with, as house sign, a Marian column with its statue of the Virgin. It was erected in 1706 by its owner the painter, Kristián Luna. He was responsible for the pilgrimage church at Bílá Hora (see p. 186). Number 48/171 has a charming, late Baroque façade. Called At the Gold Star, it was erected around 1730 probably by Alliprandi. The façade is not very satisfactory; perhaps the design is a little heavy. Alongside, the Town Hall staircase rises to the Hradčany Town Hall. The statues at the roadside were put up in 1714 by a nobleman who, wishing to curry favour with the Habsburgs, chose two favourite Habsburg saints – St Joseph, by Francesco Santini and St John Nepomuk, by M. J. Brokof. Ahead of you the serpentine walk to the castle was constructed about 1640. Before Úvoz Street was constructed in the 14C, there had been a rough, steep track or else visitors mounted by the Town Hall staircase.

Úvoz Street becomes Nerudova Street and on the right at 47/233 was the home of the writer and poet Jan Neruda. This house has early Baroque gables. Neruda's best known work is the *Malá Strana Tales*, in which he evokes the atmosphere of this district of his childhood. Note the attractive fountain on your left, 'The Toilet', by Jan Štursa, 1908.

Úvoz Street is of medieval origin and was of importance when the kings of Bohemia processed from the Royal Court in the Old Town (see p. 131) to St Vitus' Cathedral for their coronation. Note the flagpoles on the houses. Many of the houses were given new façades in the Renaissance and then again in the late 17 and 18C. On the right is Bretfeld Palace (33/240), built in 1765 by Wirch, the same architect who rococofied the Archbishop's Palace (see p. 56). Note the fine iron balcony. Here, in this house, Mozart and Casanova met in 1787.

Beyond this palace, turn to your right down into the Italian quarter by following the stairs of St John's Hill (Jánský vršek) to the bottom. Behind the gates on the left was the main cemetery of the Italian quarter, now largely built over and the tombs removed. Many of the court artists and architects, inhabitants of the Italian quarter, were buried here, including such luminaries as Spranger and Heintz, both painters for Rudolf II, and the Baroque architect Santini. Indeed, Spranger's tomb still rests in the cellars in an adjoining house (2/322).

Take the street straight ahead into Šporkova Street. The Sporck Palace (12/321) formerly belonged to the Piccolomini family. Jan Testa Piccolomini had the garden façade rebuilt by Santini de Bossi, probably in the 1660s, but the main front is late Baroque, *c.*1730. The Emblem of the Holy Trinity (10/320) belonged to the Guild of the Stonecutters and there used to be a statue of a stonecutter above the door. As each separate town in Prague had its own town hall and guild system, such guild buildings proliferate. There are good Rococo mouldings on four floors of this five-storey building. Only the façade is worth looking at: like so many other houses, this one was turned into flats in the 19C. The 18C owner, one Ondrej Kranner, carved the statue standing beside the pavement. At 8/319 stands the enchanting former garden pavilion of the house.

Continue down Šporkova Street, into the heart of the old Italian quarter. On the right (14/335), is the Italian Orphanage. As you will see from the plaque on the wall, this was founded by the Italians as the Congregation of the Virgin in 1575. Farther along on your left is the hospital (23/339) built in 1602 by Domenico de Bossi and within it is an early Baroque church, St Carlo Borromeo also by de Bossi. The interior, now a lecture theatre, has stucco decoration from the mid-17C. The complex of buildings belongs to the Italian Embassy.

Italian names appear sporadically in the royal accounts from the end of the 15C. But it was only after the accession of the Habsburgs to the throne of Bohemia in 1526, that the trickle became a flood of immigration. These Italians came mainly from the north of Italy, the area of the lakes and the valleys along the Swiss border. They were, in the main, architects and stuccoists, and a flourishing colony was established by the middle of the 16C. The Italians had a virtual monopoly in the building trade until the 1680s.

Opposite the hospital is the stunning façade of the German Embassy, once the Chinese Embassy and originally the Lobkovic Palace (19/347). It was built in 1702–8 for František Karel Přehorovský, by Giovanni Battista Alliprandi, a pupil of Fischer von Erlach. The façade was originally more interesting, with the side bays being one floor lower than the central block. The side wings were raised to the height of the main block in 1769 by I. J. Palliardi, when the Lobkovic family owned the palace. Tommaso Soldati was the stuccoist for the beautiful *sala terrena* – a sort of cross between a *porte cochère* and atmospheric garden room – and frescos were carried out by J. J. Stevens of Steinfels when, in 1717–24, the palace was in the hands of the Kolowrats of Liebstein. The *sala terrena* is visible from the street. The statues on the pediment and in the gardens are by Lorenzo Mattielli from Vienna. The terraced gardens, haven of thousands of East German refugees in 1989, were planned in 1703 in the Italian style by J. J. Kapula. In 1793, following the latest English fashion, a picturesque park was laid out. Here, the Lobkovic founded one of the earliest botanical gardens in Prague. You can still see vestiges in the upper terraces of the early Baroque garden. These comprise a bear pit, hothouse and aviary. Next to the palace is the famous Lobkovic *vinárna* or tavern, serving wines from its vineyards at Mělník, north Bohemia.

Leaving the Lobkovic Palace, walk on down the hill to the American Embassy (15/365) formerly the Schönborn Palace (15/365) whose original owners, the Colloredo, were important militarily during the Thirty Years' War. It was built in 1643–56 by Carlo Lurago, although it was probably Giovanni Battista Alliprandi who enlarged the building in 1715–18. In 1917 Franz Kafka lived here. The *sala terrena* is decorated with giants from the Braun workshop and is visible from the road as part of the reception area of the embassy. In the garden there is a fine staircase of 1715 just visible through the gate.

In front of the American Embassy is a house of 1704–5 (2/303), At the Figure of Jesus, possibly by Santini, with a wonderful rolling façade, but now alas in a poor state of repair. The historian František Palacký lived here. He was one of the leaders of reform during the nationalist revival. Turn up the small lane beside it, leaving the Santini house on your left. In this dark medieval labyrinth is the restaurant Baráčnická Rychta, meeting place of the newly formed Society of the Friends of the Malá Strana.

Tunnel your way out into Nerudova Street again. Opposite is the Church of Our Lady of Unceasing Succour at the Theatines, 1697–1717, possibly designed by J. B. Mathey, with its façade completed by Santini. This was a convent owned by the Theatines, the first of the crusading Orders founded before the Jesuits in 1524. The interior contains fine Baroque sculpture on the High Altar by M. V. Jäckel, and a painting by J. V. Callot. The sculpture on the side altars is by J. O. Mayer, and there are paintings by M. Halwachs, F. X. Balko and others.

Next in Nerudova Street is the great high Baroque palace of the Thun-Hohensteins (20/214), again by Santini but with the collaboration of the great sculptor, M. B. Braun. His is the magnificent portal with the two eagles – the crest of the Kolowrat family, the original owners of the palace – and the statues of Jupiter and Juno. This palace is fairly typical of the building development in the Malá Strana. The plots of land can first be dated to ownership in the 13C, hence the aggrandizing owners of the 17 and 18C had to build on whatever space was available, gradually buying up their next-door neighbours. The other part of this palace, belonging originally to the Hradec family, faces on to Thunovská Street. The palace came to the Thuns of Hohenstein in 1768 and it is now the Italian Embassy.

Farther down Nerudova Street, No. 18/213, the House at St John Nepomuk still sports fragments of the original sgraffiato dated 1566 and just visible now under the crumbling Rococo stucco. Note that the emblems on the houses down this street are most attractive. The house signs, used for identification before Josef II ordered conventional house numbering around 1784, often referred to the occupation of the inhabitants. One house belonged to a goldsmith, Bartolomej Schumann at 16/212; another, at 12/210, to three generations of violin-makers called Edlinger, whose founder family member was Tomáš who lived in 1662–1729.

At No. 5/256 is the Morzin Palace, again by Santini, with the happy collaboration of Brokof who sculpted the fine moors supporting the balcony in 1713–14. The modelling of these moors – a reference to the family crest – repays study. Above the two side doors are a beautifully modelled Day and Night. The Morzin Palace is now the Romanian Embassy.

On the corner, before you enter the Malostranské náměstí, refresh yourself with a Pilsner beer at No. 2, the House of the Black Cat. Beware, however. After you have placed your first order, further half-litres come willy-nilly and are put in front of you, until you decline. You pay your bill on the way out.

Moving into the hub of the Malá Strana, you go from a fascinating labyrinth into the world of town planners – those of the 13C who were extraordinarily farsighted. The large Lichtenstein Palace (2/258) of 1791 opposite the Church of St Nicholas has seen many a change of political fortune. In 1848 Prince Windischgrätz turned it into the headquarters of his General Staff; it then became a special school for the Communist Party and is now being restored as the Academy of Music.

Opposite is one of the greatest Baroque churches in Prague, the Church of St Nicholas, and the Jesuit College. The church and monastery divide the Malostranské náměstí in two. In front of St Nicholas' is the Column of the Holy Trinity of 1715 by J. O. Mayer and the architect Alliprandi. The angels round the base are an addition of 1772. The column was erected after a plague epidemic of 1713 and the angels after a famine of 1772. It should be noted that there is a church of St Nicholas in each of the parishes in Prague as St Nicholas was the patron saint of the law, the poor, and business, all of which flourished.

The Jesuit College of the Malá Strana was founded in 1628,

under the patronage of Albrecht Wallenstein. Prior to this, on this site in the Middle Ages stood twenty burghers' houses, with the Romanesque Church of St Wenceslas at one end, and the Gothic Church of St Nicholas, which had heard the preaching of some of the great 14C reformers, at the other. The Jesuits, in spite of starting their building from scratch, retained the medieval dedication to St Nicholas.

The Church of St Nicholas was built in two stages as the money came in. In the first building campaign, Kryštof Dientzenhofer built the W façade and the first few bays of the nave in 1702–11. His son Kilián Ignác continued the work from 1737 until he died in 1751. The exterior was completed in 1755. This building programme from W to E meant that the Gothic E end was retained until the last moment. St Nicholas' was the first example in Prague of the late Italianate style of Baroque. The broken pediments and the play of convex and concave mass recall something of Borromini in Rome and Guarini in Turin, both architects seminal for Bohemian Baroque. The Kolowrat family gave money for the church as one of their family belonged to the Jesuit Order and it was here they chose to be buried. The voice of the Jesuits is heard on the façade, with the Doctors of the Church at gallery level, and the Jesuit saints, St Ignatius and St Francis Xavier with SS Peter and Paul in between them, higher up. All were carved by J. B. Kohl–Severa. The whole glorious façade is topped by St Nicholas with the victorious Habsburg double-headed eagle beneath. These grand buildings, both seminary and church, set in one of the most important squares in the city, could not have been a clearer statement from the victors of the Battle of the White Mountain.

As you enter the church, note the pure drama – the darkened nave leading you to a burst of light at the E end. The sense of theatre is heightened by the glorious colour scheme of pale pinks, greens and creams mixed with gilded, gesticulating figures. The pulpit is sheer fantasy. Touch the 'marble' and discover that it is not what it seems but beautifully painted plaster – scagliola.

Starting on the right of the w door is the Chapel of St Anne. Beneath the floor is the family vault of the Kolowrats. The high Baroque altar with its twisted columns in varied marbles is by members of the Platzer family. On the altar is a Flemish painting of moderate quality of the Virgin, Child and St Anne. Note that the remainder of the decoration of this peanut-shaped chapel is in scagliola, and warm to the touch. Joseph Redemayer and Joseph Hager carried out the frescos.

The first three bays leading round from the w door are by Kryštof Dientzenhofer and the remainder of the nave to the crossing is the work of his son, K. I. Dientzenhofer. The fresco in the nave of the Celebration of the Life of St Nicholas was painted in 1761, by Jan Lukáš Kracker, a Hungarian. It comes as no surprise to learn that he was trained in Vienna in the Maulbertsch workshop. It is a *tour de force* of *trompe-l'œil* and a strange mixture of secular and religious themes. Behind you is a magnificent organ above which is a fresco dedicated to the Life of St Cecilia. Around the organ pipes putti abound and those playing French horns make playful silhouettes. In 1787 Mozart played on the organ here.

The altarpiece in the next chapel depicts the Marriage of St Catherine by Ignác Raab, himself a Jesuit. Platzer again was responsible for the statuary and it was from the Platzer workshop too, in the mid-18c, that the Jesuit saints flanking the nave came.

Next is the chapel of St Francis Xavier, with the painting of the death of the saint in China by Frans Xavier Balko; St John Nepomuk painted by Ignác Raab and a Virgin and Child, possibly German of the 16c.

At the crossing under the dome the walls bulge into the side chapels; look at the saints on the piers of the crossing, including St Gregory and St Basil. The painting on the altar is the Death of St Joseph by Kracker, with a St John the Baptist and a St John the Evangelist sculpted by Platzer. The High Altar is topped by a copper St Nicholas surrounded by putti. The St Ignatius and St Francis Xavier on either side are of wood. Note the good altar rails.

The N transept is dominated by a Visitation by Kracker. There is also a copy here of the Black Madonna of St Foy, brought from Belgium during the Thirty Years' War. St Wenceslas and St Vitus stand up on the cornice with Adalbert, the first bishop of Prague, and St Procopius, the patron saint of the Slavs. Above the Visitation is the statue of St Sigismund, the patron saint of the Luxemburg dynasty, and St Ludmila, grandmother of St Wenceslas who persuaded the king to become a Christian. The painting in the dome celebrates the Holy Trinity, the spandrels beneath hold a painting of the Virtues. The pulpit, one of the highlights of the interior, is by Richard and Petr Prachner of 1765. Its swirling form makes the early stages of the building look positively staid. At the top of the pulpit, putti hold back gilded curtains, while the remainder is of scagliola of different colours and textures. The iconograpy concerns the life of John the Baptist. In the upper section he is prepared for his beheading and there is a fine Salome; below, in the vase of the pulpit, the saint preaches and baptizes Christ in the River Jordan. Faith, Hope and Charity sit precariously on the edge.

Walking westwards to the early chapels by Kryštof Dientzenhofer, the space is much less fluid. Next comes St Michael's Chapel with a painting of the saint by Solimena and an Ignatius and a St Elijah by Raab. Then the Chapel of St Barbara, the earliest part of the church. Its shape is so different from the Chapel of St Anne opposite. The fresco of the Last Judgement is by Josef Kramolín. This chapel holds the best painting in the church, The Crucifixion by Karel Škréta of 1646. The Jesuits commissioned a series of canvases of The Passion from Škréta, the remainder of which has now come to rest in the S gallery at the W end. You can just see them from where you stand now; they are tantalizingly inaccessible to the public.

The church took 150 years to build, with the decoration completed last in 1775. One can only feel for the Jesuits: when their Order was dissolved in 1777, they had only enjoyed the finished church for two years.

Leaving the Church of St Nicholas, on your left across the square, you can see a tunnel through a grand palace (12/259); this was one of the four gates of the Malá Strana. The others were situated on the Charles Bridge, at what is now the Italian Embassy and at the Wallenstein Palace. The gate facing you is the one through which the troops from Passau invaded Prague in 1611 on the orders of Matthias. The owners of the palace were the Hartig family and it was built about 1700 by Alliprandi. You will note that it is a typical example of Viennese Baroque – so much more severe than Prague Baroque.

Turning your back on the Church of St Nicholas, turn right up Zámecká, the narrow cobbled lane beside the House of the Black Cat. You are now facing a building (18/183) currently owned by the Red Cross. This was rebuilt and served as the German Embassy during the Nazi occupation of Prague. Masaryk, as a professor of Charles University, lived here before becoming president. Ahead is the New Castle Staircase of 1674: it was planned to decorate this with statues to continue the *via sacra* from Charles Bridge (see p. 55). The niches may be seen at the top of the staircase, but the project of 1722 was never realized. Walk straight on to the Slavata Palace. This is now part of the Italian Embassy and was designed by Orsi some time after 1678. It was originally built for a branch of the Rosemberg family in the second half of the 16C.

The house at the bottom of the staircase (19/196) has the remains of some interesting sgraffiato decoration, dated 1577. This was where the painter Spranger lived. Returning to the Red Cross building, the house opposite (20/184) by F. M. Kaňka of 1720 belonged to the Hartig family. On the other side of the street is a house (13/199) with Renaissance gables in poor repair from the end of the 16C. Notice at 15/198 the 16C doorway. Facing the Red Cross building to your right, is the *vinárna* or tavern called U Palcátu, named after a form of blunderbuss used by the Hussites.

Continue down Thunovská Street which inclines steeply to

the right. Its narrowness and the buttress across the street above your head, give a true sense of the medieval Malá Strana. On the left is the Thun Palace (14/180), now the British Embassy. The British bought it from Baron Thun in 1920, lock, stock and barrel. It was formerly the Leslie Palace, built by a Scottish mercenary who, in the Thirty Years' War, was implicated in the murder of Wallenstein, one of the most powerful men in Bohemia. So powerful indeed that the emperor had him killed. The palace was rebuilt *c.*1716–27 by Giovanni Antonio Lurago. In about 1850 the neo-Gothic gate was built. This has a distinctly Venetian air. During his first visit to Prague in 1787, Mozart lived here with his wife. Follow the street to the bottom and you turn into Sněmovní Street.

The large building in front of you (4/176) housed the parliament for the Republic of Czechoslovakia up until 1938. Now it only houses the senate for the Czech State. The Republic itself has two provincial parliaments, one in Prague for Bohemia and Moravia, and one in Bratislava for Slovakia. There is a third, federal parliament. The first Czech constitution was drawn up here in 1920. All that remains of the 18C building once belonging to the Thun family are the portals by Santini. After a fire in 1801 it was rebuilt by Palliardi. In the house opposite, by Giovanni Antonio Lurago, lived the priest of the Church of St Nicholas, after 1777. Notice the traces of an oriel window. Next door to this (5/175) is the Lažanský, formerly the Wallenstein Palace, of 1740. It was built by Kaňka and shows some of the eccentricity of his designs. The next house (7/174) was owned by the Černín and later the Sterreggov family. At the end of this street is a small square called Petikostelni which means five churches; notice the 19C name on the wall. In the Middle Ages there were five churches around the square, but the only one still extant is St Nicholas. The large house on the corner is the Bylandt-Rheidtovsky Palace (13/171) built in the last quarter of the 17C. Nearby at 2/165 is a charming Renaissance house with typical Bohemian gables called the House of the Golden Swan.

With your back to this square, turn towards the Church of

St Nicholas. There is an exciting sculptural doorway on your right, by Braun, which was the entrance to the Jesuit Gymnasium (1/17). The building is by K. I. Dientzenhofer the Younger of 1726. After 1777, when the Jesuits had been banned, this became the seat of the governor of Bohemia. There are now plans for gymnasia to be reinstated as part of Czechoslovakia's educational reforms.

When you are back in the main square of the Malá Strana, imagine it encircled with medieval houses set above arcades. After the fire in the Malá Strana in 1541, these were replaced by Renaissance buildings which in turn were replaced by the palaces you see today. But the sheltering arcades stayed in place. The back of the Jesuit College, at present part of Charles University, is a plain forbidding building by Orsi of 1670. What a contrast to the earlier Carolinum, where beauty of proportion and decoration were of the essence. The Jesuit College is unmistakenly the barracks of God's army. To the right is the house of the Smiřický family (6/18). Its façade dates from the second half of the 18C and is by Josef Jägr, an Austrian from the Tyrol. It was in this house that the conspirators met to plan the Defenestration of 1618. No. 7/19 by Alliprandi belonged to the Sternberg family. Note the family crest of a crown and an eight-pointed star, symbolizing their alleged descent from one of the three kings. This was the home of Count Caspar Sternberg, friend of Goethe and one of the promoters of the National Museum. It was here that the fledgeling collection of the Society of the Friends of the Arts was first housed between 1875 and 1884, a collection which became the core of the National Gallery (see p. 58). There is a narrow inset in the façade of the building, marking where the fire which destroyed half of the Malá Strana and the castle started in 1541.

With your back to the Jesuit College, ahead of you is one of the most important buildings in the Malá Strana, the former Town Hall (35/21), rebuilt by Giovanni Maria Filippi, court architect to Rudolf II, in 1617–22. The building once had gables, destroyed in the 19C. It stands on a rusticated arcade, the windows with their mullions and transoms still have their broken triangular pediments and the bays are divided with strapwork of Mannerist design. In 1575 in this Town Hall the text giving freedom of worship to both Protestants and Catholics, the so-called Czech Confession (see p. 9) was drawn up.

At the S end of the square is the Kaiserstejn Palace (37/23), built by Alliprandi about 1700 in Viennese style. It has statues of the Four Seasons on the roof and some fine vases by Ottaviano Mosto. This was the home of the celebrated opera singer Destinová who held her salon here. It is her bust that can be seen on the façade today. Throughout the Malá Strana notice the original black and white pavements, many now in need of repair.

Cross the road at the Makarská *vinárna* and turn right into Karmelitská Street. Before leaving Malostranské náměstí, look up at the tower of the Church of St Nicholas. This replaced the Gothic spire of the old St Nicholas' in the 18C. This tower was never the property of the Jesuit Church as the town tenaciously held on to it for fire-watching. Eventually the Jesuits were able to persuade the townspeople to rebuild the Gothic tower in Baroque style, but the Jesuits were forbidden to decorate it with Jesuit saints and they were forbidden to enter the tower from the church. But the Jesuits broke the agreement; you can see the consoles on the first and second storeys which once held statues. These were quickly removed by the townspeople and the door from the tower to the church was closed and made into a street door with a house number (556) and the emblem of the town.

Continue down Karmelitská Street. At No. 25/373 is the entrance to the exquisite Vrtba Gardens. Once a Renaissance palace, after 1709 it became the property of Count Vrtba who commissioned Kaňka to rebuild it for him. This was done with the collaboration of the Braun workshop, and V. V. Reiner who painted the *sala terrena* in the garden. Nothing but the best would do for the Count. Walk through the gateway, surmounted by a statue of Atlas, and up to your right you can catch a glimpse of the *sala terrena* which tops the four terraces of the spectacular garden. The terracing was adapted from the existing vineyards, as is the case in all the palace gardens backing on to Prague Hill. The statues here are of antique gods. As a plaque points out, Mikoláš Aleš, the 19C Czech painter, lived in the garden house.

Continue down Karmelitská Street to the Church of Sta Maria della Vittoria on the right at the top of a double flight of steps. The façade is severe: under the portico is a Madonna and Child in Majesty flanked on either side by obelisks. The church was built for the German Lutherans in Prague between 1611 and 1613, after the Letter of Majesty (1609) ensured freedom of worship once more to all (see p. 9). Giovanni Maria Filippi gave this early example of Roman Baroque to a Protestant Order. The ground plan was taken from Il Gesù and the façade was to mirror Sta Trinità dei Monte, both in Rome. After the Battle of the White Mountain in 1620, the Carmelites took over the church. One Carmelite warrior had found, in southern Bohemia, a small icon of a Madonna and had taken it with him into the battle. After the Catholic victory, the little Madonna was given the credit. The Carmelites transformed the Protestant church and rebuilt its façade in 1640, to the pattern of Sta Maria della Vittoria, in Rome. The cross at the base of the obelisks is the insignia of the Knights of Malta of whom the Carmelites' patron, Balthasar Huerta, was a member. Through the gate to the right of the church you can see the position of the original façade, under the stub of the steeple.

Inside, the austere black and white of the early Baroque makes an immediate impact. The nave is of the first quarter of the 17C and the altars are of the 1670s. Through the attractive iron grille on the right is an altar *c.*1700, with a copy of the Madonna above the entrance on the façade. The next altar on the right holds Petr Brandl's Annunciation to Joachim and Anna; notice the fine treatment of the still-life on the right of the canvas. The next altar is dedicated to the Bambino Gesù who has a huge wardrobe of rich and lavish costumes. This small statue was donated in 1628 by Maria M. de Lara. The altar itself was executed by F. M. Lauermann with statues by Petr Prachner of 1776. Amazingly, this church was left untouched by the Swedish troops in 1648, a miracle ascribed to the Bambino Gesù. Thereafter the Bambino became an object of pilgrimage and there are thanks offerings all around. More impressive perhaps than the Bambino's wardrobe is the glorious cabinet he is in. It was created in 1741 by Jan Pakeniho, one of the most important silversmiths working in Prague. More of his work can be seen in the Loretto Monastery (see p. 64).

The rich carving of the High Altar is by Johann Ferdinand Schorr and although it is difficult to see without binoculars, above the High Altar is a painting depicting the victory of the Battle of the White Mountain, showing the Carmelites holding aloft the small icon of the Madonna. High above this is a copy of the original, which ended up in Sta Maria della Vittoria in Rome but was destroyed by fire in the 19C. The paintings by Petr Brandl in the church are worth looking at. They include his St Simon Stock on the third altar on the left, and other works by him include SS Joseph, Joachim and Anna. The next two altars to the N and the pulpit were created by Matthew Zimprecht around 1669. Note the good carved pews and fine confessionals of 1739 by J. A. Geiger. After passing the pulpit notice a Madonna of the 16C; she is surrounded by a high-quality silver and gilt frame of the Rococo period. On leaving the church, look at the carved Crucifixion of 1700.

Cross the road by the traffic lights and the Rohan Palace faces you (98/386). It is an attractive neo-Classical building of 1839. Inside is a good ballroom by Louis Montoyer. The palace is now part of the Ministry of Education and is not open to the public. Ahead is the Church of St Mary Magdalene of the Domenican nuns. In the 13C a cloister was founded then, in the 17C, Caratti designed the first octagonal cupola in Prague for the Order. This became the church of the Michna family whose palace was close by. Incidentally, both the Dientzenhofers were originally buried in this church. Under Josef II, in the 1780s, the church was given to the army and the bodies were removed. The Dientzenhofers were reinterred in the Malostranský Old Cemetery at Košiře in Prague 5 (see p. 179). The church is now part of the State Archives.

Continuing along Karmelitská Street, to your left is the late Renaissance Michna Palace (450/40), now the Museum of Sport, with some good plasterwork in the interior. Ahead is the funicular railway to the Petřín Hill (see p. 66). Here, if you have time, is the moment to make a detour to the Kinský Summer Palace and Gardens, now the Museum of Costume. Continue down Újezd Street, past the first Soviet tank to enter Prague in 1945. Turn into Holečkova and ahead, in the gardens, now part of Petřín Hill, is a small, severely Classical villa begun in 1825 by Koch. The hothouses on the left now house people not plants. These gardens were laid out by J. Braul and Josef Thomayer, the most important gardeners in 19C Czechoslovakia. Beyond the wall behind the house is a huge neo-Baroque school for the deaf. There are two curiosities in the grounds, both of which were left behind after an important ethnographical exhibition held in 1895. One is found at the side of the house – a tiny timber campanile. The other, farther up the hill past the waterfall and surrounded by a protective fence, is a beautiful timber church covered in shingles and with turned balustrading and three onion domes. It dates to about 1780 and looks as if it has landed by magic carpet. Instead, it represents a small forgotten corner of Czech territory. It is from Zakarpatská Ukrajina, the Czech Ukraine or sub-Carpathian Ruthenia, first annexed by Hungary and later taken by the Soviet Union and never given back at the end of the war in 1945.

If you are wearing sensible shoes, it is possible to join the path up through the woods on Petřín Hill, past some of the 16 and 18C walling now made into lookout towers, with lovely views over the city. Continue to Nebozízek restaurant and the funicular station.

Along the Banks of the Vltava

Maltézské Square – the Nostic Palace – Kampa Island – Na Kampě – the Museum of Musical Instruments – the Church of Our Lady under the Chain – the Church of St Joseph – the Church of St Thomas – the Wallenstein Palace – Vojanovy Sady – Charles Bridge

If you are short of time, continue along Harantova into Maltézské náměstí, or Maltese Square. In the 17c this area was out of the jurisdiction of the town and was solely in the hands of the Knights of Malta, an honour which dates from the 12c. The Nostic Palace (1/471), now the Dutch Embassy, must have one of the richest façades in Prague. It was begun between 1658 and 1660 by Francesco Caratti for the Nostic family. The palace contained one of Bohemia's finest picture collections and here was not only a picture gallery, but also a collection of graphics, a most important library, and a collection of sculpture put together by Count Jan Hertvík Nostic in the 17c. In common with some of the other great families of Prague, Nostic bought from the Vienna branch of the Antwerp dealer, Guillermo Forchondt. The collection also increased when he inherited 90 paintings from Count František Antonín Berka of Dubá. He mainly collected Italian and Flemish paintings of the 16 and 17c and it appears that some of the paintings were bought from the Kunstkammer of Emperor Rudolf II. The library can still be seen despite the rebuilding of *c.*1735. The interiors were by Ambrozzi, the statues on top of the cornice balustrade are by Brokof the Younger, and 1765 is the date of the main portal and the first floor by A. Haffenecker. The family were patrons too of the historian Pelcel and Josef Dobrovský, a pioneer in the study of Bohemian history and language and the author of the first dictionary of Czech. His bust may be seen in the gardens of Kampa Island. Film buffs may like to know that Forman's *Amadeus* was filmed here in the Nostic Palace.

From the Nostic Palace continue round the back of the

Buquoy Palace, now the French Embassy, and into the narrow Nostic Street where, at 2/465, Kilián Ignác Dientzenhofer was born. There are also two attractive houses designed by him at 5/466 and 7/467. Return to the site of the former Nostic Garden with the Riding School on your right and one of the many 14C mills originally powered by the artificial canal, the Čertovka or Devil's Stream. Crossing the bridge, look back at the romantic view of the palaces backing on to the canal. The public park on Kampa Island consisted, until 1940, of private gardens belonging to these palaces. Surprisingly, it was the Nazis who made a gift of this public park to Prague. Look out from the embankment along the River Vltava to Charles Bridge and across to the far bank of the Staré Město with its neo-Renaissance water tower, now the Smetana Museum. Farther right is a house with a tower where Oskar Kokoschka lived and painted.

Walk around Kampa Island to the Sovovy mill, a fine neo-Gothic building destroyed by fire and left a ruin. There are now plans for a hotel here. Across the stretch of water are the three other islands, the Střelecký, where archers trained in their craft; the Dětský or Jews' Island, now given over to a children's playground; and the Slovanský which used to have a fine dance hall. Walk through the early Baroque gate returning to the Čertovka, viewing the back of the Michna Palace. This was built before 1650 and contains good stucco in the interior by Domenico Galli which seems rather wasted as the palace is now a Museum of Sports. The palace was never finished and eventually became the property of the powerful Schwarzenberg family who created a beautiful formal garden on the site. At the end of the 18C it became an arsenal. In 1922 it was rebuilt and adapted for Sokol. This was an international body one of whose founders, the Czech art historian Miroslav Tyrš, believed in the classical ideal of the human body being in harmony with the universe. Sokol was seen by the Austro-Hungarian Empire, and later by the Nazis, as a device to promote national education. Such was its power that both the Empire and then the Nazis dissolved it.

There follows a white villa which was the Jesuits' summer house. This area of the canal was used as Prague's first public swimming pool as the water was gin-clear up until 1950. Notice the bust of Dobrovský standing in front of the charming garden house which the Nostics gave him in the last years of his life. Round the corner, back in the street, you will see in the garden wall of 7/501, a bust of Zdeněk Wirth, founder of the movement for the preservation of historical monuments in Czechoslovakia. At different times Jan Werich the actor and Vladimír Holan the poet also lived in the house.

At 4/506 stands the imposing Lichtenstein Palace. It is so different now from when it was built in 1690 as a charming summer palazzo of only two floors. The neo-Renaissance height and grandeur were added by a mill owner, Odkolek. It was the same man who built Sovovy mill in neo-Gothic style. The Gestapo took over the Lichtenstein Palace during the war and it is now being refurbished for the federal government.

Return via a beautiful oblong square, Na Kampě, full of late 17 and early 18c houses. This was formerly the ceramic market and there are still a few potters' stalls at the far end near Charles Bridge. On the right-hand side is No. 512/11 where the composer Martinů lived. Just before the neo-Gothic staircase to Charles Bridge, on your left is a palace (1/498) designed by Bartolomeo Scotti in 1732 and originally built in 1604 by the pharmacist Jan Jiří Dyrynk of Rottenberg, the mayor of Malá Strana.

Keeping the palace on your right continue round the square and turn right into the narrow Hroznová Street. Ahead of you is the small house (1/500) from 1761 by Matthias Hummel, adapted in 1896 for Pavel Švanda ze Semčic, the theatre director. Just across the bridge on the right is the site of the originally Gothic Velkopřevorský mill. This part of the canal is being restored and the mill-wheel will be replaced. Gradually this whole area of Prague's Venice is being restored to its former elegance.

Ahead, leading off Hroznová Street and flanked by plane trees, is the charming Velkopřevorské Square. At No. 1/490 is the Renaissance Mettychů z Čečova Palace behind its Mannerist gate. The composer J. B. Foerster was born here in 1859. On the other side of the street, behind the John Lennon Wall, is the Maltese Garden where, in summer, concerts and plays take place. The John Lennon Wall was an important scene of student protest in the months running up to the 'Velvet Revolution'. The police had a continuous battle to keep the wall clear of anti-Communist posters and graffiti. The French Embassy is housed in the Buquoy Palace (2/486). Founded on the site of three houses in 1719, it was totally rebuilt by J. G. Aichbauer (half-brother of K. I. Dientzenhofer). The interiors were redesigned in the neo-Baroque style in 1896 by the versatile J. Schulz. On the other side of the road at No. 4/485, behind the Braun workshop portals, is the Grand Prior's Palace of 1725–9 by Bartolomeo Scotti. Within the emblem of the Knights of Malta are two vine pruners added by the Diettrichstein family who were owners of extensive vineyards. This lovely interior houses the important Museum of Musical Instruments. It used to display a fine series of Flemish tapestries but these were 'gifted' to von Ribbentrop, Hitler's foreign affairs advisor, never to be seen again.

As you walk round the corner to the museum entrance, notice the fine gateway to the left where Adrian Vredeman de Vries lived. Next to the museum is the Maltese Church, known as Our Lady Under the Chain. It is now a shadow of its former self. The church was founded to guard the Romanesque bridge across the Vltava, chains being placed across the route. The Romanesque origins are clearly visible in the W towers, the remaining wall of the nave and in the chancel. What parts of the church that were finished were damaged by the Hussites. The Renaissance W door sits strangely with the Gothic. The nave has gone and the tiny church in the former choir was adapted by Carlo Lurago in 1640–50. On the main altar is a Škréta painting of Our Lady with the old chains of the bridge hanging above Her head.

In front of the church we return to Maltézské náměstí. A statue of St John the Baptist, patron saint of the Knights of

Malta, stands in the centre. He once stood proudly in the centre of a fountain of 1715 by F. M. Brokof. Opposite, the Rococo Turba Palace (6/477), now the Japanese Embassy, was designed by the Austrian Josef Jägr. So pleased was he with the results, that he built his own house – the so-called Muscon – next door (475/5) around 1765. The yellow façade at 8/480 was the main post office in Prague. This lucrative sinecure was owned from 1554 to 1723 by the Thurn-Taxis family. There were many hotels in the area in the past. Leading off the corner of the square, in Prokopská Street is a house (3/625) whose strange apsidal shape reveals its origins as a church. In the other corner of the square is the famous *vinárna* U Malířů (At the Painter's) which belonged to a painter in the 16c, hence its name. It serves s Moravian wines and is closed on Sundays. Its neo-Renaissance interiors date from 1937.

Walk back through the square and past the Church of Our Lady Under the Chain to Míšeňská Street. In the corner is the Sternigov Palace (9/289), rebuilt around 1720, with some good interiors of 1740 decorated with frescos by P. Molitor. At the House of the Golden Unicorn (11/285) is the hotel where Mozart stayed in 1789, followed by Beethoven in 1796. No. 4/287 was the site of the Convent of the Knights of Malta, built in 1728–31 by Thomas Haffenecker and containing good stucco by Carl Antoni. It now houses the Institute of Oriental Studies. No. 6/286 with a classical façade of 1840, was the site of V lázni, one of the most famous of the Prague hotels. Its guest list included Peter the Great, Suvorov, Chateaubriand and Bismarck.

Now turn left into Mostecká Street. On the left, the house at No. 3/55 was given to Duke Rudolf I of Saxony by the Emperor Charles IV, and it stayed in his possession until 1409. There are remains of the medieval building on the first floor, but its present appearance as a Renaissance house is due to late 16c work, probably by Campion de Bossi. Nearby on the same side of the street is a building with a yellow façade and a fine Rococo balustrade (15/277) which belonged to the Kaunic family. It is now the Yugoslav Embassy. Jan Adam Kaunic was an adviser to Maria Theresa. The house was built in 1773–5 by Anthony Schmidt and its sculpture is by I. F. Platzer.

Turn right into Josefská Street. At the end of this street rises the dramatic S façade of the Church of St Thomas. In narrow spaces like these it is easy to see why Prague Baroque had to be more dramatic with a greater sense of movement, light and shade than its Viennese equivalent. Now walk through the Post Office on your right and you will come to the cloisters of the Carmelite nuns, beyond which you can see the top of the pediment of the Church of St Joseph. Return to the street and farther along you come to the W façade of St Joseph's. The monastery was founded in 1665. In 1686 Mathey began building unusually far back from the road. The reason is not hard to find. On the left is the Lobkovic Palace whose courtyard, if the nave originally planned had been built, would have been deprived of light. Lobkovic wrote to his emperor protesting, and had the plan of the church changed. Leopold II, obviously feeling guilty about the inconvenience to the church, gave both money and his own architect, Abraham Parigi to design the interior. This Flemish Jesuit façade is unique in Prague: with its banded rusticated columns and swags of fruit, it would be more at home in Antwerp. The famous M. V. Jäckel created the statues of St Joseph accompanied by St Theresa and St John of the Cross in 1691. The interior is centrally planned and organized on the lines of the Pantheon in Rome. Rich black and gold altars in the high Baroque tradition abound. The High Altar and those flanking it date from the 1690s and are decorated in polychrome with good quality sculpted figures, again by Jäckel. Brandl painted the Holy Family on the main altar and the picture of St Theresa. The gilding must look particularly fine by candlelight.

Now continue to the remarkable Gothic and Baroque Church of St Thomas, both the S and W façades of which were designed by K. I. Dientzenhofer after 1723 with statues of SS Augustine and Thomas by J. B. Kohl-Severa of 1684. The church was founded by Wenceslas II in 1285 and finished around 1379 for the Augustinians. From this time date the ground plan, the bell tower and the original cloistral buildings. It was rebuilt during the Renaissance and the main portal dates from 1617. During the reign of Rudolf II, St Thomas became the court church. In the 18C many of the greatest craftsmen and artists in Prague worked here; it was in fact, the artists' church and many of them donated paintings and were buried here.

Inside, the nave is full of fine frescos of 1730 by V. V. Reiner of St Thomas Aquinas and St Augustus. The mass of altars both against the walls and on the piers are of high quality. In the first chapel on the right is a St Thomas of 1671 by Karel Škréta, with white painted figures on either side and good scagliola. There are some beautifully carved picture frames to the left. Indeed, throughout this church the woodwork is marvellous, especially the confessionals, pews and pavement. Adjacent to the first pier is a Crucifixion by Zimprecht. Beneath this lies the most splendid embalmed St Justin in his contemporary costume with fine wire work and embroidery. His opposite number, St Boniface, is equally finely bedecked, but is given the dignity of a plaster mask over his skull. On the right of the nave is a portrait of a donor with the Madonna and Child of 1619. On the altar opposite the pulpit is a silver ciborium of 1768 by Jacob Ebner. Walking towards the High Altar there is a fine Assumption of the Virgin by Karel Škréta and to the right is a St Roch by F. X. Balko from 1767. Note the fine grilles at gallery level on either side of the chancel which enclose on the right, the private chapel of the Lobkovic family and on the left, that of the Wallensteins.

But the glory of the church is found in the High Altar. For this, Abbot J. Svitavský commissioned Rubens in 1673 in Antwerp to paint the Death of St Thomas and St Augustus. The original is now in the National Gallery. The High Altar itself was carved by K. Kovář, who was also responsible for the pulpit in 1731. The figures are the work of Quitainer. Note Brokof's six statues of Bohemian saints on the altar. These were originally in silver but the silver has now gone. There is also a beautiful altar rail decorated with ears of corn, grapes, etc. – all references to the Sacrament. Opposite the St Roch painting is an altar dedicated to St Sebastian by Spranger and another dedicated to the Holy Trinity by Karel Škréta of 1644.

Look back now to the magnificent organ. To the left of the High Altar is the entrance to the sacristy, through an attractive 16C grille and past delicate frescos of the 14C. The sacristy, with its noteworthy keystone, has been ascribed to the workshop of Peter Parler. Here, against the walls, are fine examples of cabinet work of the 1670s. The cabinets contain an important collection of vestments, but if you wish to study them, it would be wise to write in advance of your visit.

Leave the church and turn right into the simple 17C cloister. It is now a retirement home. Note the 17C tombs against the wall. To the E is the door to St Barbara's Chapel of 1597, originally the chapter house. There is a painting of SS Catherine and Barbara by J. Heintz (1600) on the altar.

In Tomášská Street continue right past No. 4/26, the House of the Golden Deer of St Hubert of 1726. The house was designed by K. I. Dientzenhofer and the vision of St Hubert above the main entrance was created by F. M. Brokof. The original owner of the house was a professor at the University. There is some fine modelling on the façade although the drainpipes now spoil much of the effect. Tomášská is a most picturesque street lined with houses of Renaissance origin with Baroque façades. At its end, the street opens out into Valdštejnské náměstí (Wallenstein Square) with the great Valdštejn (Wallenstein) Palace on the right. Here is the first example in Bohemia of an early Baroque palace. It is no wonder that the emperor thought Albrecht Wallenstein a threat. The architect was Andrea Spezza; the two men who carried on the work after his death, Vicenzo Boccaccio and Nicolo Sebregondi, followed his designs. The main façade was built from 1621 and is a strange concoction of northern Mannerism and Italian Baroque. Around the three main doors (only that on the left is real) are designs from the pattern book of Vredeman de Vries by Caspar Bendl.

The palace is famous for three things: the great painted hall taking up two storeys, on the left of the façade, the important and beautiful garden, and its builder, Albrecht Wallenstein, who fascinated the German dramatist Schiller. He was a Protestant mercenary from Moravia who foresaw Habsburg victory and joined up on the side of the emperor. He was made imperial generalissimo in 1625. He was a remarkable soldier and for his pains was given a domain at Jičín (where he re-planned the town), the dukedom of Friedland and the duchy of Mecklenburg. That was not all: he was quartermaster for the army and when Ferdinand II could no longer pay his bills, Wallenstein was given leave to create his own mint, a privilege normally unique to the emperor. The wealth created during his five years of printing money permitted him to buy and then demolish, 27 houses and three gardens to make a site for his palace. His power eventually became a threat, so the emperor had him taken prisoner and murdered in 1634 at Cheb (Eger) by two of his own officers, the Scot Leslie and the Italian Piccolomini, both of whom were rewarded with palaces of their own (see pp. 81 and 152). However, the palace remained in the hands of the family until 1945.

Even if you do not have time to go in, at least note the quality of the window grilles. The palace is now the Ministry of Culture and it is possible to visit the gardens and Great Hall between 1 May and 30 September. Inside there are five courtyards, one of which contained the family apartments and was originally connected to the garden and the great *sala terrena* by a door in the wall facing you. Above the family apartments was Wallenstein's observatory. On the top floor ahead of you, you may be able to see some painted ceilings of astrological subjects. The courtyard to the right was for servants and that ahead for horses. The household included 700 servants and 1,000 horses.

The main hall is stuccoed by A. Spezza to a design of 1630 by B. Bianco, and shows Albrecht Wallenstein as the god Mars. The marble wall facings here are of 1853. To the E is the Hall of Knights with an equestrian portrait of Wallenstein of

1631 by F. Leuxe. The ceiling paintings here are of the 19C. The chapel is splendid with an early Baroque altar carved by A. Heidelberger. The altar bears a painting by J. Schlemüller depicting the murder of St Wenceslas by his brother.

Wallenstein's patronage of the arts extended to gardens, and his is one of the most important Baroque gardens in Prague. It was restored in 1950 so its formal vistas can again be enjoyed. The very fact that Adrian Vredeman de Vries's series of bronzes were taken from the garden by the Swedes in 1648 to decorate Drottningholm is some measure of Wallenstein's patronage. But it was not only the work of Vredeman de Vries that made this garden so remarkable. The great classical arcades of the *sala terrena* which date from 1624–7 were designed by Andrea Spezza with Giovanni Pieroni overseeing the work. The *sala terrena* is decorated with stucco and frescos of the Trojan Wars by Bianco (1630), continuing the warrior theme already found in the decoration of the palace. A bronze fountain of 1630 now stands in front of the *sala terrena* and on it is a copy of a Venus by B. Würzelbauer, cast in 1599. The original was returned from Sweden and now rests in the Castle Museum. Even more spectacular is the grotto decorated on a grand scale with tufa stalactites by N. Sebregondi and G. Pieroni. The interior and garden should be seen as one great theatrical whole. At the bottom of the garden is the huge Riding School, now an exhibition space for the National Gallery, and entered from Klárov Street.

Opposite in Valdštejnské náměstí is the Ausperg Palace (16/1) of 1670, perhaps rebuilt by Caratti. There follows the Ledebour Palace (3/162) by Palliardi in 1787. Behind these palaces rise a series of fine gardens up to the castle itself. Among the finer are those of the Palffy Palace (14/158), designed in 1723 when the palace became the property of the von Fürstenburgs. Karl Egon von Fürstenburg, who died in 1757, was a president of the first Academy of Sciences. The Palffys owned the building in the 19C. The Ledebour garden has a fine *sala terrena* by Alliprandi of 1710, with a fresco by V. V. Reiner, now alas covered with sgraffiato about the Red

Army. Sadly too, in the 1950s, restorers used disastrous materials for restoration – concrete and iron – and the gardens are now closed for the foreseeable future.

The Little Černín Palace (12/155), originally by J. J. Wirch but rebuilt in 1952, has a lovely garden beyond it. In front is the Kolowrat Palace (10/154) of the 1780s, by Palliardi. It is now the Ministry of Culture but during the Munich crisis was the seat of Beneš and the government of Prague. Some of the houses in this neighbourhood belonged to industrial barons, and even a few of the aristocrats played a leading part as entrepreneurs. The Kinskýs manufactured glass for instance, and one of the Wallensteins was a pioneer in textiles. Until the Communists took power, Czechoslovakia was one of the most advanced industrial nations in Europe, supplying up to 70 per cent of the needs of the Austro-Hungarian Empire, all from an industrial base started in the 1840s and 1850s. Note by the way the fruits of all this in the Gothic Revival grille surrounding the early Baroque palace (8/153) and gardens on your left, bought by the industrialist, Karl Egon von Fürstenburg. It is now the Polish Embassy. The Embassy of India (8/153) of 1917 is set behind this, and the Belgian Embassy in Valdštejnská Street offers a fine example of Rococo Revival. Valdštejnská continues round to the National Gallery exhibition gallery in the Valdštejn Riding School. There are statues from the school of Braun outside. The garden next door to the metro station is of the early 1970s by Otokar Kuča.

From the junction of Letenská Street and the Mánes Bridge along the U lužického semináře, keeping the river on your left, to Vojanovy Sady, formerly the gardens of a bishop's palace destroyed by the Hussites. Go through the entrance in its high wall and up a narrow internal staircase to a viewing platform. Here you will be met with an expanse of orchard and lawn stretching to the rear of the Church of St Joseph (see p. 92). In a niche in the wall is a statue of St John Nepomuk by I. F. Platzer. The tiny chapel in the centre of the gardens is by K. I. Dientzenhofer. But the most intriguing thing is the Beata Electa Chapel which doubles as a mausoleum and grotto. It is centrally planned and decorated with frescos and stalactites and, I fear, graffiti. Along from the garden entrance is a seminary (13/90) by Dientzenhofer the Younger.

Carry on to Mišeňská Street and notice the sign on the wall in Russian, indicating the route their tanks took in 1945. This enchanting street of small houses brings you out at Charles Bridge by the Hotel of the Three Ostriches (1/76), one of the most famous hotels in Prague. The fresco on the exterior illustrates the name of the hotel, but it derived its name from the fact that the original owner made trimmings for hats from ostrich feathers. Sadly, the hotel has become a base for large groups of tourists.

All this area is beginning to show the fruits of assiduous restoration and gradually the whole Čertovka waterway and Kampa Island will be restored. Ahead note another of the magnificent Prague gaslamps of the 1860s. Behind that, sitting rather severe, are the offices of the Minister of Finance (7/63), built in the thirties by F. Roith, a pupil of Otto Wagner. Now look up at the towers guarding the entrance to Charles Bridge. The smaller of the two is Romanesque and was part of the original bridge of the 1170s. This was largely restored in the 16C. The other tower is 15C and apes that at the other end of Charles Bridge.

4
THE STARÉ MĚSTO AND THE JOSEFOV

Because of the wealth of monuments in the Old Town (Staré Město), this walk is divided between the area around the Charles Bridge (Karlův Most) and that close to the Jewish Town (Josefov). The one naturally dovetails into the other, but the walk starts at the Malá Strana end of Charles Bridge, the beginning of the Staré Město.

Charles Bridge from the Malá Strana

Charles Bridge – the Old Town Gate – the Church of St Francis – the Church of St Salvator – the Church of St Clement – the Clementinum – the Clam-Gallas Palace – the Palace of George Poděbrady – the Church of St Giles – Malé Náměstí (Little Square) – Staroměstské náměstí (Old Town Square) – the Týn Church – the Church of St Nicholas

Charles Bridge is one of the most important and romantic sights in Prague. Apart from two fords across the Vltava River, Charles Bridge was, until the 19C, the only link between the castle (Hradčany) and the Lesser Town (Malá Strana) on one side, and the commercial area of the ghetto (Josefov) and the Old and New Towns (Staré and Nové Město) on the other. An earlier bridge on this site, the Judith Bridge, had been built in 1170 by Vladislav II but was destroyed by flood in 1342. The Praha Bridge, later called Charles Bridge, was begun in 1357 or, to be more exact, on 9 July 1357 at 05.31 a.m. Not only was this St Vitus' Day, but the ascent of Leo was in the appropriate conjunction with the sun and Saturn, and the date and time of 1357.9.7.5.31 was deemed numerically prophetic. The astrologers have been proved right: the bridge was only closed to traffic in 1950. The only visible damage over the years has been to its statuary.

The present appearance of the bridge owes much to the Counter-Reformation, its famous gallery of sculpture transforming it from an ordinary thoroughfare into a *via sacra* (see p. 55). Before the 17C there were two statues on the bridge, one of the Crucifixion, which Elizabeth of Bohemia (the Winter Queen) foolishly insisted should be torn down as she said it looked like a naked bather, and the other of the moderate Hussite king, George Poděbrady.

The Emperor Leopold stayed in Prague in 1680–1 during a plague epidemic in Vienna. It was probably his wish to turn Charles Bridge into something similar to the Ponte St Angelo in Rome which started its transformation. The first statue to be put on the bridge was that of St John Nepomuk, by Jan Brokof the Elder in 1683. It stands alongside the spot (now marked by a bronze cross) where Nepomuk was thrown into the river on the emperor's orders (see p. 215). His statue was followed in all by 31 more dating from the 17 to the 19C, most of which were paid for by aristocrats, the University and religious orders throughout Bohemia. In 1848 the bridge was damaged by the artillery of Prince Windischgrätz and many of the original statues were put into the Lapidarium (see p. 193) and were replaced by new statues by the Max brothers. At the beginning of the 20C the sides were raised and in 1950 the bridge was closed to road traffic.

Walk from the Malá Strana end of the bridge past the first six pairs of statues listed below, then look down over the edge to your right over Kampa Island. You can see from here the statue of Roland of Bruncvík, a 19C copy by L. Šimek of an earlier statue. Roland is the emblem of the Old Town: he does appear to be trespassing, but the Old Town originally paid for the upkeep of the bridge, so they are here staking out their territory. According to tradition, if Prague is threatened, Roland will go and fetch St Wenceslas who will march with his

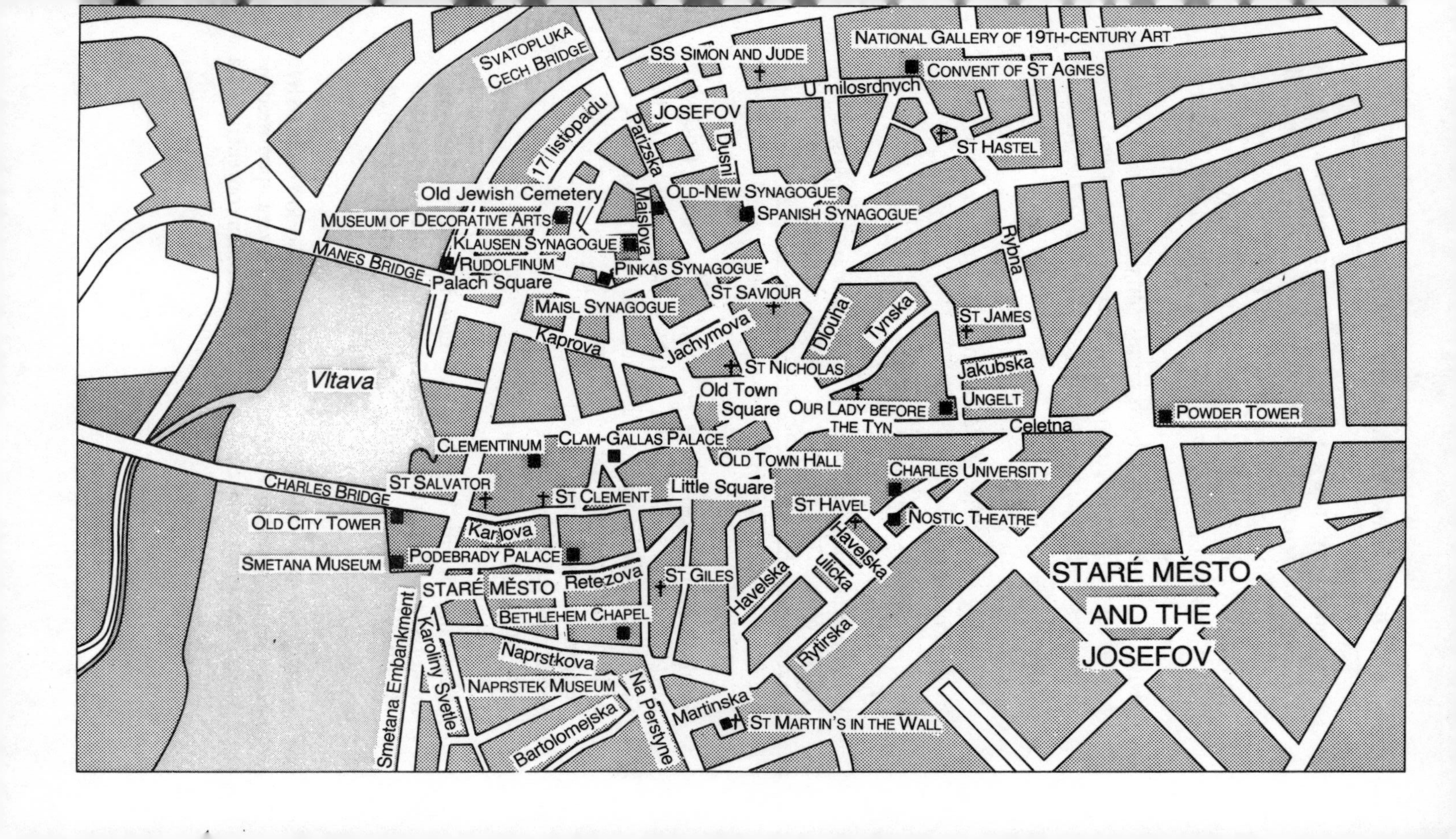
STARÉ MĚSTO AND THE JOSEFOV
National Gallery of 19th-century Art
SS Simon and Jude
Convent of St Agnes
Svatopluka Cech Bridge
U milosrdnych
Josefov
St Hastel
17 listopadu
Parizska
Dusni
Old Jewish Cemetery
Old-New Synagogue
Maislova
Spanish Synagogue
Museum of Decorative Arts
Rybna
Klausen Synagogue
Manes Bridge
Rudolfinum
Pinkas Synagogue
Palach Square
St Saviour
Maisl Synagogue
Dlouha
Tynska
St James
Kaprova
Jachymova
Vltava
St Nicholas
Jakubska
Old Town
Square
Our Lady before the Tyn
Ungelt
Powder Tower
Celetna
Clementinum
Clam-Gallas Palace
Old Town Hall
Charles University
St Salvator
Charles Bridge
St Clement
Little Square
St Havel
Nostic Theatre
Old City Tower
Karlova
Havelska
Podebrady Palace
Smetana Museum
St Giles
ulicka
Staré Město
Retezova
Bethlehem Chapel
Rytirska
Smetana Embankment
Karoliny Svetle
Naprstkova
Naprstek Museum
Na Perstyne
Martinska
St Martin's in the Wall
Bartolomejska

army and save the town. Beyond Roland are the earliest of the Malá Strana watermills, dating back to the Middle Ages. Still on the right and at eye level on Kampa Island are the eaves of the House of the Virgin Mary, where a painting of the Virgin which was said to have come floating downstream has been used as a house sign and a cult object. On one occasion, the owner of the house got both hands caught in a mangle. He prayed for help to the Virgin and was released unscathed. Note the rollers of the mangle carved on either side of the window frame.

Walking from the Malá Strana, the statues on Charles Bridge are as follows:

Right	*Left*
SS Salvator, Cosmas and Damian of 1709 by J. O. Mayer, sponsored by the Faculty of Medicine	St Wenceslas of 1858 by K. J. Böhm, sponsored by the Society for the Blind
St Filip Benicius of 1714 by M. B. Mandl, Braun's teacher from Salzburg. This is the only statue of Salzburg marble, the rest being made of sandstone. Sponsored by the Serviten Convent	Copy of 1709 of St Adalbert by J. M. Brokof, sponsored by the Lord Mayor of Prague, M. Joanelli
St Cajetanus of 1709 by F. M. Brokof, sponsored by the Theatine Convent	St Luitgarda of 1710 by M. B. Braun, sponsored by the Cistercian Convent of Plasy, w Bohemia
St Augustine of 1708 by J. B. Kohl–Severa, sponsored by the Augustinian Convent of St Thomas	Copy of St Nicolo Tolentino by J. B. Kohl–Severa, sponsored by the Augustinian convent in Malá Strana

St Jude Tadeas of 1708 by J. O. Mayer, sponsored by F. Mitrovský	St Vincent Ferrara and St Procopius of 1712 by F. M. Brokof, sponsored by the Abbot of Sazava Convent (note the Counter-Reformation propaganda as regards conversions, such as 25,000 Jews, 8,000 Saracens)
St Anthony of Padua of 1707 by J. O. Mayer, sponsored by F. Mitrovský	St Francis of Assisi of 1855 by E. Max. Thanksgiving gift of F. Kolowrat for the rescue from an attempt on the life of Franz Josef I
St John Nepomuk of 1683, after a sketch by J. B. Mathey and a wooden model by M. J. Brokof; execution by J. W. Heroldt of Nuremberg. Sponsored by M. Wünschwatz. This was the first statue on the bridge and the only one in bronze	St Ludmila of 1730 by M. B. Braun, replaced the 1754 St Wenceslas Statue
SS Norbert, Wenceslas and Sigismund of 1853 by E. Max, sponsored by the Strahov Monastery	St Francis Borgia of 1710 by Brokof, sponsored by František of Collato
St John the Baptist of 1857 by J. Max, sponsored by J. M. Gemerich of Neuberg	St Christophorus of 1857 by E. Max, sponsored by the Mayor of Prague, V. Wanka
SS Cyril and Method, Slav saints of 1928 by Karel Dvořák, sponsored by the Ministry of Education	Copy of 1711 of St Francis Xavier by F. M. Brokof, sponsored by the Faculty of Philosophy
St Anna of 1707 by M. V. Jäckel, sponsored by Robert of Lisau	St Joseph of 1854 by J. Max, sponsored by J. Bergmann

A 1629 copy of a 14C Calvary from the Dresden workshop of H. Hilger. Statues by E. Max, 1861. Pedestal *c.*1700

A Pietà of 1859, by E. Max

Madonna with St Domenico and St Thomas Aquinus of 1708 by M. V. Jäckel, sponsored by the Domenican Convent of Prague

SS Barbara, Margaret, and Elizabeth of 1707 by F. M. Brokof, sponsored by J. V. Obytecky of Obytec

1709 copy of the Madonna with St Bernard of Clairvaux by M. V. Jäckel, sponsored by the Cistercian Convent of Osegg, N Bohemia

Copy of 1711 of St Ivo by M. B. Braun, sponsored by the Faculty of Law

At the end of Charles Bridge you come to the beautiful gateway into the Old Town built between 1370 and 1410 by the workshops of Peter Parler. The W façade was destroyed by the Swedes in the fighting in 1648. Walk through and look up at the Parler net vaulting with the crown of Bohemia on the boss. The E façade, facing the Old Town, is beautifully decorated with symbols of the Luxemburg monarchy and its links with Bohemia, its patron saints and the wealth of the Holy Roman Empire. The statues (the originals are in St George's) are of Charles IV and his son, Wenceslas IV with St Vitus. Above them are SS Adalbert and Sigismund. Among the shields are those of Bohemia, Moravia, Silesia and Upper and Lower Lusatia, the states that went to make up the lands of Bohemia. Dotted all over you can see the symbol of Wenceslas IV – a kingfisher and a towel. There was an attempt on his life while he was bathing, but the would-be assassin was foiled by the shrill, warning cry of a kingfisher and the quick action of the bath girl, Zuzana.

To the right of the gateway stands the monument to Charles IV put up in 1848 to mark the quincentenary of Charles's founding of the Carolinum (see p. 4). It was cast by E.

Hahnel of Dresden and depicts, under the portrait of Charles IV, the four faculties of the University. The small garden in which this monument stands and indeed, this entire embankment was laid out in 1848–9. At the same time the railway came to Prague and there were plans to make the river navigable.

Farther to the right is the Church of the Order of the Knights of the Cross of the Red Star, 1679–89, by J. B. Mathey, dedicated to St Francis. This was built, as was so common in Prague, on the site of a Gothic church. Some may find the external colours of the dome surprising, but apparently these reds, blues and creams are faithful to the colours that were there at the end of the 17C. The angels with the symbols of the Passion on the cornice are by M. V. Jäckel but there are strange symbols in the metopes, presumably relevant to the Order. On the façade is a statue of St Francis, the patron saint of the Knights of the Cross by Quitainer, with Bohemian saints and St Mary and St John Nepomuk by R. Prachner (1758). On the corner of the street is a statue of St Wenceslas by J. J. Bendl of *c.*1678.

The interior of the church is centrally planned and rich with ceiling frescos of the Four Evangelists and the Glory of the Cross by V. V. Reiner. Quitainer carved some of the statues on the walls but some, more classical-looking, are by the two Süssner brothers from Bavaria. The High Altar was carved by M. V. Jäckel and J. K. Liška painted the fine Stigmata of St Francis here, and also the Finding of the True Cross on the altar to the N. The Assumption of the Virgin on the right-hand altar is by Willmann, and it is his Expulsion from the Temple over the W door. The magnificent picture frames over the W door are of 1701 and are from the Jäckel workshop. Quitainer carved the pulpit and the interior was finished by 1720.

The choir of the church was so famous in the 17 and 18C that its music attracted many great composers. Glück played the organ here, between 1732 and 1736 and in 1860, so did Dvořák.

Return to the gateway by Charles Bridge. This was the site

chosen by the Jesuits for their complex of College and churches when they arrived in Prague in 1556. They took over the Gothic Domenican Church of St Salvator and that of St Clement around the corner, and gradually accumulated a huge parcel of land here. In fact, 32 houses, 3 churches and 2 gardens were taken over for the building of the Clementinum or Jesuit College.

Between the last years of the 16C and about 1653, they rebuilt the Church of St Salvator making it the first church in Prague of the Counter-Reformation. Part of the staggered building campaign may be seen in the Mannerist W door set into the very Baroque triumphal arch which comprises the remainder of the W front. You will note that the triumphal arch meets the traveller straight off the Charles Bridge. At a time when this was the only bridge in Prague, such a meeting would have made an impression. The architect was Carlo Lurago with Domenico Galli responsible for the rich stucco decoration. The statues on the façade are by J. J. Bendl: his St Mary sits above the door, and above her is the Salvator Mundi flanked by Evangelists with SS Francis Xavier and Ignatius Loyola. Above them are the Doctors of the Church and some wonderful vases.

Entering the church you can see that during the first building period of 1578–81, the E end up to the crossing was constructed; then the nave was continued in 1600–61. The stucco and the spandrels of the cupola date from 1648–9. The beautiful grille in front of you is partly of 1620 and partly of 1760. The main altar is of the 18C but there is also a very beautiful modern altar of 1985 by Karel Stádník made from glass and metal, symbolizing the cosmos. Note the confessionals with statues by J. J. Bendl of 1675 and the fine altarpieces by J. Heintz and J. J. Haring.

Come out of the church and to the left you can see one façade of the Clementinum. It is unfortunate that this street Křižovnická is so busy as it is difficult to see. Its fine architecture decorated with giant banded pilasters have more than a hint of northern Mannerism in spite of the fact that they were finished as late as 1653. The public entrance to the Clementinum is now off Karlova Street.

The Jesuits had been thrown out of Prague between the Defenestration of 1618 and the Catholic victory at the Battle of the White Mountain in 1620. On their return they were given the Charles University which they absorbed into the Clementinum, and the emperor became their protector. Estimates vary but it is thought that in 1574 the population of Prague was 5 per cent Catholic. By 1648, at the end of the Thirty Years' War, Catholicism held total sway. Carrot and stick were used in this transformation. In 1621 all Protestant ministers were compelled to leave the country, and in 1627 Emperor Ferdinand ordered all his Bohemian subjects to choose between Catholicism or exile. The carrot took the form of education and the Jesuits saw the potential for music and the theatre to get their message across to the masses. They set up the first important theatre in Prague in the Clementinum with the Czech language as its medium.

Opposite St Salvator, in Karlova Street, is the Colloredo-Mansfeld Palace (2/189) of *c.*1730, designed by Francis Ignatius du Prée for Prince Vinzenz Paul Mansfeld-Fondi. The portal is from the workshop of M. B. Braun. There is a good ballroom inside, but the building is now used by the Academy of Sciences and is not open to the public. Next, at 4/188, is The House at the French Crown. Between 1607 and 1612, the German astronomer Kepler lived here, and there are remains of sgraffiato decoration, a Renaissance portal and arcades in the courtyard. At No. 8/186, with the Sternberg star over the door, was the palace of the Pötting family during the first quarter of the 18C. The architect was F. M. Kaňka. Ahead, where the street forks, is the House at the Golden Well (3/175) with fine stucco reliefs by J. O. Mayer of 1701 of patron saints who, hopefully, protected the occupants from the plague.

Before you visit the Church of St Clement and the Clementinum, you might like to stop for a cup of coffee at the House of the Golden Snake. This was the first coffee house in Prague, founded by an Armenian, Deodatus Damajan, in 1714.

The Church of St Clement is one of the three churches within the Jesuit College. It now belongs to the Greek Orthodox Church and serves many of the Ukrainians who came to Prague after 1918. It is open to the public at 17.00 on Fridays and on Sunday mornings, or you can apply at the sacristy. The architect was K. I. Dientzenhofer but his plans may have been executed betwen 1711 and 1715 by F. A. Lurago. The statues inside of 1715–21 are all by M. B. Braun; many from the hand of the master himself are quite magnificent. These include the work on the side altars, the four Evangelists in niches in the nave and the confessionals. Some painting is by the Jesuit painter, Raab, but do note that the first altar on the right was painted by Brandl. The main altar of 1760 is by J. Kramolín and portrays St Clement himself. Kramolín was a pupil of Andrea del Pozzo, best known for his work in Il Gesù in Rome and his speciality of *sotto in sù* painting. The fresco of 1711–15 is by Jan Hiebel, another follower of Pozzo. It depicts the Life of St Clement. The other objects worthy of note are the lovely modern screen by Karel Stádník, the papier mâché crucifix on the right wall as you leave, and the magnificent organ decorated with vases and putti by Braun.

When you leave this fine church, note its entrance and beautiful grille designed by K. I. Dientzenhofer. On your immediate right is the tiny, oval Chapel of the Assumption built in 1590–7 as the Chapel of the Brotherhood of Italian Painters, Sculptors and Masons. It was the first centrally planned church of its kind in Prague. Its similarity to Vignola's oval-planned Sta Anna dei Palafrenieri in Rome (begun in 1570) has been mentioned in the literature. This church is still the property of the Italian State.

The entrance to the Clementinum (1/190) is a few steps farther down, on the same side of the street. If you wish to visit this as an individual, I suggest that you write in advance of your visit. It is easier to book in as a group of four or more, by telephoning in advance, 26-65041 ext. 212 or 262.

The Clementinum was built by the Jesuits from 1653 to 1748 after a plan by Carlo Lurago and his follower, G. D. Orsi.

The craftsmen used throughout were almost all Italians. The only way the magnitude of this building may be grasped is by seeing the model of Prague in the Prague City Museum (see p. 158). Enter by the porter's lodge; if no one is there go to the door in the first courtyard on the left and someone is bound to come to your aid. From the porter's lodge, a long passage stretches before you, off which is an attractive antechamber with water stoups, busts and something of the atmosphere of a grotto. This corridor is by Orsi after 1660 and the stucco is by Galli. The scenes, some damaged after a fire, are of the Coming of the Jesuits to Prague. The adjacent refectory is a monumental room of *c.*1660 by Lurago. This is now the main reading room of the State Library, open every day. It is difficult to imagine how readers concentrate while putti and the Vices and Virtues gaze down upon them. Both end walls have paintings of 1710 by the Jesuit, Tausch, a copyist who worked on the cartoons of the Italian fresco painter, Andrea del Pozzo. Holding its own in the space is a fine stove of 1760. The neo-Baroque bookcases were given by the opera singer Destinová.

Now go upstairs to the Mathematical Hall by K. I. Dientzenhofer, where there are good Rococo tables and a collection of clocks made in the Clementinum. Most have astronomical mechanisms in addition, as astronomy was an important part of Jesuit education.

By far the most exciting room in this complex, not surprisingly, is the library. It has been open to the public since 1787 thanks to the efforts of Count Kinský, although its collections have not been added to since 1721. This was the second largest library in Prague after that at Charles University. After the Battle of the White Mountain the Clementinum absorbed the books from the University. The paintings are by Hiebel, with the subject-matter influenced by Diderot and the Enlightenment. The bookcases date to 1727. In 1948, when the Communists took power, there was a directive to remove the theological sections; by some miracle, however, they remained. The other important feature of the room is the series of geographical and astrological globes, made here from the 1570s to the 1670s. There is one exceptionally fine scagliola globe. Among the books in the library is the Vyšehradský Codex of 1085, decorated in the scriptorium at St George's Monastery. There is also a collection of Wycliff's writings brought over at the time of England's Queen Anne.

Returning to the ground floor once more, visit the last interior in the Clementinum to be finished. It is the Hall of Mirrors or the Marian Chapel, the private chapel of the Brotherhood of the Holy Mary, designed by K. I. Dientzenhofer in 1724. The room gains its secular name from the mirrors in the ceiling – a well-known Rococo device. Indeed, this room represents the very beginning of the Rococo in Prague. The ceiling is frescoed by Hiebel, and V. V. Reiner painted four canvases for it. These have been taken down for conservation and it is hoped to replace them with copies. There is also a very beautiful floor. It is rather tempting to think of this room as a boudoir rather than a chapel. Since 1936 the Hall of Mirrors has been used as a concert hall.

Do not retrace your steps on leaving, but carry on past the observatory tower, completed by Anselmo Lurago and a reminder of the prominence of the Jesuits in the sciences. In the 18C the astronomer J. Steepling founded the meteorological observatory at the top of the tower. Records have been kept there for two hundred years.

Under the reforms of Josef II, when the Jesuit Order was abolished, the Clementinum became a seminary under the supervision of the archbishop of Prague, and in 1799 it became the first Academy of Fine Arts. Between 1928 and 1930, L. Machoň, a pupil of Jan Kotěra, adapted it as a State library. Sadly, in the past, the authorities did not produce adequate postcards and guide books for the Clementinum, but there is now a video of its history lasting about an hour, which can be viewed in a seminar room by booking in advance.

Leave this seat of learning and you come into the newly renamed Marianské Square. To your right is the back of the Clam-Gallas Palace (see p. 111), ahead is the New Town Hall

(2/2) by O. Polívka, 1908–11, and to your left is the Municipal Library of 1926–30 (98/1) by F. Roith. For a short time in the 1920s this library housed the collections of the National Gallery. It still retains exhibition rooms for the Gallery's use.

Turn into Husova Street and find on your right the wonderful façade of the Clam-Gallas Palace. The street is too narrow to take in the full glory of the design by Fischer von Erlach but the two doorways immediately make an impact, with their wonderful straining Hercules bent under the weight of the door entablature. Further decoration is of scenes from his Labours. The sculptures bear all the hallmarks of the Braun workshop and date from 1713–19. In fact, Braun was responsible for all the sculpture in this sumptuous palace. The present palace follows the ground plan of an earlier one built for the Margrave of Moravia, Jan Jindřich, brother of Charles IV. It was originally designed for Johann Wenzel Gallas, a diplomat and viceroy of Naples who bought up neighbouring houses and by 1715 was ready to start building. The façade is more classical than is usual in Prague, but it is nevertheless true Baroque – a Baroque that is more used to being displayed in the wider streets of Vienna. Gallas had wished to buy the row of houses opposite, demolish them and create a fine square in front of the house. But he was told that he would have to pay rent for the land until the end of time, so he gave up the idea. The palace now houses the Prague City Archives.

If you go in, look at the magnificent staircase and follow it up two floors to enjoy not only the staircase itself, with its figures by Braun, but the frescos by C. Carlone. The subject of the first-floor frescos is The Triumph of Apollo and the main halls on the second floor were painted with the Gathering of the Gods on Olympia and the Coronation of the Arts and Sciences (1722–3). There were minor additions made to the decorative scheme in the 19C.

Farther down the street on the left is the Central Bohemian Gallery (21/156). The gallery, which charges an entrance fee, puts on good quality exhibitions some of which are commercial. Follow the steps down to the cellar which was the original first floor of the 12C house. Continuing down Husova Street, notice the house emblems on the right. Turn right into Řetězová Street and at the end of the street find the gate to the fascinating Romanesque palace of the Lords of Kunštát and Poděbrady (3/222). The most remarkable member of this family was George Poděbrady who was first regent, then king of Bohemia (see p. 6). He set out from here, Poděbrad Palace, for his coronation in St Vitus' Cathedral in March 1458.

The house was built some time in the second half of the 12C or beginning of the 13C. The ground floor, now the cellar, has retained its original three rooms with vaulted ceilings. In the centre room there is an impressive sexpartite vault supported by two piers. Remains of fireplaces and windows may be seen. Here are held temporary art exhibitions. The present ground floor (the medieval first floor) must have been similar in construction. The first rooms here contain very fine collections of stove tiles from the medieval period and the Renaissance. The quality of craftsmanship and interesting shape of the tiles designed to convect heat shows that even at this early date, the room stove was an important decorative object as well as an efficient source of energy. In subsequent rooms there is an interesting exhibition about Poděbrady's life. He tried to set up the League of Princes, an international peace-keeping force aimed primarily against the Turks, and the exhibition shows the route of the journeys he made to other countries to promote the idea.

Return to Husova Street and to the Church of St Giles (St Jiljí), first built in 1339–71 by John of Dražice and Arnošt of Pardubice, who had it built as a hall church. This became the church of the Domenican Order when the Domenicans had to leave the Clementinum. Monastic buildings were added to plans by Carlo Lurago and the church was redesigned by F. Špaček from 1733–5. As an ensemble the effect is rich and exciting, but the paintings are not of top quality. However, the paintings on the side altars at the E end and the frescos on the vaulting are by V. V. Reiner who is buried in the church. The

1. *(left)* Charles Bridge from the Malá Strana. The lower tower *(right)* dates from the 12th century. The higher tower *(left)* was built by George Poděbrady in 1464. The gateway between was added under Wenceslas IV. In the background, the Old Town Bridge Tower, the dome of the Church of the Knights of the Cross *(left)* and the façade of the Church of St Giles *(right)*.

2. *(below)* The Malá Strana seen from the garden of the Lubkovic Palace up to the Castle and the Cathedral of St Vitus.

3. *(left)* The south transept of the Cathedral of St Vitus (1366–1419) by the workshop of Peter Parler. In the foreground the Golden Gate (1366–7). Above its gothic arches a mosaic of Bohemian glass set by Venetian craftsmen and window tracery by K. Hilbert.

4. *(below)* Vladislav Hall (1486–1502), built for Vladislav Jagiello by Benedict Reid.

5. *(left)* Statue of St Wenceslas in St Wenceslas Chapel, Cathedral of St Vitus. By the workshop of Peter Parler, painted by the court painter Oswald.

6. *(right)* Diamond Monstrance in the Treasury of the ›retto Monastery by ıdsmiths M. Stegner ınd J. Känischbauer. ›sign by J. B. Fischer von Erlach.

7. The Sala Terrena in the gardens of the Wallenstein Palace, the Malá Strana. Statues are copies of the originals by Adrian de Vries.

8. Theological Hall of the Strahov Library, Strahov Monastery.

9. Chinese Pavilion at Cibulka. A marvellous example in Prague 5 of a garden influenced by the English landscape garden.

10. The west towers of Our Lady before Týn seen over the roof-tops of the Staré Mešto.

11. The façade of the Hradčany Town Hall, Loretánská, illustrating typical sgraffiato decoration of the 17th century.

12. House sign in the Malá Strana at 'The Three Fiddles'. This house in Nerudova belonged to three generations of violin makers.

13. The Villa Bertranka in Smichov, Mozartova, today the Mozart Museum. Mozart stayed here as the guest of the Dušek family and wrote *Don Giovanni*.

14. Church of St Thomas, Malá Strana. West façade by K. I. Dientzenhofer.

15. The Nostic Theatre, Staré Mešto. Site of the première of Mozart's *Don Giovanni*.

16. Vyšehrad Cemetery. Memorial to the outstanding personalities in Czech cultural life in the 19th and early 20th centuries.

17. An example of Prague's unique Cubist architecture by Josef Gočár, 1912. Tychon Street, 268/6, Prague 6.

18. *(right)* The Hanavský Pavilion from the Jubilee Exhibition, 1897, now on Letná, Prague 7. Architects Otto Heiser and F. Hevcík, constructed by Z. E. Fiala.

19. *(below)* The main station, Wilsonovo, Prague (1901–9). Designed by Josef Fanta and executed by Vincenc Gregov.

20. *(above)* Villa Müller, Prague 6, by Adolf Loos (1928–30).

21. *(below)* Veletržní Palác (Trade Fair Palace) (1924–8) by J. Fuchs and O. Tyl. The site of the Museum of Modern Art, Veletržní Street, Prague 7.

22. *(above)* The Church of the Sacred Heart (1928–32) by Jože Plečnik, George of Poděbrady Square, Prague 2.

23. *(below)* Pařížská Street, east side, by K. Mašek, E. Dvořák and J. Vejrych, *circa* 1906. Prague 1, Josefov.

24. A Cubist street lamp in the foreground (1913) with the gateway to Our Lady of the Snows of the 14th century in the background, Jungmann Square, Nové Mešto.

best parts of this interior must be the sculptures. On the NE altar is a good 14C sculpted crucifix. There are outstanding furnishings and sculptures by M. Schönherr, J. A. Quitainer and F. I. Weiss, and fine confessionals of 1765 by Prachner. There is a tomb of 1835 by Schwalnthaler of the lawyer Mráček.

Leaving the Church of St Giles, turn right and continue to the Little Square (Malé náměstí). In the 12C this belonged to a community of French merchants. In the centre of this busy square is a beautiful fountain of 1560 with its original wrought-iron canopy. All around are medieval houses with later façades, some with sgraffiato decoration. At 2/143 is a Gothic portal; at 12/458 is the House at the Golden Lily of the 15C with a later façade by K. Dientzenhofer before 1700. It still retains a medieval shop window. (There are many medieval and Renaissance shop windows, complete with shutters, throughout the city.) No. 3/142 has a façade decorated by Mikoláš Aleš for the ironmonger, Rott, and the chemist at 13/457 has a most interesting 19C interior. The Rechter House (11/459) dominates this small square with its neo-Classical façade. This is deceiving however, as it was originally two Romanesque houses, one of which was Prague's first pharmacy owned in 1353 by Augustin of Florence. Ahead is the Town Hall and past that is the famous Old Town Square (Staroměstské náměstí). If you can resist the temptation of going straight into this wonderful square, turn right into Melantrichova Street where, at the House at the Green Tree (12/472), behind the neo-Classical façade, is a Gothic house which retains at ground level a vaulted hall of the 14C. No. 15/463 preserves a large Renaissance courtyard with arcades, as does 1/475, The House at the Two Golden Bears with its good 16C portal. This house is where the famous journalist, E. E. Kisch was born and is now part of the Museum of the City of Prague. At 17/971, first right through the archway are the remains of the Monastery and Church of St Michael, an important church for the followers of Jan Hus, where many of his friends preached and where the sacrament was given *sub utraque specie*, in both kinds (see p. 6). The Baroque church is at present used as a warehouse, but note the fine windows.

Now go into the Old Town Square (Staróměstské náměstí). Commerce was the *raison d'être* of the Old Town and possibly as early as the 10C it embraced a huge mix of nationalities. The Romanesque foundations of so many of the houses in this area bear witness to its size and wealth. The first marketplace was on the site of Široká Street. Later Old Town Square became important as it was convenient for the customs house at Ungelt near the Judith Bridge – the forerunner of the Charles Bridge – and Vyšehrad. The walled Havelské Město (the Gall Town) to the E, was founded in 1232–4 and its free citizens granted their privileges to the older settlement as well. In the 13C, recognizing the importance of the Old Town, the royal family founded two major monasteries here – the Convent of the Blessed Agnes and the Monastery of St James. In the next century, Charles IV set up his university, the Carolinum, here. This was the seat of the king's magistrate and its main parish church, St Nicholas', had a second use as an assembly hall for the town representatives. In 1338 the right was granted to have a town hall, built on its present site. Work also started on the main church, Our Lady Before the Týn, which was the great Hussite cathedral until the Battle of the White Mountain. The royal court was in the Old Town in the 15C and the Jesuits recognized its stategic importance by building the Clementinum here. Looking around Old Town Square, it is a remarkable survival for a capital which was rich in the 19C and which could have been rebuilt then. But Prague has been lucky with its citizens, and time and again informed voices have been heard above the clamour of the developers.

The square has recently been renovated although people complain that it is like a film set and the houses are still crumbling behind their façades. It looks timeless but there have been changes. One of the most notable gaps is the missing part of the Town Hall to your left. There is still a large space where it received a direct hit at the end of the war, destroying much of the city archives. Apart from this, Prague was relatively untouched, visually, by the war.

It is difficult now to imagine this square without the powerful bronze of Jan Hus gazing upon his church with his followers holding the chalice which was so significant in his religious arguments (see p. 6). This testing commission was designed by Ladislav Šaloun in 1900–15 in conjunction with the architect A. Feiffer. It was unveiled on the quincentenary of Hus's burning at the stake, amidst much controversy and anti-Habsburg demonstrations.

There used to be a fine Marian statue of 1649 by Bendl to the S of the square. In fact it was the earliest in Bohemia and was based on the column erected in Munich by Elector Maximilian I to commemorate the victory of the Battle of the White Mountain. When Czechoslovakia achieved its independence from the Austro-Hungarian Empire in 1918, it was considered too redolent of the Habsburgs and sadly was destroyed.

There are guided tours lasting approximately an hour round the Town Hall. There are some interesting furnishings and paintings of the Gothic, neo-Gothic and of *c.*1910 to be seen. The Town Hall (1378) was created from private houses: that nearest the Clock Tower dates from the middle of the 14C with Renaissance windows of 1520–8. The next has a pseudo-Renaissance façade by A. Baum, 1879–80, and the third is from the early years of the 19C with arcades beneath. Today these are exhibition halls. At the corner the House at the Minute has sgraffiato from the 17C. The most remarkable feature of these houses is, of course, the mechanical clock, still with its original mechanism created in 1410 by Mikuláš of Kadaň and perfected by Master Hanuš in 1490. The calendar, painted with roundels of the Labours of the Months, is a copy of 1864 by J. Manés of the original now in the Prague Museum (see p. 158). It depicts idealized peasants involved in seasonal countryside activities. Czechs monopolized agriculture as Germans did the towns so this decoration is much concerned with idealizing the Czechs at the expense of the Germans. Note too the rich decoration round the clock and the portal of the Town

Hall by Matěj Rejsek, *c.*1475. Turning the corner, the bay window of the Town Hall chapel is a reconstruction of the one that existed before 1381. Note the 14C Madonna on the corner.

On the façade facing the Old Town Square is the list of 27 Czech nobles, professors and burghers who were executed in 1621 after the Battle of the White Mountain. The crosses in the pavement mark their place of execution. Their heads were impaled on Charles Bridge as a warning to others and their families were sent into exile and their lands given to Ferdinand's Habsburg supporters, mainly Germans. The other plaques on this wall refer to Dukla which was an important pass eventually taken by the Russians in 1944 during their advance into Czechoslovakia. Note too, the bronze hand held up in blessing commemorating a place of execution by the Nazis.

Continue round to your right. At 20/548, the House at the Golden Unicorn, there are some late Gothic details in the entrance hall and a good net vault. In 1848 the composer Smetana established his first music school here. At 18/550 is a fresco depicting St John Nepomuk. This house was the venue for a famous salon held by Mrs Berta Fanta in the early 1900s. Kafka was a guest, so too was Albert Einstein in 1910 when he spent a year at Charles University. At 17/551 is The House at the Stone Ram. Originally Romanesque, like so many houses around this square, but later added to in Gothic and then early Renaissance style at the beginning of the 16C. The original very Bohemian house sign still exists. No. 16/552, Štorch's House, has a façade of 1897 with a painting of St Wenceslas by M. Aleš. It is a fine example of Bohemian Renaissance Revival. Before entering the Church of Our Lady Before the Týn, look in front of it at the Týn School, which is in Gothic style with 16 gables and a strange bulging turret in the centre of the façade. Here the architect Matěj Rejsek taught in the late 15C.

Beyond, fortress-like, rises the Church of Our Lady Before the Týn built by the workshop of Peter Parler in the second half of the 14C. The late Gothic gable of 1463 originally held a gold chalice, symbol of the Utraquists, and a statue of King George Poděbrady, their supporter. The Týn was the metropolitan church of the Utraquists from 1348. After the Battle of the White Mountain and the executions of 1621 opposite in the square, the symbol of the Utraquists – the chalice – was melted down and recast as a Madonna in 1626. The N tower was completed in 1466 but rebuilt after a fire in 1835; the S tower is of 1511. The times of opening are Monday to Friday 14.00–16.00, Saturday 10.00–14.00, Sunday 10.00–13.00 and 20.30–22.00.

At first when you enter, the church seems forbidding and rather a muddle. This is perhaps because the later accretions are somewhat dwarfed amid the towering Gothic architecture. Looking up you will see that the whole of the clerestory of 1457 was replaced after a fire in 1679, although the side aisles still have their original quadripartite vaulting of the 1380s. It is a church that repays study. Of the same date as the vaulting in the nave are the organ and many of the side altars decorated in black and gold. The High Altar, dated 1649, was the first example in Prague of this Baroque style. It enfolds a 1649 painting of the Ascension of the Virgin and a Holy Trinity by Karel Škréta. Also at the E end is a fine Calvary of the early 15C and sedilia of the Gothic period. On the nave piers are statues of the Apostles by F. Preiss of *c.*1700. Magnificent is the fine stone canopy which once stood over the tomb of Bishop Lucianus by Matěj Rejsek, 1493. Now it shelters a neo-Gothic altar. The pulpit too, is Gothic with Gothic Revival additions by J. V. Hellich of 1847. Behind it is the marble tomb of the Danish astronomer Tycho de Brahe, of 1601, who worked for Rudolf II. Ahead is more sculpture – a magnificent altar of St Wenceslas by J. J. Bendl with a painting by A. Stevens of 1664. Other highlights include the lovely Madonna and Child of *c.*1400 at the end of the S aisle to your right and the John the Baptist altarpiece by Master I. P. This sculptor is thought to have arrived in Prague around 1520. Characteristic of his style is his intensely naturalistic carving of man and nature; the carved drapery folds seem to take on a life of their own. His work shows the influence of the Danubian School, but little else is known of him. More of his work is in the St George's Gallery.

Against the walls, the Stations of the Cross were painted by Führich, in a similar style to the Nazarenes. He was director of the Academy of Art. At the W end on the N wall is a balcony with a grille which led into the palace next door. On a pier to the left of the entrance is a painting of St Adalbert of 1648 by Karel Škréta. On the wall next to the entrance to the sacristy is the Renaissance memorial to Václav Berka of Dubá. Just before leaving, glance up to the left to see the glazed window through which Franz Kafka gazed upon Catholic services in church from his parents' flat next door.

Leave the church and return once more to the W façade. To the left is The House at the Stone Bell (15/605) which was originally Romanesque and which, until recently, retained an 18C façade. This has now been stripped back to its appearance of 1340. It is fair to speculate from archaeological finds that both John of Luxemburg and his son Charles IV lived here while Prague Castle was being made habitable. Now concerts are held here, and also exhibitions of contemporary art.

At No. 12/606 is the gloriously rich façade of the Goltz-Kinský Palace. This was built in 1755–65 by Anselmo Lurago. The Platzer family was responsible for the sculptures. By the end of the 18C the Kinský family had left and the palace became a gymnasium which educated Kafka among others. From its balcony, in 1948, Gottwald declared the introduction of Communist rule. The palace is now home to the National Gallery's collection of graphic art.

The N side of the square was redeveloped when the Josefov district was demolished, and the only building to escape was the Pauline Monastery (7/930). This was designed in 1684 by J. D. Canevalle and in 1696 M. V. Jäckel carved the statues. The monastery was connected with St Saviour in Salvátorská (see p. 126). By a quirk of fortune, a mint was here in the 18C. At 6/932, is a neo-Baroque house by O. Polívka, built after 1900. Note the lively sculpture of the roof line, one figure looking as if he is smoking a hubble-bubble or earning his living as a snake charmer: in fact he is a fireman! The building was put up by an insurance company.

Cross Pařížská Street, to the Church of St Nicholas where the Benedictines replaced the Gothic church of the German merchants with K. I. Dientzenhofer's bold design of 1732–5. The detailing on the Pařížská Street façade is of 1910–14. The S façade facing the square with its twin towers is decorated with sculptures by A. Braun. Inside it is evident from its simplicity that this church belonged to the Hussites. But the walls of the interior still retain their rich stucco by B. Spinetti, Braun's workshop decorated the dome, and there are paintings depicting Old Testament scenes by C. D. Asam in the octagonal cupola. There is a fine crystal chandelier of the 19C and do note too, the metalwork on the doors. The buildings of the monastery were demolished in 1897 and only the porch remains of Dientzenhofer's work. Behind is the flat where Kafka was born in 1883. The second half of this walk starts on the embankment and the area around the late 19C institutions that played such an important role in Czechoslovakia's eventual independence. We carry on to the old Jewish quarter (Josefov) and continue around to the E through the former Jewish ghetto, skirting the Old Town Square.

The Jewish Quarter (Josefov)

The Rudolfinum – the Museum of Decorative Arts – the Old-New Synagogue – the Old Jewish Cemetery – the Maisl Synagogue – the Church and Hospital of St Simon and St Jude – the Convent of St Agnes (Gallery of 19C Art) – the Church of St James – the Ungelt – the House of the Black Madonna – the Powder Tower – the Carolinum – the Nostic Theatre – the St Gall area – the Bethlehem Chapel – the Náprstek Museum – the Divadlo Na zábradlí – the Smetana Museum

From Old Town Square, turn left into Kaprova Street and continue to Palach Square. The embankment and many of the buildings and gardens along its length were begun by the farsighted Count Chotek, governor of Prague in 1826–43. By the 1870s, ideals of nationalism, public education and culture were translated, with the aid of industrial wealth, into a grand series of public buildings in every possible historical style. Although most of the architecture you see before you would be more at home in Vienna, the impetus for development came from committed Czechs like Count Sternberg and the architect of the Ring in Vienna, Josef Hlávka, who used his vast wealth to become patron of Bohemian everything. To make matters tidy, Prince Rudolf of Habsburg was placed at the head of the committees to promote Bohemian culture. As the Renaissance was seen as the most enlightened period in European history this was the style chosen for the following colourful buildings. On your left at 3/80 is the Academy of Applied Arts of 1884, which was organized by Gustave Schmoranz, and where Kotěra was professor until 1910. Then comes the Faculty of Philosophy (2/55) of 1928–9. The Rudolfinum (1/79) by J. Zítek and J. Schulz is on the far side of the square. It was set up between 1876 and 1884 as a combined concert hall, gallery and art school, and until the war, it also served to house the parliament. It is now the home of the Czech Philharmonic Orchestra and the Prague Spring Music Festival takes place here. It is roughly on the site of the main ford across the River Vltava.

On the other side of the street, dressed in French Renaissance Revival style, is the Museum of Decorative Arts (4/73), founded in 1897 by V. Lanna the industrialist as an inspiration for new design. The museum was built after a plan by Josef Schulz and with an interior richly decorated with stucco and paintings by B. Schnirch and A. Popp. The collections were founded in 1885 and were housed first in the Rudolfinum. Many of the objects were donated by businessmen and craftsmen. The museum suffers from shortage of space and there is talk of its contents being moved to another site. However, in spite of that, the range of decorative arts on display gives an insight into the intense creativity of Bohemian craftsmen and the workshops of Prague. The exhibits are on the first floor.

As you go up the stairs, note the fine terracotta vases from the Trója Palace (see p. 194). The first room contains the late medieval and early Renaissance collection. Notice the fine *commessi in pietra dura* (hardstone plaques) inset into furniture. This technique was brought from Italy by Giovanni and Cosimo Castrucci for the delight of Rudolf II, and serves as a reminder of the mineral wealth of Bohemia. You will also see the products of the Miseroni workshop. The Italian Ottavio Miseroni was in Prague from 1588 to 1624, where he specialized in cutting gemstones. Cutting gemstones developed into the cutting of Bohemian glass, now celebrated throughout the world. The Miseroni family worked in Prague for three generations. Worthy of note too, are the cabinets made at Cheb and the fine examples of Baroque furniture, much of which was designed by architects like K. I. Dientzenhofer and the craftsmen working with him. There were no clear distinctions between the fine and the decorative arts in Mannerist or Baroque Prague.

The collections here include metalwork, goldsmiths' work, ceramics and textiles from the Middle Ages to the middle of the 19C. The galleries are arranged in chronological order. As in so many museums, the stored collections – including photographs and costume – are more extensive than those on display. Specialists are advised to get in touch with the museum to arrange to see items held in store.

Leave the Museum of Decorative Arts and walk along to the Svatopluka Čech Bridge of 1906, by J. Soukup and J. Koula. Look over to the platform high on the opposite bank of the river where once loomed a huge statue of Stalin, which the Communist Party ordered to be destroyed in 1962. This proved difficult and Josef Vissarionovich had to be blown up little by little over a period of two weeks. The sculptor Švec committed suicide. To the left of the bridge, on this side of the river, is the Faculty of Law. This building (7/901) was planned as early as 1914 by Kotěra, but was not finished until 1929, by his pupil, Machoň. It is worth paying a visit to the interior urtyard to see the impressive design and use of materials. A milar building, housing the faculty of Theology, was proposed for the other side of the road, but instead we have the not very edifying Intercontinental Hotel of 1974 by K. Filsak. On the other side of the square is a fine Art Deco block, built in 1921 as homes for schoolteachers by O. Novotný.

We are now in the middle of the Josefov, the former Jewish quarter or ghetto. The ghetto, founded in the 13C, grew up in the area between the Old Town Square and the River Vltava near the ford. It was ideally placed for commerce. Alas, little now remains of this once-thriving community, which made such an important cultural contribution to Prague, and indeed to Judaism. (The first Hebrew was printed in Prague in 1512.) Louis Léger, writing in 1907 of the clearance of the ghetto, pointed out that 'Les amateurs du pittoresque sordide peuvent le regretter; les amis de l'hygiène, du confort et de la lumière ne peuvent que s'en réjouir.' There is a school of thought that claims that the ghetto was cleared for commercial rather than health reasons. This is the only area of central Prague that has so suffered.

Jews settled in Czechoslovakia as early as the 10C, but it was not until the 13 and 14C that a small Jewish community became a feature of every large town. By the mid-15C as a result of epidemics, pogroms and wars, urban Jewish settlement virtually disappeared, but by the middle of the 16C there were about 1,000 Jews living in Prague. As money lenders, they enjoyed comparative political freedom and were directly subject to the Royal Chamber without any restriction imposed on them by the guilds. They were however compelled to wear the yellow Star of David. Ferdinand I threatened them with expulsion, but the Dutch humanist Erasmus successfully intervened. Finally, in 1571, the Emperor Maximilian II and his wife paid a visit on foot to the Jewish quarter, and were welcomed under a traditional canopy by the Rabbi and the mayor, Mordechai Maizl.

When in 1574, Rudolf II made Prague the capital of the Holy Roman Empire, he gave the Jews yet greater security. In

1580, he allowed them to trade freely and repealed a restriction applying to furriers, but he still insisted that Jews wear the yellow star. The last years of the 16C saw a blossoming of Jewish intellectual life, the central figure of which was Judah Loew ben Bezalel (see below). In 1689 there was a fire which destroyed much of the ghetto and in 1848, when the Jews were given civil rights, the ghetto walls were removed.

The 20C has not been kind to the Jews and the community in Prague has never recovered from its suffering at the hands of the Nazis. In the Pinkas Synagogue you will find the names of 36,000 of their victims from Prague alone. Those who were children during the war recall with horror how, one by one, their Jewish classmates disappeared. Under Communist rule, as with other religions, services were permitted but no cultural or educational activities. Since President Havel's visit to Israel in 1990, 'The Friends of Jewish Culture' has been founded. Its aim is to promote a reunion of Czech Jews for the first time since the war.

At the turn of the century Paris caught people's imagination. Pařižská Street with its buildings dating from 1900–10 cuts a swathe through the picturesque Jewish ghetto. In this area you can see the fruits of the 19C art schools – jewels of mosaic, stained glass and tiling, Art Nouveau figures. Make your way along Pařižská Street from the river and you will pass on your right a fine statue of Moses by Bílek (1906) in the gardens beside the Old-New Synagogue. Behind the statue at 18/250 Maislova Street is the Jewish Town Hall, built in the late 16C by the ever-generous Mayor Maizl, and given a Rococo façade by J. Slesinger in 1765.

There were once 9 synagogues in the ghetto; now the Old-New Synagogue is one of only two in Prague still serving the tiny Jewish community. It is one of the capital's earliest Gothic buildings, dating from the second half of the 13C, and is one of the earliest surviving synagogues in Europe. (The synagogue in Toledo dates from the 12C.) Its striking brick gables are of the 14C. The interior is fascinating, with twin vaulted naves and a women's gallery. Some of the details are similar to those found in St Agnes' Convent. The original seating has been preserved and there is some fine, late Gothic ironwork in the centre around the *bimah* or reading platform. Note the banner (much restored) given to the Jews of Prague by Charles IV in 1358. In the 19C the synagogue was restored by Josef Mocker and its picturesque qualities attracted many architects and painters during the Romantic period.

Opposite its entrance is the High Synagogue, completed in 1568 and paid for by the mayor of the ghetto, Mordechai Maizl. It was he who extended the graveyard and established the famous Rabbi Loew in the Talmudic school here. He had received a special trading privilege from Rudolf in 1592 and became the richest man in Prague. The High Synagogue now houses a textile museum and you may buy tickets here for all the museums in the ghetto.

At the end of this street is the Klausen Synagogue constructed by Rabbi Cohen in 1694. It has a fine room with a barrel vault. Most interesting is the three-tiered Ark built in 1696 by Samuel Oppenheim. The synagogue now exhibits Hebrew manuscripts and prints. Alongside the synagogue is one of the most remarkable sights in Europe, the Old Jewish Cemetery, where the famous and the infamous are squeezed together, the crowded headstones looking like so many crooked teeth. The gate lodge, built in 1906 in a neo-Romanesque style, has a moving display of drawings by children from Terezin concentration camp.

There were originally medieval Jewish cemeteries in the Malá Strana and the New Town but these had gone by the 15C. Some of the headstones were later discovered and moved to this cemetery but the oldest grave here is that of Abigdor Karo, (d.1439) who was a poet and scholar at the court of Wenceslas IV. The list of people buried here is long and includes Judah Loew ben Bezalel (Rabbi Loew d.1609), a philosopher who was interested in the supernatural in traditional Jewish teaching, and whose notorious *golem* or artificially created servant, was said to lie in pieces in the attic of the Old-New Synagogue; David Gans, the first Jewish historian to write a history of the gentiles which was published in Prague in 1592; Josef Salomo ben Elias del Medigo de Candia (the Wandering Jew), who was born in Crete, studied at Palermo, was a pupil of Galileo, and finally practised medicine everywhere from Cairo to Prague; Mardochee who founded a most important printing press in Prague and who was one of the founders of the Brotherhood of the Dead who until this century kept vigil at the cemetery. The headstones here were used as models all over central Bohemia. You will note that Jewish pilgrims to the graves leave pebbles and messages on paper. At dusk you will be warned to leave by the ringing of a handbell around the tombstones.

After 1787 the graveyard was no longer used and the Jewish community buried its dead in the cemetery in the Žižkov quarter. This is where many of the founders of industrial Prague rest. Franz Kafka, amongst others however, is buried in the New Jewish cemetery in Prague 3, in use from the end of the 19C (see p. 176), where some of the headstones are carved by leading Czech sculptors.

On the edge of the Old Jewish Cemetery is the Pinkas Synagogue, founded by the Horowitz family in 1479. This was enlarged both in 1535 and in the early 17C. It is now a memorial to all the Jews in Bohemia and Moravia who were killed by the Nazis – a staggering 77,297.

Turn into Maislova Street from Široká Street and at No. 18/250 is the Town Hall which was once accessible from the High Synagogue. Continue up Maislova to the Maisl Synagogue at 10/36. It was once the most lavish Baroque building in the ghetto but was burnt down and rebuilt in the neo-Gothic style between 1883 and 1913. It is now the Museum of Jewish Silver.

Near the Town Hall there is a good, cheap kosher restaurant and there are several others in the area, notably U Golema and U Matyáše. Turn left into Jáchymova Street, across Pařižská Street and into Kostečná Street to visit the Church of St Saviour in Salvátorská of 1611–14, by J. Christoph of Graubünden. In 1910 it was modified and given a sparse interior for the Czech Brothers who today, are the inheritors of the ideals of Jan Hus.

Turn right into Dušní Street and then into Salvátorská where O. Novotný, later professor of the School of Applied Art, designed No. 8–10/931 for the Štenc Publishing House, a publisher specializing in art history books and magazines. The building is an exciting example of 1909–10 Art Deco, using a wide range of materials including brick, and it has a long glass gallery at roof level. It is now in a poor state of repair, but note many of the original fittings still *in situ*. Nearby is the Church of the Holy Ghost, evidently of the 14C. Opposite is the Spanish Synagogue, 1868, the last synagogue to be built in this area, on the site of the earliest known synagogue or Old Shul. The exterior was designed by Josef Niklas and the remarkable Moorish interior was designed by Josef Niklas with decoration by A. Baum and B. Münzberger. At the moment it is closed but normally it displays a rich collection of textiles.

Follow Dušní Street to your left towards the river, turning right into U milosrdných and passing the Church of SS Simon and Jude of 1615–20 on your left. The whole complex of church buildings which includes a hospital, founded by the Milosrod ní Bratři (the Merciful Brethren), and a famous pharmacy, was transformed into the Baroque style by J. Hrdlička in the mid-18C. The High Altar was painted by J. Hager in 1773 and the patron saints are by V. V. Reiner. There is also a fine St John of God by J. R. Bys of 1691. Both Haydn and Mozart played the organ here. There is a proposal to turn part of the building into a museum of pharmacy; at the moment it still functions partially as a hospital. Continue to the end of U milosrdných and turn right into Haštalská Square where the Church of St Gastulus sits in the middle. It dates from the second half of the 14C. Inside there is a fine double nave, the first example in Prague. In the northern nave is a Calvary of 1716, by the followers of F. M. Brokof. The church is open on Sundays at 17.00 during Mass.

Adjacent to this in the area known as Na Františku (Franciscan district) is the entrance to the Convent of St Agnes, now the

National Gallery of Nineteenth-Century Art. St Agnes was founded in 1233 by King Wenceslas I for the mendicant orders at the instigation of his sister Agnes of Bohemia (St Agnes). There are two monasteries on the site comprising two cloisters and three churches dedicated to St Francis, St Saviour and St Barbara. The Franciscan monastery of St Francis (the first north of the Alps) was almost totally destroyed by the Hussites, and only the choir, the Salvator Chapel remains. St Agnes introduced the Poor Clares into the Convent of St Saviour and became their first abbess in 1235. It is the Convent of St Saviour that forms the present complex. The Church of St Francis was probably finished by 1249 and was built by craftsmen trained under the Cistercians. The Salvator Chapel was incorporated in 1285 and is considered one of the most perfect examples of its type in Central Europe. After a period under the Domenicans, the Poor Clares returned once more to their convent but the buildings then suffered from the fire in the Old Town in 1689. The convent, as with most of those in Prague that were not considered useful, was closed by Josef II in 1782. During the 19C this and the surrounding area fell into decay and the cloisters were actually divided horizontally to provide two sets of slums.

In the 19C the entire area of the Na Františku became an idyllic subject for Romantic painters and writers of the day. In the redevelopments of the 1880s Na Františku came under the same threat of destruction as the ghetto but was saved by the efforts of the Association for the Rehabilitation of the Convent of the Blessed Agnes. It was finally rebuilt between 1964 and 1982 as the present-day art gallery.

The development of 19C painting in Czechoslovakia follows that elsewhere in Europe, but here it is imbued with the same emergence of a national consciousness which can also be seen in literature and architecture. Among the painters of this time to note are Antonín Manés, whose fine Romantic landscapes are signed 'Bohemus', and the landscapes and still-lifes of Josef Navrátil who also painted house interiors. A fine example of his interior decoration may be seen in the rooms he decorated for Václav Michalovic in his house, now the Postal Museum (see p. 157).

The central hall in the gallery is dedicated to the work of Josef Manés who produced a wide range of subject-matter including fine portraits of the rising bourgeoisie. There are also some decorative arts scattered around the museum, and one wishes there were more. Of note is the fine quality of porcelain and, of course, Bohemian cut glass. There are concerts held in the museum every month. The magnificent sculpture collections of the 19C are all held in the Castle of Zbraslav (see p. 181).

Leave Haštalská Square by Rybná Street and take the third right into Jakubská Street to visit the beautiful Church of St James. This was founded by Wenceslas I for the Order of Friars Minor and was considered so important that it was rebuilt by John of Luxemburg and Charles IV. During the Hussite period the church was used as a meat store and so suffered relatively little damage. Jan Pánek transformed the original Gothic into Baroque but then, after a fire in 1695, the craftsmen returned between 1736 and 1739 to redecorate the interior. However, much remains of the earlier Baroque building.

The W façade is remarkable for its monumental stucco reliefs over each of the three W doors. These include the Apotheosis of St Francis, St Anthony of Padua and St James. They are all by the Paduan Ottaviano Mosto. Inside, the plan and much of the elevation of this vast Gothic basilica remains. The pace of the building quickens towards the E end, where at gallery and later at clerestory level, gesticulating putti balance on Rococo vases, turning towards the High Altar. The overall impression is one of great wealth and the craftsmanship is superb. The scagliola work is by K. Schartzmann; Abondio Bolla carried out the stucco decoration and Ferdinand Drack, the wood carving. The frescos on the vaulting are by F. Voget. The altars are all of *c.*1680, with frontals painted to look like brocade. The altar paintings vary and many seem in need of restoration. There is an Assumption of the Virgin in the first chapel on the right, and a St Joseph nearby, both by Petr

Brandl. The other paintings are by Peter Keck of 1705, and offer nothing very exciting. There is however, a fine canvas on the High Altar, the Apotheosis of St James by V. V. Reiner with a tabernacle by Platzer. There are two other objects of note; one is a Pietà of *c.*1380 from the Peter Parler workshops and the other is the magnificent monument to the Lord Chancellor Count Mitrowitz, made in 1714–16. The designer was Fischer von Erlach and the sculptor was F. M. Brokof.

The church had important links with the butchers of Prague and they were given the first chapel on the left at the W end in honour of their defence of Prague, once in 1611 against the troops from Passau, and again in 1648, against the Swedes. Across the nave from this chapel, hanging up on the W wall, is something looking very like an old chicken-bone. Thereby hangs a tale. One night a thief broke into the church to steal jewels from the Madonna on the High Altar. As he grabbed, his hand stuck to the statue and he remained imprisoned there until found the following morning. The angry congregation cut off the offending hand, and that is what dangles up there today, 400 years on.

If you go out of the W door and immediately right you come to the fine cloister of St James.

Many nationalities traded from the Jewish quarter and an area called the Ungelt or Customs House developed in front of the Church of St James. Built around a courtyard, it originally housed craftsmen, but later became the main market and customs house for Bohemia. There are plans to turn it into a hotel, leaving visible the original Romanesque and Gothic buildings, including the Týn Court. Notice here the Granovsky House (12/639) of 1560 with remains of Renaissance sgraffiato decoration; this is one of the finest houses of its type in Prague. The land was given by Ferdinand I to the chief of customs in 1558. The maze of small streets behind the Týn Church is still a bustle of small picturesque houses. From Jakubská Street follow the Malá Štupartská to Týnská Street on the left. Walk around the outside of the N transept of the church whose fine tympanum relief is now in St George's

Gallery. Opposite is the site of the house belonging to the painter Karel Škréta. Ahead is the Old Town Square, but we turn left into the important royal route of Celetná.

Celetná Street is one of the most attractive in Prague and is flanked by important buildings. Follow it to the Powder Tower at the far end. At No. 2/553, the first floor of the Romanesque house is preserved in the basement. From 1567 this house belonged to Sixt of Ottersdorf who, as Chancellor of the Old Town, played a part in the anti-Habsburg uprising of 1547. Its present Baroque appearance dates from the early 18C with the statues on the attic attributed to the workshop of Braun. The Prague coffee house, At the Three Magi (3/602), is an unusually complete example of a late 14C house. Franz Kafka lived here for a time. Next door (5/601) is the Týn Presbytery. In the 15 and 16C this was the seat of the Consistory of the Utraquist Church which administered the Týn. Until 1820 the house was surrounded by a graveyard. Continuing to the right at 12/558 is the Hrzán Palace, built in 1702 by Zikmund Valentin Hrzán of Harasov, perhaps by G. B. Alliprandi. The sculptural decoration on the façade is from the workshop of F. M. Brokof. Across the road at 13/597, again with Romanesque foundations, is a Baroque palace built in 1756 by Count Jan Caretto Millesimovský and designed by Anselmo Lurago. It was used as the Library of Culture for the Communist Party and is now the teachers' training faculty of the University.

Across at 20/562 is the Buquoy Palace, once lived in by the widow of Count Karel Buquoy, a general of the Imperial troops at the Battle of the White Mountain in 1620. It was bought by Charles University in 1762 and they had it rebuilt by A. Prachner. Next door No. 22/563 again belongs to the University. Its neo-Classical façade dates from 1804 although the foundations of the houses are Gothic. Opposite, the shop at 15/596 is a fine example of Constructivism designed by J. Gočár and built in 1933–4 for the Baťa Company. At No. 17/595 the Schützen Palace was rebuilt *c.*1700 and completed after 1706 to a design by V. Kaňka. The sculpture of St John Nepomuk on the façade is of this date. The decoration of the interior is by P. Molitor of 1736. In the courtyard is a wooden statue of Hercules from the second quarter of the 18c, attributed to L. Widmann. At No. 30/567 is a house of 1897 designed by Friedrich Ohmann, Professor of Applied Arts within Prague. Across at Solomon's, 23/592, the design of *c.*1730 has been attributed to Kaňka and the Madonna is from the workshop of M. B. Braun. Opposite at 34/569 is the House of the Black Madonna, a superb example of uniquely Praguian Cubist architecture by J. Gočár, built in 1911–12.

On the corner across Ovocný trh is No. 36/587. In 1420 during the Hussite Wars the Old Town acquired the building and installed a mint there. Apart from a short period, the mint was in operation until 1784. The present house was built in 1755 to a design by J. J. Wirch. The balcony above the main door has figures of miners on either side. These are by Platzer of 1759 and serve as a reminder of the wealth of the silver mines in Bohemia and Silesia. In 1784 the house was remodelled and was finally given its neo-Baroque features in 1860. The first tussles of the 1848 revolution took place here when it was the military headquarters. It was here that the wife of Prince Windischgrätz was killed by a stray bullet and this caused the prince to react with unnecessary violence against the protesters. Opposite was the site of the Royal Palace lived in by the kings of Bohemia from the Hussite Wars in 1419, until King Vladislav reasserting the rights of kingship in 1484, returned to the castle. The corner house on the other side of the street (31/585), the Pachta Palace, was rebuilt in the 1730s probably to a design by K. I. Dientzenhofer. During the ownership of the Pachta family of Rajov, the stucco busts of Maria Theresa and Franz of Lorraine in medallions over the first-floor windows were added.

Take a detour to the left from Celetná Street into Králodvorská to the wonderfully grim Communist Party hotel. Opposite is the Paris Hotel. This was designed by J. Vejrych in *c.*1901. Although not in the top league of hotels, it is one of the most pleasant hotels in Prague and retains many of the original fixtures and fittings.

Ahead is the late Gothic Powder Tower, built for Vladislav Jagiello, the Polish king, as a wedding gift from the city of Prague. It was originally the main town gate, built by Matěj Rejsek in 1475–83, and decorated in a marvellously intricate style. This virtuoso decorative carving is a typical feature of late Gothic architecture in Bohemia. When Vladislav moved to the castle, the tower was left incomplete and was subsequently used for the storage of gunpowder. In the 19c Mocker finished the tower and added the statues of Vladislav and his son.

Facing the Powder Tower, turn right into Ovocný trh to visit the Carolinum or Charles University, founded by Charles IV in 1348 and therefore one of the earliest universities in Europe. The founding of the university was important in Charles's attempts to make Prague a cultural centre and to foster an interest in Slav history. He commissioned from Beneš of Weitmil the *Cronica Ecclesiae Pragensis*, and the *History of Bohemia* from the Italian Giovanni di Marignola. Writing in the vernacular, both in Czech and German, was encouraged; the chronicles and lives of saints, as well as the Bible, were translated into Czech, and a Czech encyclopaedia and Czech-Latin dictionary were compiled. The use of the vernacular encouraged much freedom of thought. In 1390 one of the major figures of the Reformation, Jan Hus, studied at the Carolinum and became rector in 1409, although he was later ordered to cease preaching and was excommunicated (see p. 218).

The Carolinum is a muddle of buildings from the Gothic period onwards. Much still remains of the earlier medieval university and downstairs you can wander through a maze of beautiful simple passages and rooms with quadripartite vaulting. By far the most interesting room in the complex is the Great Hall on the first floor, where degrees are conferred. It is basically 14c but was modified in the late 1940s by J. Fragner. The tapestry on the main wall depicts Charles IV in front of St Wenceslas. This, as well as the paintings on the organ loft are by V. Sychra. The statue of Charles IV is by K. Pokorný of the

1950s. The room has a comfortable 1940s feel about it apart from the oriel window of the chapel *c.*1385 which is a beautiful and important example of high Gothic.

A passion for the revival of the Czech language was behind the founding of the Nostic Theatre, on the corner of Železná and Rytířská Streets. Reach it by turning left from the Carolinum. It was built from 1781–3 by Anthonín Haffenecker and was redesigned in 1881 by A. Wolf. Its sponsor was Count Nostic who leased it to various theatrical societies from the end of the 18C for the performance of Bohemian drama. It was under the protection of the Estates and was also known as the Estates Theatre. In 1787 it saw the première of Mozart's *Don Giovanni*, with Mozart conducting, and in 1791 his *La Clemenza di Tito*, commissioned for the coronation of Leopold II as king of Bohemia. Carl Maria von Weber held the post of opera director here in 1813–16.

Farther down Rytířská Street is the Kolowrat Palace (4/579) by G. D. Orsi of 1674. Still in Rytířská Street, on the right at No. 20/536 is the Klement Gottwald Museum. Its collection of Communist propaganda is now being dismantled. The one good thing about the display is that it did not damage any of the glorious neo-Renaissance interiors, originally designed as a bank by A. Weihl in 1892–4.

On the other side of the road at 18/402 is a house of 1770 by Palliardi and next door was the site of a famous bookshop and printer's, Kramerius. Farther along on the same side is the tower house of the 13C and still farther along there is a good market hall of 1895–8 by J. Fialka, the original iron struts of which may be seen through the modern ceiling.

Turning right into Havelská Street you will find yourself in the middle of the St Gall area of the Old Town, part of the ancient marketplace founded in 1232 by Wenceslas I. In the 15C the marketplace was split in two by the building of stalls between today's Rytířská and Havelská, hence the grand houses set on arcades in Rytířská and Havelská and the street of low houses between. These old shops are still in business today, selling second-hand clothes and materials. There is a flower market here every morning and it is one of the most atmospheric areas of Prague.

The Church of St Havel with its Romanesque foundations was surrounded by the houses of wealthy merchants. The reformer, Konrad Waldhauser preached here, packing out the church so often that he was sometimes forced to preach in the square. Jan Hus followed his example in 1404. The church then came to the Order of the Shod Carmelites who built a monastery and rebuilt the church from 1723–38. The architect was P. I. Bayer, with interior decoration by V. V. Reiner. There is a remarkable Calvary Chapel here by Ferdinand Brokof of 1719–20 and the church is also notable for being the burial place of Karel Škréta. It is open on Sundays at 17.00.

Leaving the church behind you, walk round either side of the square to Uhelný trh, the site of the old coal market. In the centre a fountain was set up in 1797, with a statue by F. X. Lederer, an allegory of fruit-growing and viticulture. On the left is the first tenement block to be built in Prague in 1813–47 and designed by J. Hausknecht. The flats are set around a spacious courtyard with shops at ground level. It is also known as Plateys House.

To the right of the tenement is the Church of St Martin's in the Wall. In the 13C this was the line of the Old Town wall. The church is basically of the 12C with 14C additions. As you will see from the detailing, it was restored from 1905–7 by K. Hilbert for the Czech Brothers. There is a plaque on the wall to recall that all the Brokof family of sculptors are buried here. From Martinská Street turn right into Na Perštýně and at 7/345 is the Perštýn house or the old beer hall The Two Bears, where V. V. Reiner lived after marrying the innkeeper's daughter.

At the beginning of Bartoloměјská Street, on the left, is the forbidding door of the main police station in Prague. At first glance, Bartoloměјská looks like a street full of picturesque houses. So it is, but each house is part of the police station. Continue down Na Perštýně Street, turning left into Bethlehem

Square. The Bethlehem Chapel stands on the site of the original donated by Hans von Mühlheim, a follower of one of the reformers, and consecrated in 1394. The vaulting, influenced by the S porch of St Vitus', was in its turn the prototype for hall churches with net vaults of the late 14 and early 15C. Jan Hus preached here between 1402 and 1413 and later the Bethlehem Chapel became one of the centres of the Reformation. In 1609–20 it belonged to the Czech Brothers and the father-in-law of Comenius preached here. Later in the 17 and 18C the Jesuits took it over, but after their dissolution the chapel was demolished. Basing his work on archaeological finds, the chapel was rebuilt by J. Fragner from 1950–2.

On the N side the square at No. 1/269 is a low attractive building, originally a brewery, U Halánků and now the entrance to the Náprstek Museum or Museum of Australasian, African and American Cultures. The museum was named after its founder, Vojta Náprstek who, on being exiled after the revolution of 1848 went to America. Here he was impressed by America's industrial progress and in 1862 he visited London for its World Exhibition and to see the museums of South Kensington. When he returned from exile, he was fired with the wish to help his country catch up with the advanced industrial countries of the west, so he set up the Czech Industrial Museum in his family brewery. The collections grew too large and in the 1880s he added the tall building next door. His other interest, ethnographical collections, grew through his support of Czech travellers all over the world. They returned with artefacts which gradually superseded his industrial collections.

At present the Náprstek Museum is closed, but when it reopens, the American, Australian and African collections will be shown here. The Oriental collections are in southern Bohemia at Liběchov and the costume collection can be seen at the Kinský Summer House (see p. 86). Most of the industrial machinery is now housed in the National Technical Museum in Letná while all that remains in the private family apartments of the brewery is a sewing machine of 1862 by Wheeler and

Wilson from Bridgeport, Connecticut, and a large part of the library and fine photographic collection. Náprstek was also an enthusiastic supporter of the emancipation of women, and there were rooms set aside in the apartments for the American Club of Czech Women. The meeting rooms were next to his own and there is what looks like a peephole through the door. His mother was tight-fisted with the money from the brewery and he did not marry until after her death. He was a prominent member of the Prague city council and the placing of railings around the trees in the city was one of his ideas.

Continue down Náprstkova Street turning right before the end into a narrow lane, Anenská Stříbrná, leading into Anenské náměstí. On the right at 2/211,213 is a former Domenican convent with a façade of 1676, built on the site of the 12C rotunda of St Lawrence and a church of the Templars. It is now part of the National Theatre. Opposite, at 5/209, is the Divadlo Na Zábradlí (The Theatre on the Balustrade), a theatre reknowned for performing the work of dissidents, including that of Havel in 1968. At 4/208 is a small palace, now part of the theatre, with an enchanting courtyard of 1760 by Wirch and a staircase by Platzer.

Go back onto Náprstkova Street and right along Karoliny Světlé to the 12C rotunda of the Holy Cross. This stood by the important road between Vyšehrad and the Vltava fords. It was restored both inside and out in the 1860s by V. I. Ullmann and B. Wachsmann, although there are some remains of 14C frescos. It is one of three such Romanesque churches left in Prague.

Leaving the rotunda, turn right on to the embankment, Smetanovo nábřeží where there is a fine memorial to Francis II, Emperor of Austria, by J. Kranner, built 1844–6. This is a fine example of neo-Gothic taste with sculpture, 'The Homage of the Czech Estates', by the Max brothers. The Smetana Museum (1/201) is in what was originally the municipal water tower. This was built in 1885 in the Czech Renaissance style after a plan by A. Wiehl, and is decorated with marvellous sgraffiato depicting the battle with the Swedes on Charles

Bridge in 1648. The museum, containing material concerning the life of the composer, was founded in 1928. In front of the building there is a statue of 1984 of Smetana by J. Malejovský. This part of the embankment was the first to be built to the designs of B. Grueber between 1841 and 1845. There is a fine view of the castle from here.

5
THE NOVÉ MĚSTO

The very name Nové Město or New Town brings to mind the sort of showpiece architecture of the 1920s and 1930s that fills much of Wenceslas Square. Yet in spite of its name, the New Town was founded in 1348 by Charles IV and quickly absorbed the earlier settlements that dotted the area outside the Old Town, including Poříčí, Rybníček and Opatovice. There was nothing haphazard in this, and the New Town presents the most outstanding example of town planning in medieval Europe. Three main districts were designed, each with trade, traffic and aesthetics in mind. First, the central area was joined to the most modern regularized part of the Old Town, the St Gall quarter (see p. 133) about 1230 and its hub became the oblong horse market, now Wenceslas Square. To the north, the wide Hybernská (formally Horská) led to the silver-rich town of Kutná Hora and linked in with Senovážné Square, the site of the hay market. The south was dominated by the huge square of the cattle market, today's Charles Square, a rectangle of eight hectares.

The streets were laid out 18–27m wide, wide enough even for today's traffic, and the houses were built to regulation dimensions and of regulation materials. In each parish, new churches and monasteries were founded, the five most important forming a cross on the ground plan of the town. The whole area was enclosed by three kilometres of fortifications pierced by four gates and this was complete by 1350. The first architect of St Vitus', Matthieu d' Arras, has been held responsible for this extraordinary vision. Outside the walls to the south there is a fourth area of the Nové Město between the walls and the river, an area once of isolated monasteries and hospitals set amidst gardens and vineyards. The New Town, the largest of Prague's towns, remained autonomous until Josef II's reorganization in 1784.

Traditionally the New Town housed the poor of Prague and in the 15C it was the radical stronghold of the Hussites. But of the medieval New Town only the most important churches and palaces still stand. In the hands of the late 19C reformers, huge areas were flattened and rebuilt, although the earlier street plan was retained.

The New Town is divided into two districts: the so-called Upper Town in Prague 2 round Charles Square (Karlovo náměstí) and the remainder in Prague 1. A walk around the New Town reveals that it has the highest concentration of 20C architecture in the city. Our two walks cover the New Town's two districts, starting in Prague 1.

Prague 1

The National Theatre – the Convent of St Ursula – Our Lady of the Snows – Wenceslas Square – the National Museum – the Smetana Theatre – the Obecní dům – the Postal Museum – the Museum of Prague History – the main railway station – the Church of St John Nepomuk

From the Smetana Embankment (Smetanavo nábřeží), look for a moment at the Bridge of Legions (most Legií), formerly the May Day Bridge. It was designed by Antonín Balšánek between 1899 and 1901.

Leave the bridge and walk along the embankment to Národní Street and the National Theatre. The growing awareness of Czech culture was the impetus behind Czechoslovakia's desire for independence from the Habsburgs in the 19C, and the theatre has always held a special place in Czech culture. The National Theatre, built by subscription collected from both Bohemians and Moravians, became a symbol of national revival and patriotism. It was also the forcing house

THE NOVÉ MĚSTO AND VYŠEHRAD
Postal Museum
Samcova
Petrska
Tesnov
St Peter's in Porici
Biskupska
Na Florenci
Museum of Prague History and Art
Josefov
Na porici
St Joseph
Havlickova
Masaryk Station
Obecni Dum
Republic Square
Hybernska
Powder Tower
Nové
Senovazne nam
Opletalova
Stare
Na prikope
Nekazanka
St Henry's
Jeruzalemska
Vltava
Embankment
Město
Město
Panska
Jindrisska
Wilsonovo Station
Our Lady of the Snows
Wenceslas
Politickych
Smetana
Narodni
Laterna Magika
Jungmannova
Bridge of Legions
Purkynova
Vodickova
Square
veznu
Viteznehovnora
St Ursula
Smetana Theatre
National Theatre
New Stage Scene
Vorsilska
Spalena
Holy Trinity
Lazarska
Stepanska
St Wenceslas
National Museum

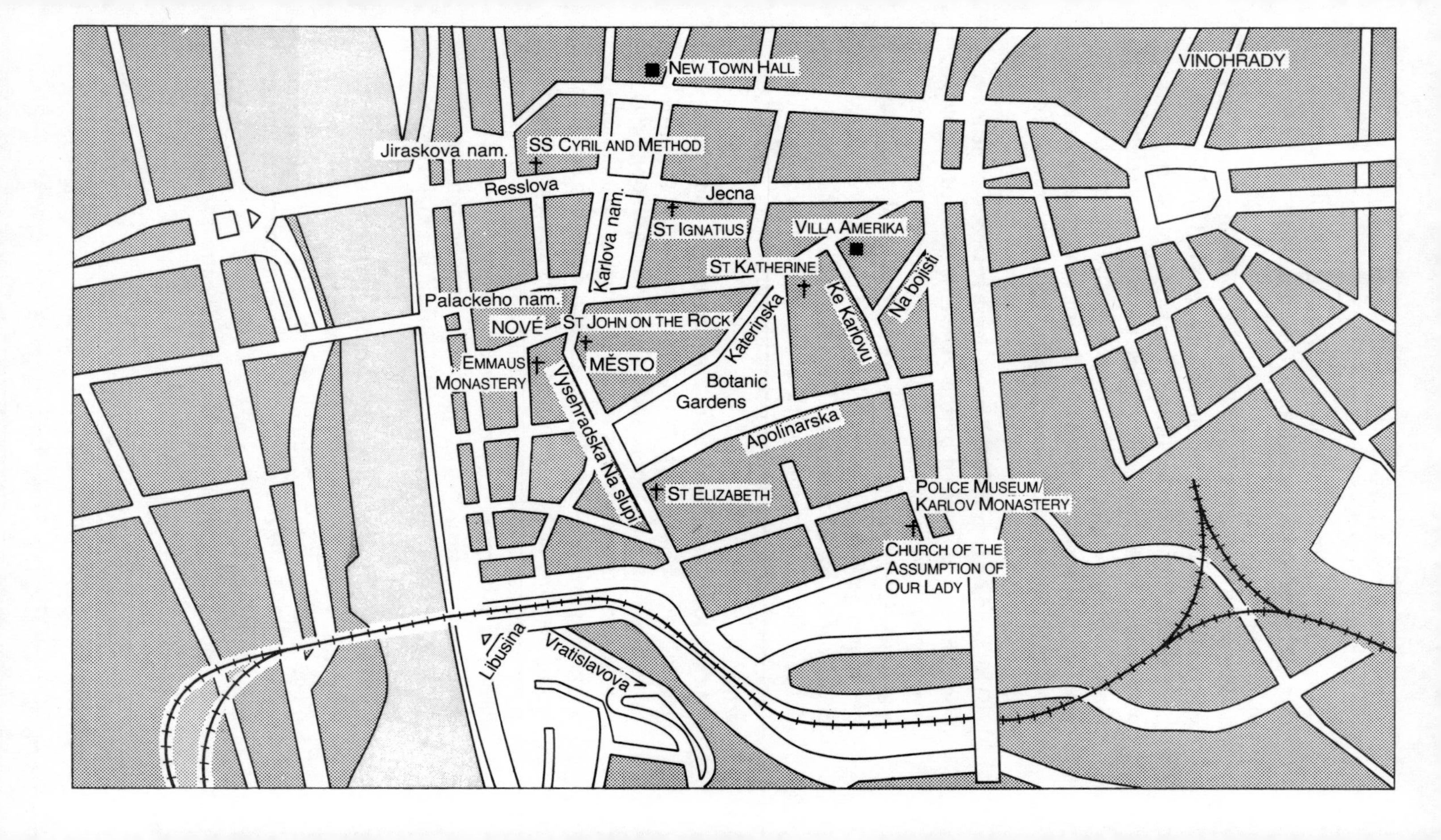
VINOHRADY
NEW TOWN HALL
Jiraskova nam.
SS CYRIL AND METHOD
Resslova
Jecna
Karlova nam.
ST IGNATIUS
VILLA AMERIKA
ST KATHERINE
Na bojisti
Ke Karlovu
Katerinska
Palackeho nam.
NOVÉ
ST JOHN ON THE ROCK
MĚSTO
EMMAUS
MONASTERY
Vysehradska Na slupi
Botanic
Gardens
Apolinarska
ST ELIZABETH
POLICE MUSEUM/
KARLOV MONASTERY
CHURCH OF THE
ASSUMPTION OF
OUR LADY
Libusina
Vratislavova

for a group of young Bohemian artists, the so-called Generation of the National Theatre, much of whose work can be seen in St Agnes.

The neo-Renaissance building was planned by Josef Zítek who had trained in the studio of Van der Nüll and Siccardsburg, the architects of the Vienna Opera. The foundation stone was laid in 1868, and other stones, brought from celebrated places in Bohemia and Moravia, were set into the foundations. Just before it was completed in 1881, there was a fire and the rebuilding, started under Josef Schulz, was finally completed in 1883.

The building is grand with no expense spared. On the main floor, the loggia inspired by the Venetians is decorated with lunettes by J. Tulka and sculptures representing epic poetry and lyrics. On the balustrade above are statues of Apollo and the Muses between chariots bearing the Goddess of Victory, all modelled by B. Schnirch. The theatre building has been dubbed the 'culminating work of Czech architecture of the 19C', but the interior too is a rich gallery of late 19C Bohemian art.

In the foyer and vestibule is a pantheon of bronze busts of people involved in Czech drama and opera, modelled by L. Šaloun, B. Kafka, J. Štursa and J. V. Myslbek among others. On the walls of the foyer is a cycle of lunettes, 'My Country', painted by M. Aleš in 1881. František Ženíšek painted the ceiling here and in the auditorium. The presidential box and its anterooms are also decorated with paintings and sculpture, largely of subjects taken from Czech history, by artists of the stature of V. Brožík and J. Mařák and by the sculptors A. Wagner and J. V. Myslbek. The curtain is a major work of V. Hynais.

Next door is the New Stage Scene, a theatre built by K. Práger in 1977–83 with a glass façade hiding the director's office and the theatre administration. Tickets for performances are difficult to get but there is a convenient restaurant in the building.

Immediately opposite the National Theatre is the Lažanský

Palace (1/1012), a severe example of Renaissance Revival built in 1861–3 by Ignác Ullmann. Smetana lived here between 1863 and 1869 and it is now the Academy of Music, Film and Theatre. On the ground floor is the well-known café Slavia where one may take a leisurely coffee overlooking the river.

Farther along Národní at 5/1009 is another large neo-Renaissance building, the former Czech Savings Bank, built between 1858 and 1862 also by Ullmann and with sculptural groups depicting Bohemia, executed by Wildt after drawings by J. Manés. The entrance hall has a bronze lion by Myslbek. In one part is the Academy of Sciences founded in 1952 as successor to the Bohemian Academy of Sciences and Arts. The latter was founded in 1890 by Josef Hlávka and played an important part in laying the foundations for a new generation of Czech scientists.

Continue down Národní třída which was laid out in 1781 along the fortifications and moat of the Old Town. The houses on the left belong to the Old Town; those on the right to the New. On the left are two superb Art Nouveau buildings from 1907–8, after plans by O. Polívka. At No. 7/1011 is the former Savings Bank of Prague, built in 1903 with the collaboration of the sculptor Ladislav Šaloun and the designer Franta Anýž. There is now an Italian restaurant in the courtyard.

On your right is the Church and Convent of St Ursula. The convent (8/139) was built in 1674–8 by Marco Antonio Canevale. Over the entrance is a carved St Ursula of 1674 by Hieronym Kohl. The rather good *vinárna* Convent is situated on the ground floor. The church was also by Canevale, and was one of the first high Baroque interiors in Prague. The façade holds figures by F. Preiss and the ubiquitous St John Nepomuk by I. F. Platzer of 1747. Enter the church by the s door. The church has been newly restored and gives a marvellous picture of early 18C decoration. The frescos are by J. J. Stevens of Steinfels, the stucco by T. Soldati and the scagliola was carried out by J. T. Baumgartner. František Preiss was responsible for the statues and the altars. The picture frames and pulpit are superb. On the main altar is a St Ursula by J. K.

Liška and the two paintings below the choir are also by his hand. The Assumption of the Virgin was painted by Petr Brandl before 1709 and there is a Nativity by the Swiss J. R. Bys and a St Joseph by J. B. Risi.

The congregation is always full of nuns. Although the convents were closed at the same time as the monasteries in 1954, the Communists found there was no one to look after the sick and the mentally ill, so some nuns were allowed to follow their vows. The Ursuline nuns returned in 1990 and, in September 1990, opened the first church school in Prague since the Communists took power.

Returning to Národní Street, turn right into Voršilská Street. At 12/140 is the neo-Baroque Valter Palace built in 1891 by a wealthy owner of sugar refineries. Its architect, Friedrich Ohmann, was professor of Decorative Arts in Prague and later became official architect in Vienna for Franz Josef. This is now the seat of the Vatican Nuncio. At the end of the street on the left at No. 10/130 is the Schwarzenberg Palace of 1787 by I. J. Palliardi.

Return to Národní Street, keeping to the right, and you will see on the corner at 10/138 the Danube Palace of 1928–30 by O. Polívka and A. Foehr.

Across the road are two houses, 15/341 and 17/349, in the early modern style from 1912 by B. Hypšman, a pupil of Otto Wagner. On the right at No. 12/118 is the Baroque Schirding Palace probably built by F. M. Kaňka from 1735–40. It was beneath these arcades that the student demonstration of 17 November 1989 was so brutally put down and the 'Velvet Revolution' began. To mark the spot, a mound of candle wax grows from the flickering candles among bunches of flowers.

Continue along Národní Street and, at the crossing with Spálená Street, at No. 9/342 is Albatros, the famous House of Children's Books built in the 1960s by S. Franc and L. Hauf. On the other side at 26/63 is the department store Máj built in the 1970s. Turn right down Spálená Street past the metro station and there are several Constructivist buildings from the 1920s and 1930s. Among the best is the Olympic store at No.

16/75 designed by J. Krejcar in 1923–6. Here the terraces and receding storeys were balustraded with railings taking their inspiration from ships. Note too, the factory production line windows which show how the architect is following the theories of Constructivism of the founder members of Devětsil in the early twenties (see p. 22). Turn left into the narrow Purkyně Street to the House of Slovak Culture (4/153) with its exhibition rooms and restaurant. It is a most attractive late Baroque building from the end of the 18C. It is here that the philosopher J. E. Purkyně died in 1869.

Walk back to Národní Street and farther down on the left is the huge façade of Plateys House (37/416) which you may have also visited from the Old Town walk (see p. 134). It was built between 1813 and 1847 by J. Hausknecht and has a fine courtyard. In 1840 and 1846 Franz Liszt gave concerts in the hall.

On the same side at 49/365 is a rather dull building, the Hypotecs Bank by I. Ullmann of 1865–6. On the other side of the street is the now shabby Špála Gallery at 30/59. This was formerly the J. R. Vilímek publishing house designed by F. Zelenka *c.*1938. Further Functionalistic buildings such as No. 32/58, the Palace Chicago of 1925 by J. Havlíček and O. Polívka and DILO at 36/38, a Co-operative for Supporting Arts and Crafts built from 1936–8 by O. Starý, rub shoulders with a late Baroque palace at 38/37, formerly the Desfours Palace brought up to date in 1794 by I. Palliardi. In the winter of 1799 the Russian commander, A. V. Suvorov, had his headquarters here.

At No. 40/36 on the corner of Jungmannova Street, is the Adria Palace built between 1923 and 1925 for the Italian insurance company the Riunione Adriatica di Sicurità after a plan of J. Zasche and P. Janák. If you don't mind risking your life, stand back to enjoy the superb Art Deco sculpture, the work of O. Gutfreund, K. Dvořák and B. Kafka. The experimental Laterna magika Theatre has worked from the basement since 1958 and from its depths, Václav Havel and his supporters planned the first stages of the 'Velvet Revolution'.

Turn right into Jungmannova. On the left at No. 30/748 is the Mozarteum, the publishing house of M. Urbánek built by J. Kotěra, 1912–13, with sculpture by J. Štursa. To its right at 29/35 is the Škoda company head office by P. Janák, 1924–6, with statues by K. Dvořák.

Return to Jungmannova Square. Here is a monument of 1878 by Ludvík Šimek to Josef Jungmann, author of the first Czech dictionary. Walk through the imposing Doric portal ahead to the beautiful Church of Our Lady of the Snows, formerly belonging to the Carmelites and founded in 1347 by Charles IV. The choir of this monumental church was completed between 1379 and 1397, but the building of the nave was halted during the Hussite Wars. However, the Hussites made full use of the building, their leader Jan Želivský preaching here until 1422. The Franciscans were given the church in 1603 and under them, restoration went ahead. At the entrance is a modern mosaic by V. Foerster and sculptures dating from 1715 of St John Nepomuk and St Peter of Alcantara by J. O. Mayer. The interior is most beautiful, the Baroque mixing well with the late Gothic. It is perhaps due to the height that such a sense of refinement is achieved. The main altar dates from 1649–51 with sculptures on the wall from 1625 by A. Heidelberger. There is also an Annunciation by V. V. Reiner of 1725 and a typical Bohemian pewter font of 1459.

Leaving the church, turn right across the small garden into the street where there is a good Functionalist design of a shop front of the House of Musical Instruments from 1938. Walk around to the N side of the church with its exquisite tympanum from the mid-14C. The iconography is complex; God the Father at the head of Christ crucified on the Tree of Life. At Christ's feet is an elegant Coronation of the Virgin and beside them are the donors – Charles IV and Blanche of Valois. The original tympanum is in St George's.

Contrasts are perhaps more startling in the New Town than elsewhere in Prague. In front of this elegant gateway at the N side of the church is a lamp straight from the studios of

Cubism, probably made in 1913 by V. Hofman. Walk through the passage ahead into Wenceslas Square.

This must be the most photographed public space in Prague. Its dimensions were laid down by Charles IV in 1348 and it has remained the city's main thoroughfare, shopping centre and hotel area. The combination of live music playing in the square and circles of melting candles piled on the ground around images of those killed by the last regime, remind us that this is also the centre of social and political life. So many of Bohemia's revolutions have begun here – in 1848, 1918, 1948 and 1989. Since 1680 a statue of Wenceslas has overlooked the square. The earlier statue by J. J. Bendl, has been moved to Vyšehrad. The present equestrian statue of Wenceslas surrounded by the Czech patron saints Adalbert, Procopius, Ludmila and Agnes now stands at the SE end of the square. In 1894 J. V. Myslbek, the founder of modern sculpture in Czechoslovakia, won the competition for the design of this group. His fine free modelling work has echoes of that of Sir Alfred Gilbert in England. The equestrian statue was erected in 1912 but the Czech patron saints were added later in 1923. The design of the base was by A. Dryák with decoration by C. Klouček. The whole was sponsored by the Academy of Arts and Sciences, the Bank of Bohemia and the City of Prague. It was here that the Czech student from Charles University, Jan Palach, set fire to himself in protest at the arrival of the Russian tanks in Prague in 1968, and now the candles and flowers here also commemorate the revolution of 1989. A wooden theatre, the so-called Hut, solely for the performance of Czech plays was situated at the N of the square from 1786 to 1789.

Since the beginning of this century, Wenceslas Square has become a showplace of architectural movements. All is here from the last vestiges of 19C Romantic Revivalism, to the new Brutalism of the 1960s. For a long time the Revivalist styles of the neo-Baroque and Renaissance ran a parallel course with Art Nouveau, aptly named as the art of the new century and the first architectural style to break with the past. Prague's most original and exciting contribution to this architectural lexicon, its unique style of Art Deco, is not well represented in the square although there is an example (12/777) of the architecture of Jan Kotěra, one of the main protagonists of Art Deco, whose later severe use of brick and concrete was considered too rationalistic by some of his contemporaries. Kotěra had studied architecture in Vienna under the great Otto Wagner and became a lecturer at the Art-Industrial School in 1898 and then Professor of the Academy of Fine Arts in Prague. He trained Jaromir Krejjar, architect, designer and theorist of the later Devětsil (see p. 22).

For those who do not have a great interest in 20C architecture, I would suggest an amble up to the statue of St Wenceslas under the National Museum. By night the throngs of people and the circles of glowing candles transform this forbidding place. There are plenty of good hotels offering refreshment. The Europa Hotel is highly recommended as the interior is superb, but it is not cheap.

However, for those who would like to see something of the Modern Movement in Prague, both before the First World War, with its Art Nouveau and Cubism, and from 1918–39 when the Devětsil's Constructivism was the rage, start in the NW corner. At 4/773 is Lindt's House, built in the Constructivist style in 1926–8 by L. Kysela. Next, at 6/774, is the Baťa shoe store, again by Kysela, 1928–9. (Baťa began his rise to fortune in the 1920s by applying industrial methods to the production of shoes. He believed in profit-sharing for the workforce and set up an advanced school of design. His beliefs were contrary to those of the Communist regime.) Less aggressively functional is 8/775, Adam's Apotheke, designed by M. Blecha and J. Králíček, with fine statues of Adam and Eve by A. Waigant of 1911–13. No. 10/776 goes by the unlikely name of the Holy Trinity, an administrative office building for trade – the function of so many of the buildings around this square. It is an example by A. Dlabač (1899–1900), with sculpture by the excellent L. Šaloun and V. Amort. At 12/777 is Peterka House, built to fulfil both residential and commercial needs after a project undertaken by Jan Kotěra between

1899 and 1901, and actually signed by him. The decorative Art Nouveau stucco is by Sucharda and J. Pekárek and contains good detailing. At 22/782, Juliš House is a Constructivist house by Pavel Janák, built in 1930–2. At 28/785 is the Alfa Palace by L. Kysela and J. Jarolím, with a passage through it to the Semafor Theatre, reknowned for its avant-garde plays. No. 30/788 demonstrates that the battle of the styles – the 19C versus the 20C – continued to the outbreak of war and beyond. This neo-Baroque building was erected between 1914 and 1916 by J. Sakař and O. Polívka.

Cross Vodičkova Street and continue along the square. No. 34/792 is the very colourful Wiehl House (1895–6) in the Bohemian neo-Renaissance style by the architect A. Wiehl with paintings by M. Aleš, J. Fanta and L. Novák. It houses the main offices of the Academia publishing house. At 36/793 is the Melantrich House constructed after a project by B. Bendlmayer and modified about 1930 by J. E. Koula. It is now the offices and publishing house of the Socialist Party newspaper. From the balcony, President Havel and others spoke to the demonstrators in November 1989. Next, at 38/794–5, is a Modernist building of 1911–13 by M. Blecha and E. Králíček.

Turn right into Štěpánská where the vast Lucerna Palace at 61/704 was built to the designs of V. Havel, grandfather of President Havel, between 1907 and 1921. This pleasure complex includes a cinema and large concert and dancing hall in the basement. It is notable for being the first building in Prague to use reinforced concrete. Return to the square and at 42/796 is the grim-looking Czech State Savings Bank, a Constructivist building by F. Roith of 1929–31. It has a splendid main hall.

To the SE of the square visit 54/802, the Fénix Palace which was built for trade and administration by B. Ehrmann and J. Gočár from 1928–9. In the passage there are mosaics by R. Kremlička. You will now be alongside the Wenceslas Monument looking back down the hill. Towering over the square is the National Museum (68/1700) in the place of the Horse Gate. The whole idea of a national museum was the brainchild of Count Caspar Sternberg in 1818 but the collections did not have a purpose-built home until a public competition in 1884 for the design of a building was won by Josef Schulz. The museum was inspired by Perrault's E façade of the Louvre (1665) and was completed in 1890. The decoration owes little to France however and the statues personifying every imaginable Bohemian and 19C-approved virtue, art and science are by A. Wagner, J. Maudr, B. Schnirch and A. Popp. You will notice that the stonework has been damaged by gunfire. In 1968 the Warsaw Pact troops attacked the building, mistakenly thinking that it concealed the radio station. The lavish interior with its splendid staircase was decorated between 1895 and 1902 by well-known painters such as V. Hynais, V. Brožík and F. Ženíšek. The staircase is lined with the busts of those responsible for the founding of the museum. In the Pantheon there are wall paintings of important episodes in Bohemian history, further allegories of Science, Power, Art and Inspiration by V. Hynais, and more busts of great Czechs by the leading sculptors of the day, including many who worked on the National Theatre. If you wish to see displays which have hardly changed since they were first installed, it is well worth a visit to the beautifully laid out mineorological rooms. The museum also has an interesting, if curious exhibit showing the relationship between the portraits carved by Peter Parler of the royal family in St Vitus' and the reconstruction of their features from their skulls, demonstrating that they were portraits from life.

When you leave the National Museum, notice the street at the side leading to the Radio Station. It is known as the street of Political Mistakes because its name has been so frequently changed according to the vagaries of politics.

From the National Museum turn right to the Federal Assembly at No. 6/52 on Vítězného února Street. It was built as the Stock Exchange in a neo-Classical style in 1936 by J. Rössler and was given its strangely shaped but practical addition in 1973 by K. Práger, J. Albrecht and J. Kadeřábek. The statue Atomic Age is by V. Makovský from the Brussels Expo '58.

Next to it at 8/101 is the Smetana Theatre, formerly the Deutscher Opera which was built in competition to the National Theatre. It is in the neo-Renaissance style by the Viennese firm Fellner and Helmer with statues by O. Mentzel and T. Friedl. The interior is a delight, pure *fin de siècle* Rococo in white and gold with paintings by E. Veith.

Return to Good King Wenceslas and walk down the square on your right. Remember to keep a lookout for the many good, very cheap record shops. At 45/818 is the Jalta Hotel, a neo-Classic design by A. Tenzer of the fifties with a good cocktail bar on the balcony, but where service can be slow. At 41/820 is Letka, another administrative and trade building in the Constructivist style by B. Kozák of 1924–6. One of the glories of the square is the Europa Hotel (29/826), a splendid Art Nouveau building designed by B. Bendlmayer in 1903–5 with the collaboration of B. Hypšman and A. Dryák. The interiors have managed to retain their glory. The building at No. 21/831 – a 1970s example of Czech Brutalism – leaves a different taste in the mouth. The bank at No. 19/832 employed Franz Kafka while he was working on *The Trial*. It was built by F. Ohmann and O. Polívka with decoration by S. Sucharda, B. Schnirch and A. Procházka.

Wenceslas Square is a centre for publishing. The Praha Palace at 17/834 was the office of the Práce publishing house and printers. Its glazed façade by R. Stockar dates to 1927–9. No. 15/835 was the printing house of Politik newspapers, built in 1906–7 by M. Blecha and E. Králíček. The Práce bookshop at 13/838 was built by J. Sakař with decoration by C. Klouček. The same architects were involved at No. 7/839, the Golden Goose Hotel, built between 1909 and 1910. There is a very ugly passage modernized in the 1930s by L. Machoň. He also adapted the popular restaurant the Koruna next door, which was originally built as offices and shops in 1912–13 by A. Pfeiffer. The sculpture was done by V. Sucharda and the frescos by V. Foerster.The lower part of Wenceslas Square is called Můstek which is also the name of the metro station beneath the buildings. On the corner by the metro station is the

1983 building of the ČKD engineering works (1/388). This was one of the first examples of post-Modern architecture and has been influential for the young generation of Czech architects. Farther along is a late Baroque building of the 1780s (12/378) and the Prague Bank (13/377), erected in 1902 by Matěj Blecha with Art Nouveau decoration by C. Klouček. There is a good café in the building above the metro station.

At the end of the square turn right into Na příkopě built on the site of the Old Town defences. This must vie with the most interesting streets in the capital, and is quite different in mood from Wenceslas Square. Starting on the right you come to No. 4/847, the House of Elegance, Prague's oldest department store built between 1869 and 1871 after a plan by Theophil Hansen of Vienna. It has a façade meticulously designed in the north Italian style with, surprisingly for a shop, sculptures of the Virtues carved into it. Unfortunately, all the original fixtures have gone apart from the staircase. On the other side of the street the State Bank (3/390), formerly the Wiener Bankverein, was built in 1906–8 by Josef Zasche and Alexander Neumann with sculpture round the door by Franz Metzner. On the right at No. 10/852 is the Sylva-Taroucca Palace, formerly belonging to the Piccolomini family. It is the fruit of collaboration between K. I. Dientzenhofer and Anselmo Lurago between 1743 and 1751. Inside there is a fine staircase decorated with stucco by C. G. Bossi, as well as sculptures by I. F. Platzer and frescos by V. B. Ambrozzi. Between 1895 and 1905 the ethnographic collections from the National Museum were shown here. On the same side is the House at the Black Rose (12/853). Its façade dates from 1847 and it was one of the first buildings in Prague to have proper plumbing.

On the site of the State Bank (14/854) was the house where the Czech writer Božena Němcová died. She is considered the Czech George Sand or George Eliot. She wrote the first truly Czech novel, *Babička* (Grandmother) in 1850, a book for children which has always been important for Czech nationalism. One of her patrons was Vojta Náprstek (see p. 135). Opposite at 15/583 is a further Constructivist house by L.

Kysela of about 1927 and if you turn left into Havířská Street, No. 4/397 is interesting: it is a building of 1930 by A. Foehr with reliefs from an earlier house of 1794.

Now return to Na příkopě. On your right on the corner with Panská Street is the Church of the Holy Rood, an unusual example of neo-Classicism built between 1819 and 1823 by J. Hausknecht. The simple furnishings date from 1824. The church was part of a gymnasium and college in Panská Street (1/892) built in 1766 by A. Müller and adapted in the 1860s. There is a 1766 fresco in the interior by J. Hager. The gymnasium gained a reputation for its high academic standards and many Czechs of note studied here. Turning into Panská Street, at 5/891 is the Neuburg Palace remodelled probably by Kaňka some time before 1747. The palace once contained a famous private collection of antiquities which was moved in 1892 to the Applied Arts Museum. Next at 7/890 is the Kaunic Palace, probably designed by Alliprandi in 1716–24. It was remodelled both in 1782 and 1843 when the great hall was decorated with frescos in the Romantic style. At 6/895 is the Stahlburg Palace, built in the Rococo Revival style by Josef Maličký and at 8/896 – the home of the Mladá Fronta newspaper – is another Revival style building, this time one in Renaissance Revival by I. Ullmann of 1861.

Return to Na příkopě and banks once more come to the fore. On the same side of the Holy Rood church is the former State Bank (18/857). This is interesting as an example of the mix between late historicism and Art Nouveau. It was designed in 1909–11 by O. Polívka with sculptures by C. Klouček and L. Šaloun, and mosaics by J. Preisler. On the ground floor is the information centre of Čedok, the Czech national tourist office. It is connected by a sort of Bridge of Sighs to a much earlier building, the Živnobanka or Investment Bank (20/858). Look at the side portal on the right in Nekázanka Street – a good example of high Baroque executed by M. B. Braun about 1735. You will notice the new keystone above the doorway with Polívka's portrait. In 1845 it was the property of the Nostic family and they gave shelter to the collections of the National Museum here until 1890. The bank itself, with its entrance on Na příkopě, is well worth a visit as a reminder of the wealth and industrial power of Czechoslovakia within the Austro-Hungarian Empire at the end of the 19C. Czech neo-Renaissance was the style chosen by O. Polívka in 1894 for its remodelling, and the reliefs on the façade are personifications of Technology, Agriculture, Industry and Trade by C. Klouček. M. Aleš prepared the cartoon for the mosaics and in the vestibule there are wall paintings by M. Švabinský of 1896. The staircase by F. Hergessel is pompous with decoration and paintings by K. Klusáček and K. V. Mašek. On the first floor, overlooked by the torch bearers of B. Schnirch and the statues of the Czech regions by S. Sucharda and Schnirch, you may find it difficult to resist cashing a cheque.

Next door is the former Vernier Palace (22/859) of the 17C. In 1873 the interior was adapted to a German casino and it is now a restaurant with a non-stop bar on the ground floor. On the other side of the street, at 29/583, is the first building in Prague with an all-glass façade, built in 1960. At 29/988 is the Sevastopol Palace with a cinema and Constructivist passageway of 1937. This was the site of the famous Café Corso, Prague's first Art Nouveau building in 1897. There was another famous café – the Café Français – on the site of the 1930s Escompt Bank at 33/969. It was one of Franz Liszt's favourite watering places. Between 1945 and 1960, the bank was the home of the central offices of the Committee of the Communist Party.

Now you come again to the Powder Tower (see p. 132) which was the gate from the Old Town to the New. Vladislav Jagiello's Royal Court was just next door on the site of the magnificent Art Nouveau Obecní dům or Representatives' House (5/1090). This is still one of the most important concert halls in Prague and here the Prague Music Festival begins with Smetana's *Má Vlast* (My Country) in May every year. Antonín Balšánek and O. Polívka won the commission for the Obecní dům in 1903 and it was built between 1906–11. Its richly modelled façade was decorated by a number of official artists including L. Šaloun and J. Mařatka among others. The mosaic Hommage à Prague is by Karel Špilar. Inside is one of the few important interiors of this period left untouched in Europe. Even the lifts date to the first decade of this century. In the basement is the *vinárna* and on the ground floor a most attractive café and restaurant with mosaics by J. Preisler. A grand staircase carries the concertgoer to the first floor and to the Smetana Hall, the largest of the concert halls in Prague. Here the wall paintings are by K. Špilar. The sculptures of Bohemian Dances and Vyšehrad are by L. Šaloun and the medallion of Smetana was modelled by F. Hergessel. Around the landing on the first floor are individual salons. The most celebrated is the so-called Lord Mayor Salon decorated by Alfons Mucha. In the Reiger's Salon are wall paintings by M. Švabinský. The Sladkovský Salon is decorated by V. I. Ullmann and Grégrs's Salon by F. Ženíšek, but the best examples of Art Nouveau are the Palacký Salon decorated by J. Preisler and the Moravian Salon with its fountain by J. Pekárek. There is even a neo-Classical sweetshop. There can be no doubt that the Obecní dům is one of the city's most important cultural and social centres.

Leaving the Obecní dům, ahead, in Republic Square, is St Joseph's Church of the Capuchins, dating to the first half of the 17C. The barracks at 1/1078, still in use, are an attractive example of Gothic Revival of 1860.

On the other side of Obecní dům, at 4/2037, is U hybernů, a dour-looking building offering a rare example of Prague Empire architecture. This was a style that was to prove influential for the Constructivists in the 1920s and 1930s. It was built between 1808 and 1811 by Jiří Fischer as the Prague Custom House, but since 1940 it has been an exhibition centre. The street name of Hybernská is earlier however. On this site a Benedictine monastery was founded by Charles IV, which was then given to a Franciscan Order from Ireland, the Hibernians. The monastery was abolished by Josef II.

On the corner between Na příkopě and Hybernská Street, at

28/864, is the State Commercial Bank built by F. Roith in 1938. Before this, it was the site of the famous Blue Star Hotel, where Tchaikovsky and Chopin lodged and where the peace treaty between Prussia and Austria was signed in 1866. From here continue up Hybernská Street. To the left at 3/1036 is the Sweert-Sporck Palace. The early 18C palace was adapted in 1783 by Antonín Haffenecker, and the lower part of the building was added in 1793 by Palliardi. The sculptured portals are by the Platzer workshop. Josef Gočár achieved the difficult task of adding sympathetically to this building in 1923–4 for the Anglobank. At 7/1033, in the former Losy Palace, is the Lenin Museum whose future must be under review. The building dates to the middle years of the 17C with Carlo Lurago as architect. F. Heger adapted the street façade in a neo-Classic style in 1798. In 1912 the sixth conference of the Russian Democratic Party, under the leadership of V. I. Lenin, was held here and it remained the Central Office of the Czech Social-Democratic Party until it was forced to merge with the Communists in 1950. It became the Lenin Museum soon after this, and reliefs depicting Lenin's life were installed on the façade. At the time of writing it is the Socialist Party's Central Office.

On the other side of this busy street at 10/1001 is the Central Hotel, an Art Nouveau building of 1898–1900 by F. Ohmann and Q. Bělský. At one time it was the home of the famous cabaret Red Seven, then subsequently, in 1929, it was adapted to become the Chamber Theatre. Round to your left at 9/1030 Hybernská Street is Lanna House, a neo-Gothic building of 1857 by J. Ripota and J. Kranner. The interiors were famed for their collections of the art patron Vojtěch Lanna, one of the founders of the Museum of Decorative Arts (see p. 120). Retrace your steps to the corner leaving Masaryk Station (2/1014), the earliest in Prague of 1843–5, on your left, turning left down Havličkova then right into Na poříčí. Here at 24/1046 is the Legiobank of 1921–3 by Josef Gočár, with sculptural decoration by J. Štursa and O. Gutfreund.

Turn left into Biskupská Street to St Peter's Church in Poříčí in Petrská Street. In the Middle Ages Poříčí was the area of the German merchants and the church belonged to the Order of German Knights. Later, in 1235, the church was given to the Knights of the Cross with the Red Star. The original basilica was built in the middle of the 12C, then reconstructed twice in the 14C. Josef Mocker took a hand between 1874 and 1879 resulting in the neo-Gothic main door with a relief by L. Šimek. Inside, V. V. Reiner painted the High Altar with Christ and St Peter in 1730, the side altar of St Florian is by P. Molitor, and at the W end stands a statue of St Peter by M. V. Jäckel of 1722. There is a font of 1544. The belfry is late Gothic of 1598, but has a Baroque dome.

Continue to the embankment via Samcova Street. Looking over to the Šverma Bridge on your left, you will see a number of ministries and offices of industrial companies from the twenties and thirties. Below the Gothic water tower there is the small white building of the Vávra Mill (2/1239) which was one of several mills in this area. Originally 16C, it was rebuilt in 1840 and is now the Postal Museum. It is well worth a visit even if you are not a philatelist. The house belonged to Michalovic who commissioned Josef Navrátil to decorate his living-rooms upstairs. The stamps are an interesting reflection on some aspects of history and also on the attitude to artists in Czechoslovakia. Many of the foremost artists in Prague, including Mucha were commissioned to design the stamps. They are easily accessible in well-designed cabinets and include stamps from all over the world, but those from Czechoslovakia reveal politically interesting periods in the country's history. The first stamps found here date from 1918; they are Austrian, overstamped in Czech. Some commemorate the Czech Legion which fought against the Communists in Russia at the end of the First World War. Many of these men and their families had to escape through Japan. During the Communist regime this episode tended to be ignored. Also of interest are those stamps printed in London by the Czech government in exile in 1945.

Upstairs, in the first-floor living-rooms, the series of

decorative paintings are charming. Here the armchair traveller may surround himself with European Alpine scenery without moving a step, or he can travel through time with scenes from Czech history and theatre. There is also a self-portrait of the artist Navrátil, and some of the lovely still-lifes for which he is best known.

Returning to the embankment, the ministries continue with No. 12/1222, the grim Ministry of Transport (1927–31) which later became the headquarters of the Communist Party and which has now returned to its original role. Round the corner at 17/65, is the Ministry of Agriculture by F. Roith of 1927–30. Moving farther upstream, cut off by the motorway is Těšnov with the Museum of Prague History and Art (1/1554). The motorway cutting through this area is a marvellous example of bad planning. The planning authorities have attempted to appease the public by laying out an apology for a lapidarium under the carriageway. The elegant classical building housing the museum and surrounded by a small park was built in 1898.

The displays start upstairs on the first floor. On the landing is the original clockface by Manés from the Town Hall in Old Town Square, showing idealized Czech peasants at work in their fields (see p. 115). The exhibits contain many treasures from the Middle Ages including a very beautiful Man of Sorrows, originally from the New Town Hall of 1510–20. It is interesting too to see material from the guild halls and to remember that as each town of Prague was autonomous until the reign of Josef II, each had its own guild system and town hall.

But the most important item in the museum is the famous model of Prague, the so-called Langweil Model of 1826–34. Here, made to exact scale from paper, is the castle, the Malá Strana, the Old Town and the New as they were in 1834. What is so remarkable is to see how little has changed: the cathedral has not been finished, the Marian statue still stands in Old Town Square but the statue of Jan Hus does not, the river has not been embanked and the Josefov is seen in all its picturesque glory. As if in an aircraft it becomes really possible to appreciate the vastness and importance of the Clementinum, looking somewhat like the Escorial, or the spaciousness of the garden city of the Malá Strana in comparison to the Gothic huddle of the Old Town. And on a more practical level, this unique model has been most useful as a reference for the protection and conservation of ancient monuments.

Return to Masaryk Station, passing under the motorway by way of Těšnov and Na Florenci. Turn left into Havlíčkova Street, left into Hybernská, then right into Opletalova. Then cross Vrchlického Sady passing the small Art Deco tobacco shop (*c.*1920) to reach the main railway station. It was once named after Franz Josef and is now named Wilsonovo after President Wilson. It was built between 1901 and 1909 by J. Fanta but, as is obvious, it was richly decorated by the protagonists of Art Nouveau. The doorways and lateral towers were decorated by S. Sucharda, Č. Vosmík and H. Folkmann, and the vestibule by J. Fröhlich. The construction of the main hall from 1901 by J. Marjanka and P. Kornfeld was one of the most important examples of technical architecture in Prague at this period. Alas, the fine station restaurant has been destroyed. The new station beneath was added in the 1970s and works efficiently if not stylishly. Walk back across the park and at 29/1337 Opletalova is a further example of 1920s neo-Classicism in the Automobile Club of Czechoslovakia. Turn left into Jeruzalémská Street and at 5/961 is the Jubilee Synagogue. When three synagogues in the Josefov were demolished in 1898, a society for the construction of a new synagogue was founded. The granting of civil liberties to the Jews in 1848 meant that many left the ghetto to settle in other parts of Prague, so a synagogue was needed here. Alois Richter was commissioned to build this one in 1906 to the design of Wilhelm Stiastný. It is built in the richly exotic Islamic Revival style then so popular in Europe. This one and the Old-New Synagogue (see p. 123) are the only synagogues that still serve the Jews of Prague.

Shortly before coming to the junction of Jeruzalémská

Street with Jindřišská and the ancient hay market, is a Constructivist building (3/1321) for an electrical company by F. A. Libra of 1928. To the left is St Henry's Church, founded at the same time as the New Town in 1348. The exterior has the machine-cut feel of the 19C and indeed in 1875–9 J. Mocker busied himself here. However, the statues on the front of the church, of St John Nepomuk and St Jude date from 1709 and are from the workshops of Brokof. The tower was completed at the end of the 15C and there is a Renaissance porch of 1526.

The interior is worth a visit. In the porch there are wall paintings of 1535. The Gothic interior was given a Baroque facelift between 1737 and 1749, but retains the original furnishings from both the 17 and 18C. There are several important paintings in the church. At the W end, on the right, is the altar of St John Nepomuk where there is a 15C panel painting of the Madonna. Again on the right, in the Chapel of the Virgin, V. V. Reiner painted a Transfiguration and an Immaculate Conception. At the E end is the Annunciation by Trevisano of 1675, and on the High Altar are the patron saints, SS Henry and Cunigund by J. J. Heintsch of 1689 with statues by Bendl of SS Adalbert and Wenceslas. Also in the chancel is a St Cecilia by Heintsch. Karel Škréta's Holy Trinity is in the N chancel with further canvases by J. J. Heintsch. There is a font of 1487.

Return to the street and note the 15C belfry standing apart; this was 'done over' by Mocker in 1879. Turn right into the square, náměstí Senovážné, (the Hay Market). No. 29/866 was formerly the Stock Exchange, built in 1894 and now the offices of Czech Television, and the Ministry of Machine Industries at 32/976 was built in 1912 by J. Zasche. Make your way back along Jindřišská Street and on the left at 20/939 is the Harrach Palace of 1765–70. This is a good piece of architecture by I. J. Palliardi camouflaged by the horrible modern colours on its façade. At 9/1308 is the Art Deco building of the Exico company, built in 1923 by J. Gočár, with plastic decoration by K. Dvořák. No. 19/880 should be noted as the birthplace, in 1875, of Rainer Maria Rilke, the poet. To the right, on the corner of Panská Street is the Palace Hotel. This has been newly refurbished in Art Deco style and is one of the plushest and most expensive hotels in Prague. It has a good dining-room and coffee house, all in Art Deco style. Opposite, at 14/909, is the Central Post Office built 1871–4. The large hall inside has painting by K. V. Mašek from 1901. In the 14C this was the site of the botanic garden of Angelo de Firenze, apothecary to Charles IV. It is probable that this was the first botanic garden in Europe. During their visits to Prague, in 1350 and 1356 respectively, Cola di Rienzo and Petrarch stayed in the house of the owner.

Round the corner, by the Post Office in Politických vězňů are two attractive examples of neo-Renaissance palaces at 7-9/936 and 9/1531 by I. Ullmann, and at 11/1419 is a modern building by Jan Kotěra of 1923–4. To follow the next walk, return to Jindřišská and walk straight along it to Wenceslas Square and into Vodičkova Street.

Prague 2

Charles Square – the Church of St Ignatius – the Church of St Katherine – the Karlov Monastery – the Police Museum – the Church of St John on the Rock – the Church of SS Cyril and Method – the Church of St Wenceslas

On your left is the Lucerna Palace (see p. 149) and on the right at 35/708 is a palace by K. I. Dientzenhofer of *c.*1726. At 31/710 is a Cubist house by J. Čapek, now a well-known shop selling Bohemian garnets. Turn right into Palacký Street where, at 7/719 stands the Mac Neven Palace built by I. Palliardi where the historian F. Palacký lived and died. Returning to Vodičkova, it is difficult to miss the Art Nouveau Novák House at 10/699 built by O. Polívka in 1903 as a department store. The mosaics depicting Trade and Industry were designed by J. Preisler. The building is now the Variety cinema and the modern building was added in 1930 by the same architect. At the end of the street, the most important building here is covered in Bohemian sgraffiato. It was the first girls' school in Prague and was designed by I. Ullmann, 1866–7. At 18/681 is the Modernist Security Company building of 1929 by A. Foehr.

If you follow the street round to the left, a little way up the hill and marked by a long queue of people, is the shop selling the best ice cream in Prague. However, by bearing right into Lazarská, at 4/82 you pass the picturesque Cubist house Diamant of 1913 by M. Blecha and Králíček. Turning right into Spálená Street is a fine statue of St John Nepomuk by Brokof from 1717, and the Holy Trinity Church of the Trinitarians founded in 1712 by I. J. Putz from Adelthur. It was built by O. Broggio and finished in 1713. Inside, the most important painting is that on the High Altar by F. A. Maulpertsch of the Holy Trinity. The font is of 1552 and the frescos by A. Schlachter were completed in 1779. Return to the street and turn left up Spálená Street to Charles Square and Prague 2.

Charles Square was founded in 1348 as the cattle market and as the central area of the upper New Town. In the centre of the square Charles IV built a chapel to display the Bohemian crown jewels. By 1382 these had been removed and the Chapel of Corpus Christi was built on the site. In 1473, the pact between the council of Basle and the Hussites was proclaimed here and the text was written on the walls of the chapel (see the facsimiles in the Museum of Prague). The chapel was finally demolished in 1791. Between 1843 and 1863 the public park here was planned by Josef Thomayer, the most important garden designer of the second half of the 19C and whose work you can see on Petřín Hill. There are several memorials here including those to the poet Vítězslav Hálek (1881 by B. Schnirch), to the writers Karolina Světlá (1910, G. Zoula) and E. Krasnohorská (1931, K. Vobišová), to the botanist, B. Roezl (1898, Č. Vosmík and G. Zoula) and to the physiologist, J. E. Purkyně (1961, O. Kozák and V. Štrunc). Farther E is the statue by M. V. Jäckel from 1698 of St Joseph, the patron saint of the Habsburgs.

The N side of the square has the Law Courts of 1901–3 by the Viennese, E. Forster. But perhaps more interesting is the old New Town Hall (1/22), dating from the second half of the 14C. The façade facing the square, with its delightful gables, was built in 1411–16. The belfry was built on earlier foundations in 1451–5 and all was 'modernized' by Benedikt Ried in 1520–6. No restoration work has been carried out since 1905. Now some conservation of both the exterior and the interior with its wonderful high Gothic hall and Baroque chapel is being planned. In front of the Town Hall is a memorial to Jan Želivský, Hussite priest and leader of the revolutionary wing of the Hussite movement. It was from the Town Hall that the first Defenestration of Prague in 1419 took place (see p. 6). Walk past 24/671 where the sculptor M. B. Braun died in 1738, and past the hospital and across Ječná Street to the Jesuit New Town College and its former Church of St Ignatius, with its striking façade.

The church was built in 1665–70 by G. D. Orsi and was finished by M. Reiner in 1671. The distinctive portico is by P. I. Bayer and the belfry is later, dating from 1686–7. The most remarkable feature of this church is the quality of the stucco decoration, both inside and out, carried out by T. Soldati between 1697–9. The interior is grand, based on the ground plan of St Ignatius in Rome. The High Altar has a Celebration of St Ignatius by J. J. Heintsch of 1688, and it was he who painted the Death of St Wenceslas in the church four years later. The statues are good, with the Apostles by M. V. Jäckel and a Calvary by J. A. Quitainer of about 1765. The pulpit by R. Prachner, with its gilded figures and scagliola must have proved a rich background for Jesuit preaching when it was erected in 1760. In the mid-17C Carlo Lurago built the Jesuit College on the site of the appropriated land of 23 houses and 13 gardens. On the Order's abolition in 1773, the college was converted to a hospital. A new Jesuit college was founded near the church in Ječná Street and was in use between 1866 and 1950.

Turn left out of the door and walk to the end of the gardens.

Turn left once more into U nemocnice around Prague's oldest hospital (2/499) built in the 18C. Where the road joins Kateřinská Street, on the right, is the Church of St Katherine. This church is magnificent but has been closed for years as it is structurally unsound. It was founded in 1354 for Augustinian nuns from Bavaria in fulfilment of a vow made by Charles IV. The original Gothic appearance of St Katherine's has been preserved only in its needle-shaped tower. Left almost in ruins by the Hussite Wars, the monastery (30/468) was redesigned between 1718 and 1730, perhaps with the help of Kryštof Dientzenhofer, and the church from 1737–41 by Kilián Ignác Dientzenhofer. The interior is rich in sculpture by F. I. Weiss who collaborated with Dientzenhofer on work for the Augustinians. The sculpture here dates from 1741–3 and among the frescos is some magnificent late work by V. V. Reiner. The church now acts as a deposit for the City Museum.

Take the first right into Ke Karlovu where at 20/462 is the Michna Summer Palace or Villa Amerika, erected between 1712 and 1720 for Jan Michna of Vacínov. It is an early example of the architecture of K. I. Dientzenhofer. The railings are 19C and in spite of the garden being dotted with attractive statues by Braun, it is not what it was. Despite this, the two charming service lodges are still in place and the house, now a museum dedicated to the life of Antonín Dvořák, is a tiny jewel of the Baroque. The young Dientzenhofer treats the ground-floor rooms in an already masterly, free-flowing manner and upstairs, on the *primo piano* are superb and playful frescos by J. F. Schorr depicting the Arts and scenes from mythology. Some further frescos have been discovered and will eventually be shown. Dvořák could not have wished for a more beautiful surrounding for his life's history.

In the neighbouring street, Na bojišti, is the famous brewery U kalicha (12/1733), well-known from Hašek's novel *The Good Soldier Svejk*. Continue straight down Ke Karlovu until, on the right, you come to a neo-Gothic hospital (4/458) built along English lines in 1861. Walk on to one of the most beautiful churches in Prague, within the monastery of Karlov.

This was yet another church founded by Charles IV. Its dedication is to The Assumption of Our Lady and to Charlemagne, the patron of Charles IV. The plan is unusual – an octagon shape to emulate the emperor's chapel at Aachen. It was founded in 1350 and was complete by 1377. The church is open on Sundays and holidays from 16.00 to 17.15.

Inside, the vaulting of the choir was complete by 1498 and that of the nave – conceived by Wohlmut as a huge starfish pattern – was complete by 1575. The Baroque rebuilding began in about 1733 under F. M. Kaňka, and the artist J. J. Schlansowsky let loose theatrically and emotionally on the dramatic scenes of Christ arraigned before Pontius Pilate from a balcony on one side of the church, and on the Annunciation on the other. The Annunciation has gesticulating, noisy onlookers all in fashionable 18C dress looking out of fashionable 18C windows. They could easily be shouting over to the characters in the paintings on the other side that they want Barabas freed. Thus the beginning and end of Christ's life interact loudly from one side of the church to the other. There can be few better examples of the sheer theatre which was characteristic of both late Gothic and the early Baroque in Bohemia. Thanks to this dramatic link, the architecture of one period merges seamlessly into the sculpture of the other. The altar paintings are mainly from the brush of J. J. Heintsch *c.*1708. Beneath the Pontius Pilate scene is the Scala Santa or sacred staircase which J. Santini designed in 1708, based on that of the Lateran Palace in Rome. Behind the staircase, follow the signs on the right to 'Bethlehem' to reach the Chapel of the Nativity with a further scene by J. J. Schlansowsky from 1738. The organ loft is full of sculpted Old and New Testament figures and the Apostles. The russets and golds of their costumes, the veined marbling of the scagliola and the painted vault of the ceiling all add colour to this lively interior.

The Karlov Monastery is now the Police Museum. This former Augustinian convent was designed by Orsi from 1660–8 and then by Kaňka from 1716–19. Some of the exhibits are fairly gruesome, especially those showing the 'work' of the

Nazis. One exhibit I fear will go under the new regime is the wall on which, mounted at right angles, are square yards of revolvers taken from 'British and American spies' over the last thirty years. The emphasis is on more normal policing, with exhibits on the drug problem and football hooligans. There is even a Liverpool football team's supporter's cap among the exhibits. From the terrace there is a good view to the Gothic fortifications, Vyšehrad, the new bridge by S. Hubička and the monstrous Palace of Culture which is so vast and white it is known as Moby Dick.

Walk back to the junction with Apolinářská Street and round the Prague maternity hospital (18/441), an interesting neo-Gothic building from 1867 by Josef Hlávka, to the Church of St Apolinaire. It is yet another church founded by Charles IV, this time in 1362. The Gothic church was restored by J. Mocker but its interior still retains wall paintings from about 1390. The High Altar dates from 1740 and bears a sculptural group depicting four Apostles and the Assumption of the Virgin, perhaps by J. J. Schlansowsky.

Continue to the left down Apolinářská Street and turn left again into Na slupi where there is the complex of the former Elizabethine Monastery, now the State Hospital. Its Church of Our Lady remains, its architecture by K. I. Dientzenhofer constructed upon the ground plan of 1350, with a remarkable Rococo chapel of St Thecla (1724), and frescos of 1762 by J. L. Kracker. If time is short, don't visit this church but instead turn right up Na slupi. At the crossing with Vyšehradská Street, on the right, is the entrance to the Prague Botanic Gardens laid out in 1897. They have seen better days but do have some attractive planting of the period and they provide a moment's rest.

Continue to your right down Vyšehradská Street to the Church of St John on the Rock. This church with two w towers was built by K. I. Dientzenhofer between 1730 and 1739. He also designed the gate facing Charles Square. The statues on the staircase are of 1880. Inside, the frescos are by Karle Kovář who completed them in 1748. On the High Altar is a wooden modello of the bronze statue of St John Nepomuk intended for Charles Bridge by Jan Brokof in 1682. In front of the church is the entrance to the Monastery Na Slovanech or Emmaus, founded by Charles IV in 1347 and consecrated in 1372, for the Croatian Benedictines. The founding of so many of these monasteries had political undertones. In this case, it was both to ease political tensions and pave the way for renewal of papal privilege thus allowing the Slavonic liturgy in Bohemia. This monastery was an important cultural centre and scriptorium. In the cloisters are wall paintings of the Old and New Testament carried out between 1355 and 1360. With their expressive manner, they are among the most important and treasured of their date in Bohemia. The stunning hall church was built from 1351 and dedicated to the Virgin and the Slav patron saints. The neo-Goths restored it in 1880–5 under the patronage of the Benedictines of Beuron. Sadly, the church was one of the few casualties of 1945 and some of its panel paintings were removed to the National Gallery. Much of the work seen at the monastery today is restoration of the 1960s. It has been declared a national monument and the Institute of the Czechoslovak Academy of Science is housed here.

Return to Charles Square along Vyšehradská. At the corner of the square is the Faust House (40/502), a late Baroque palace of 1740–70. It was here that the Englishman, Edward Kelley lived; he was alchemist to Rudolf II. It was adapted to the Baroque by Count Ferdinand Antonín Mladota of Solopysky, a celebrated chemist whose experiments recall those of Faust. Continue along the left-hand side of the square to Resslova Street, past the neo-Renaissance Old Technical University (14/293) of 1867. Here you will discover two important churches. The first on the right – now the Orthodox church – is that of SS Cyril and Method, built in 1730–6 from a plan by P. I. Bayer. A poignant sight here are the bullet holes round the crypt window (see p. 23). Unfortunately, nothing remains of the original interior. On the left-hand side is the Church of St Wenceslas. Its foundations are Romanesque but it was rebuilt some time before 1399. The vaulting is of a later date, 1587. Since 1929 it has belonged to the Hussite Church. Inside, the crucifix and pews are by F. Bílek.

The Gothic water tower is evident from Jirásek Square on your right, and below is the Modernist building of the Union of Artists from 1930 by O. Novotný. This is still an important exhibition space. On the left, continue along the Rašín Embankment to No. 78/1980, built by V. Havel, grandfather of the President in 1904. In Palacké Square is a good memorial to the Czech historian, František Palacký. It is an Art Nouveau work by S. Sucharda, dating from 1905–7. There follows a complex of ministry buildings (4/375) in the neo-Classical style by B. Hypšman, a pupil of Otto Wagner. These were put up in 1924–9.

Continue along the embankment with its blocks of modern houses from about 1910 and 1920 by F. Roith, J. Kotěra and J. Zasche, to the railway bridge of 1901. On the embankment there is also a small 16C building with the town emblem and nearby is the former Town Hall of the Podskalí quarter. Before the embankment was built in 1906, this part of the river was the haunt of fishermen and sailors.

Passing beneath the bridge to the Vyšehrad quarter, it is worth looking closely at some rare examples of Cubist houses – a style unique to Prague and reminiscent of some of its late medieval vaulting. Some of these houses were designed by prominent members of the Graphic Artists' Group which was influential from 1911 until the outbreak of war in 1914 (see p. 20). Josef Chochol was responsible for the most important examples on the Rašín Embankment at Nos. 42, 47 and 71 and Nos. 6–10. There is a further house by him at 49/13 Libušina Street, finished in 1913. Also in Libušina Street, at 2/48, is an example by O. Novotný. No. 30/98 Neklanova Street (return along Libušina to Vnislavova, then turn right) is a magnificent example from 1913 by Chochol, showing how the exciting angular forms of Cubism can make as much impact as the architecture of Dientzenhofer or Kaňka centuries earlier.

Continue uphill to Vyšehrad via Vratislavova Street.

6
THE PRAGUE SUBURBS AND VYŠEHRAD

In order to walk around the extensive suburbs of Prague without too much frustration, I would recommend the excellent *Praha*, a small book of town plans published by Geodetický a kartografický podnik v Praze and easily acquired. Note that some of the street names have recently been changed.

Vyšehrad

The founding of Vyšehrad is shrouded in legends of Princess Libuše and the first Přemyslids and, accordingly, it has always been regarded as the ancient seat of the princes of Bohemia. Thanks to archaeological research first begun in the 1920s, the castle of Vyšehrad has been shown to be later in date than Prague Castle. Evidence points to foundations of the first half of the 10C, during the time of Duke Boleslav II when Vyšehrad was, for a short time, his seat. It was also important at the end of the 11C during the reign of Vratislav I. It was he who built a castle of stone in which he took up residence, set up a Chapter and erected three churches. When the court moved to Hradčany in 1140, Vyšehrad lost some of its importance but the Chapter connected with the office of the Chancellor of State remained. Charles IV was only too well aware of the symbolism of the site, and he used this knowledge to the benefit of the Luxemburgs by bringing Vyšehrad into the elaborate coronation ceremony. In the second half of the 14C new fortifications were built as well as the Royal Court and the

Chapter House. At this time Vyšehrad suffered from the occupation by Hussite troops. However, by 1476, the Town of Mount Vyšehrad was founded. As the result of the Thirty Years' War in the 17C, some of the earlier buildings were demolished and the whole was fortified anew to the specifications of two Italian military specialists, I. Conti and J. Priami. The fortifications were built by yet more Italians: Giovanni da Capauli, Carlo Lurago and Santini de Bossi. Vyšehrad remained a fortress as late as 1866, but in 1884 it became part of Prague.

Legend is sometimes more telling than fact and the 19C Romantics took this princely fort to their hearts and imaginations. Smetana composed his three-act opera *Libuše* to a libretto originally in German by Josef Wenzig: this opened at the National Theatre in 1881. J. Zeyer wrote a cycle of poems entitled *Vyšehrad* in 1879–80, and the fortress was often a subject for painters. The castle even found its way into German literature and art, for example in the poetry of Zeyer and Ebert, and the drama of F. Grillparzer. Even at the end of a somewhat cynical 20C, the atmosphere still lingers.

Although Czechoslovakia is no longer ruled by princes and kings, a visit to the National Cemetery where so many of those who played an instrumental part in the country's intellectual life lie buried, is to visit the fount of Czech ideals and power. For the walk round Vyšehrad start at the Brickwork Gate, built to the order of the Governor of Prague and the first modern urbanist, Count Karel Chotek in 1841–2. Continue by way of V pevnosti Street around the partially destroyed Church of St John the Beheaded of the 14C. Continue on to the Chapel of Our Lady of 1760 to the Romanesque rotunda of St Martin. This simple building is not only the earliest extant building in Vyšehrad, but is also the oldest of the three Prague rotundas. Built in the last third of the 11C, it was restored by A. Baum in 1878–80. The neo-Romanesque doorway and the wall paintings inside date from this period.

Bear right and then left down K rotundě and round the Old

Deanery and the remains of the Romanesque basilica of St Lawrence and the Romanesque bridge, to the Church of SS Peter and Paul. The Romanesque basilica was burnt down in 1249 and rebuilding began *c.*1369. It was modified in 1575 and again from 1707–29. These last building phases are now hidden by today's neo-Gothic building, with its two W towers designed by J. Mocker and F. Mikš. The towers are now a major landmark of Prague. Inside are neo-Gothic paintings, windows and altars. This historic church was being rebuilt at the same time as the W end of St Vitus'. There are a few earlier furnishings, such as the 17C pews in the presbytery. A Romanesque sarcophagus of *c.*1100 is in the first chapel on the right. In the third chapel is a panel painting of Our Lady of the Rain, *c.*1350.

Leave the church and enter the graveyard to the N. This unique cemetery can perhaps only be compared with the Père-Lachaise in Paris. In 1870, the original parish cemetery of the Vyšehrad Chapter was converted into a national cemetery at the instigation of two patriotic men, the deans V. Šulc and M. Karlach. The area was then surrounded by Italianate arcades – *a campo santo* – designed by A. Barvitius and completed in 1908 by Antonín Wiehl. The Slavín or pantheon to the most honoured figures of the nation was built according to Wiehl's design between 1889 and 1893. The statues by J. Maudr symbolize Rejoicing Homeland, Lamenting Homeland and Genius, and the Cross is by V. Levý. Here, among the fifty interred in the Slavín are writers, painters, sculptors, architects, singers, actors and inventors. Some six hundred more notables are buried in the graveyard and a gentle walk will discover many celebrities and interesting tomb sculpture. Note especially the work by F. Bílek, J. V. Myslbek, B. Kafka and O. Španiel, mainly from 1890–1920, as well as some interesting contemporary headstones. Those buried here include the writers Karel Čapek, Jan Neruda and Božena Němcová; the composers Dvořák and Smetana; the violinists František Ondříček and Jan Kubelík; the opera singer Emma Destinová; the painters Alfons Mucha and Mikoláš Aleš, and the physiologist J. E. Purkyně. The Prague Music Festival begins here with homage paid at Smetana's grave.

On the other side of the church, past a small building by Santini, is the Vyšehrad Park. Here you will find statues of legendary Czech heroes by J. V. Myslbek from 1881–97 which were originally situated on the Palacký Bridge. The park was laid out in 1927 on the site of the medieval castle of the Bohemian kings and princes. From the Baroque defences there is a wonderful view of the town and the River Vltava as it wends its way through the Prague Valley. Return to the rotunda of St Martin and turn right by V pevnosti Street passing three gates: the Leopold Gate which forms the inner entrance to the fortress, built by Lurago before 1678; the remains of the Gothic Špička Gate, and the Tábor Gate from 1655 forming the entrance to Vyšehrad from the SE. Continue down Na Pankráci to the Palace of Culture and the metro station of Vyšehrad, (see Prague 4). From here start your visit of the suburbs of Prague.

Prague 2

(Excluding parts of the New Town and Vyšehrad dealt with in the section on the Vinohrady quarter)

Vinohrady is situated on the terraces of former vineyards against the walls of the New Town. Today it is divided into five different administrative areas, the most important central part belonging to Prague 2.

Development along the main roads leading out of Prague began to be regulated around 1800 and the community of Vinohrady was formally created in 1849. In 1879 it was given the status of a separate town, and a town plan was devised, although the present grid system with radial avenues dates mainly from 1901–3.

Vinohrady quickly became the quarter of the bourgeoisie, upper-middle class, small entrepreneurs and civil servants. Complete squares remain in the numerous 'neo' styles of architecture or in Art Nouveau dating roughly from 1880 to 1910. There are numerous parks and gardens, such as the Riegrovy or Havlíčkovy Sady, this latter being laid out by the military purveyor Wimmer. Several fine examples of 20C architecture are also to be found.

The centre of the quarter is náměstí Míru (Square of Peace) on metro line A. At its heart is the Church of St Ludmila, a neo-Gothic brick church with W towers built in 1888–93 by J. Mocker. Over the W door is a relief of Christ by J. V. Myslbek. The interior was completely decorated by artists under the eye of Mocker.

Also in the square is the neo-Renaissance Vinohrady National House (9/820), built after a plan by A. Turek, with sculptures by A. Popp decorating its façade. In the hall are paintings by A. Liebscher. At 7/1450 the Vinohrady Theatre was erected in 1905–9 to a plan by A. Čenský, with sculptures by M. Havlíček and B. Kafka on the façade. The interior has sculptural decoration by A. Popp and A. Mára, and ceiling paintings by F. Urban.

From the NE corner of the square runs Slezská Street and at 7/100 is the Academy of Agriculture, a brick building of 1924–6 by J. Gočár with sculptures by O. Gutfreund. At 9/2000 is the Ministry of Science and Technical Progress by A. Dryák of 1926–8. Turn left to reach Vinohradská Street which runs parallel to Slezská, and you will find the Old Market Hall by A. Turek from 1902. Walk to your right along this street to the Sady Svatopluk Čecha Park to find a memorial to Čecha by J. Štursa and P. Janák of 1924. Čecha was the author of epic poetry based on scenes from Czech history. Retrace your steps to turn right at Třebízského which will lead to Riegrovy Sady of 1902–8, where there is a late Empire villa of *c.*1820 with sightseeing tower, and school and restaurants from 1931–4 by F. Marek. The garden here was founded in 1783 and was open to the public. In 1787 Mozart played here, and Washington Irving visited it early in the 19C. Along the eastern edge of the park runs Chopinova Street and at 4/1543 you find the house of the publisher Jan Laichter, by Jan Kotěra, 1908–9.

Turn left then right to return once more via U Kanálky to Vinohradská, passing the Orbis Agency Building (46/1800) by A. Dryák from 1925. At 38/1971 is a school by F. Kavalír of 1924–5, and the Czech Radio Building at 12/1049 was erected by B. Sláma in 1929–31. Farther down the street are two ministry buildings of the 1970s. Go through Škrétova Street and turn into Mikovcova where at 5/548 is the neo-Renaissance house built in 1875 by Antonín Wiehl for the sculptor B. Schnirch.

Take a No. 22 tram to Havlíčkovy Sady (Havliček's Park), a pleasant garden with grottos and fountains and a neo-Renaissance villa built in 1871–88 for the entrepreneur Moritz Gröbe by A. Barvitius and J. Schulz. It was adapted in 1953 for use by the Czech Pioneers.

Prague 3

(Žižkov and part of the Vinohrady)

To reach Žižkov, take metro line A to náměstí Jiřího z Poděbrad. The suburb was named after the warlike Hussite general Jan Žižka, to commemorate the battle he won in 1420 on the hill of Vítkov dominating this quarter. After the death of Jan Hus, the movement took on a more aggressive character and this battle was the start of the new phase of the Hussite Revolution.

This is a suburb with its origins in the second half of the 19C. Together with the coming of the railway and gasworks in 1867, urban development was well under way under the architect Karl Hartig, lord mayor of what became the new town in 1881. As in much of Europe, Prague saw a building boom between 1890 and 1900, when hundreds of tenement houses in sub-standard Revivalist styles were built, or rather thrown up. Žižkov was an area of manual workers and small tradesmen, so the general standard of building is poor and its architectural quality cannot be said to be more than average. Here, however, is an area of exceptional unity, of a type and date that has been lost in western Europe either through war damage or through urban planning of the 1950s and 1960s. The area, brought to life in Hašek's novel *The Good Soldier Svejk*, has a unique atmosphere, but a fragile one. Just how fragile may be gauged by the insensitivity shown in allowing the construction here, in spite of voluble protests, of a TV tower in 1989, designed by the architect V. Aulický.

As you emerge from the metro, you will find one of the most exciting churches in Prague. The Church of the Most Sacred Heart of Our Lord was built between 1928 and 1932 by Jože Plečnik who also worked on the castle (see p. 20). Born in Yugoslavia and trained in Vienna under Otto Wagner, his greatest loyalty was towards the Slavs. A romantic mix of historicism, nationalism, rationality and superb design is the key to his style. He was a contemporary of Kotěra in Vienna, at whose instigation he arrived in Prague in 1911 to accept the job as head of the Academy of Decorative Arts. He finally left Prague in 1935 with arguments over his changes at the Hradčany ringing in his ears. A committed Christian, he was long interested in designing churches and liturgical furnishings for the 20C. It was the Society of Architects in Prague who commissioned him to design this modern church for the Catholic rite. The most arresting feature is the exterior, with a huge stele acting as clock-tower rising at the E end, like the headboard of a giant bed. Striking too are the materials used in its construction, and Wagner's influence may be seen in the enjoyment of the functional brick. The interior is equally simple and original, showing an eye to decorative detail that was uniquely Plečnik's. It is the balance of superb design that gives this church its atmosphere of stillness. His designs were executed by D. Pešan.

You can also travel to Flora station on metro line A, to see the Olšany Cemetery. This is the largest in Prague, founded outside the walls after the plague epidemic of 1680. It was further enlarged from 1786 to become the main cemetery on the right bank of the Vltava. It covers an area of over 500,000 square metres and is divided into separate graveyards. One is in honour of the Red Army troops who lost their lives in 1945. Many remarkable Czechs are buried here including writers, painters, musicians and art patrons. As at Vyšehrad, there are some good headstones by some of the leading Czech sculptors working around 1900, although the earliest date from the late 18C and are situated around the oval Chapel of St Roch, erected in 1680 by J. B. Mathey. There is an Orthodox chapel by V. Brandt of 1924 and a ceremonial hall of 1898 by F. Velich.

The New Jewish Cemetery at Želivského station on line A was founded in 1895, and here you can see the grave of Franz Kafka. There are some excellent headstones by sculptors of the stature of A. Balšánek, J. Kotěra and J. Zasche.

Take a No. 9 tram to the Central Trade Union Council, formerly the General Pension Institute in Winston Churchill Square (2/1800). Here is a good example of Constructivist architecture built 1932–4 by K. Honzík and J. Havlíček. It was Prague's first multi-storeyed building. Its two architects were both near the beginning of their careers when they were chosen for this commission.

To reach the National Monument on the Vítkov Hill, go to Florenc station on metro lines B and C and walk along Husitská Street. In 1420 this hill was the scene of a significant battle between the Hussites and Sigismund's Imperial troops. The granite-faced National Monument was put up in 1929–32 by J. Zázvorka. The interior was decorated by famous Czech artists in the 1930s and 1950s. In front of the monument is an equestrian statue of Jan Žižka of Trocnov, leader of the Hussites, by Bohumil Kafka. The statue was planned before 1940, but was not erected until 1950. The Military Museum is housed in a building of 1927–30 in the Modernist style.

The Church of St Procopius in Jaroslava Seiferta Street, is in neo-Gothic style, erected between 1899 and 1903 by J. Mocker and F. Mikš. This is the centre of the most romantic part of Žižkov and is reached by a No. 9 tram from the National Theatre.

Prague 4

(The SE district, formerly the districts of Braník, Krč, Michle, Nusle, Modřany, Podolí and others)

This is the largest and most modern district of Prague, but from the architectural point of view is not very interesting. The earliest development is the area of Nusle, created in the second half of the 19c, and Pankrác, where there are some interesting examples of state housing including some Constructivist apartments. But there is nothing of any great beauty. Examples of this type of housing may be found in 5. května where J. Havlíček and K. Honzík were designing in 1929–30 (37–41/1120–1035). No. 6/526 Jankovská Street is a contribution of 1931 by F. A. Libra and 22–26/556 Humpolecká Street is again by Libra, this time from 1932–8.

The nearest metro station is Pankrác on line C. This is also close to the area of modern hotels and new administration centres, such as the Motokov Building of the 1970s, the Czech Television building, the Panorama and Forum Hotels or the monstrous Palace of Culture, finished in 1981.

The areas near the River Vltava such as Podolí, Braník and Modřany are best known as recreation areas. Here is the vast Podolí swimming stadium of 1965 by R. Podzemný. There are also many attractive family houses, both of the 19c and modern. The most interesting examples of these can be found in Nad cementárnou Street, at 23/331, built by K. Honzík in 1928; 12/282 Na Podkovce by K. Stráník of 1936 (Stráník was a pupil of Le Corbusier); 6/208 Hodkovická and 9 Na lysinách, both built in 1936 by L. Žák. The waterworks in Podolí were designed by A. Engel in 1923–4 in a neo-Classical style and the water tower in Baarova Street in Michle was designed by Jan Kotěra in 1906–7. The relatively clean air here is the reason for the growth of hospitals and sanatoriums in the district. There is one at the foot of the Vyšehrad in U podolského Street, built in Art Nouveau style by R. Kříženecký, 1909–10, and a large complex is to be found in

Krč, in Vídeňská Street by B. Kozák, 1926–34. In southern Prague is one of the largest housing estates in the capital. Built in the 1970s and 1980s and known depressingly as South Town 1 and 2, it houses about 100,000 people without many amenities.

Prague 5

(The sw district which absorbed older quarters from across the river, such as Smíchov, Košíře, Hlubočepy, Radlice, Motol, Chuchle and others)

Of all these quarters, the earliest is Smíchov with its centre around the metro station Anděl on line B. Do not be put off by the fact that this was the second of the Prague suburbs founded in 1838 for industry. Here were the textile mills, light industry, a ceramics factory and a brewery but there are architectural gems to be hunted out. One such reached on metro line B to Anděl or tram No. 9 is the exquisite Summer House built by K. I. Dientzenhofer in 1725 for his family, now known as the Portheim or Buquoy Summer Palace. Vestiges of the garden remain, but you need to use your imagination as the surroundings are dire. The land was originally given to Dientzenhofer by the Jesuits in gratitude for his work for them. The tiny pavilion stands at 9/68 Štefánik Street and sums up so much of the work of this genius. There were originally two symmetrical wings, one of which has been destroyed. The façade is decorated with busts of Apollo and Diana. The oval room on the *primo piano* was decorated with a marvellous Bacchanalian Feast by V. V. Reiner in 1729. It is now called Galerie D and is open during exhibitions. Above it, and the reason for the demolition of the wing, is the neo-Renaissance Church of St Wenceslas, built by the Italian-trained, Antonín Barvitius from 1881–5. Before entering, note the della Robbia-style tympanum depicting the murder of St Wenceslas. The interior decoration is the work of Czech artists, mainly professors at the Academy of Fine Arts, including J. Trenkwald and F. Sequens.

The interior is severe with a deep, coffered ceiling. Mosaics decorate the spandrels of the arcade of the nave, and the frescos are painted in a stern neo-Classical style. There is a fine pulpit. The whole has a severe beauty, only spoilt by the choice of modern lighting.

Also within easy walking distance of the metro is the famous Bertramka (2/169 Mozartova Street), a charming summer house surrounded by a lilac-filled garden. Here is the table at which Mozart is said to have been inspired to write *Don Giovanni*. Mozart appears to have slept all over Prague, but he did stay here with the Dušeks – František a composer, and Josefina his wife, an outstanding singer – during his Prague visits in 1787 and 1791. Inside, to an accompaniment of Mozart's music, you can see his life unfold as you look at the series of engravings and text on the walls. There is a translation available in English. A delightful facsimile of the libretto of *Don Giovanni* is on sale at the door, and there are displays of musical instruments and reconstructions of rooms. It is a place of great charm, with concerts held here in the summer. One friend stoked the boilers in the Bertramka for years after being convicted for refusing to join the Communist Party. He was hauled out and dusted down every now and again to conduct VIPs over the museum!

Nearby is the Malostranský hřbitov (the Lesser Town Cemetery), open from 09.00 to 19.00. Walk down Mozartova, turn left at Duškova and take the second right, passing behind the Church of the Holy Trinity (1831–7). The entrance is down some steps at the W end of the church. It was founded during the plague epidemic of 1680 and continued in use until 1884. For connoisseurs of such things, this must surely go down as one of the most romantic cemeteries in Central Europe, especially on a sunny spring evening as the light slants through the trees. Although many great artists are buried here and indeed, also sculpted the headstones, little remains that is not cracked, broken or has been reduced to a mound of ivy. But the trees and the birdsong are glorious. Still intact however, is the monument to the Bishop of Passau, Leopold

Thun-Hohenstein, cast in 1830–1 by D. Zafouk after a model by V. Prachner. He kneels in the centre. One can also pay one's respects to Sophy of Wallenstein by Prachner, and to the Ebenberg family by I. M. Platzer, or one can follow the well-worn path to the tomb of the musician F. X. Dušek and his wife Josefina. It is worth noticing that most of the inscriptions are in German. Thanks to the hard-working Germans in the area the Malá Strana was always a wealthy town.

Leave the graveyard behind you, cross the main road, Plzeňská Street, and walk straight ahead through Na Čečeličce Street into Holečkova Street where there is a complex of churches and monasteries in a neo-Gothic style, erected by the Beuronian Benedictines from 1882–91. The Postal Museum has been here at 8/106 since 1933. Walking farther down Holečkova Street you come to the Kinsky country house on the Petřín Hill, surrounded with its large park and built in 1827–31 by Heinrich Koch (see p. 86). This is one of the most important buildings of the 19C in Smíchov.

On the embankment in Janáčkovo nábřeží, reached by tram No. 9 from the National Theatre, there are fine luxury neo-Renaissance houses with rich decoration and to the S, on the edge of Smíchov, are a large number of interesting modern villas, especially on the streets U Mrázovky and Nad Santoškou. Close by at No. 10/2092 Na Cihlářce, is a house by Adolf Loos, built in 1931.

Characteristic of Prague 5 are its irregular building plots scattered over hills and valleys amidst what were vineyards, gardens and country house estates. Examples are the Clam-Gallas Garden, founded in 1757, and the celebrated Cibulka at 118 Nad zámečkem Street. Reach these by No. 9 tram to Motelstop, then turn left. This country estate was converted between 1818 and 1824 by the Bishop of Passau, Leopold Thun-Hohenstein, into a summer house set around with a large natural park in the English mode. Among its valleys and hills, a Gothic-style hermitage, a viewing tower and a charming Chinese pavilion were picturesquely sited. Sadly, the garden buildings have been vandalized and the house is now falling down, as are the charming stone dog kennels which are listed buildings.

From the end of the 19C, new houses started to encroach on the bishop's peaceful glade and, at the beginning of the 20C, it became an area of lower-middle class housing, albeit with some interesting examples. The best may be seen in Hlubočepy (bus No. 105 from metro Anděl, line B) where there is the so-called Barrandov villa quarter, named after the French geologist Joachim Barrandé who did a lot of research in the area in the 19C. It was laid out by M. Urban and contains work by a number of good architects, such as V. Grégr, R. Stockar, J. Fragner, J. Gočár and F. A. Libra. The centre of the quarter is formed by the Barrandov Restaurant in Barrandovská, remarkable for its lighthouse tower, large terrace and swimming-pool built in 1929 by M. Urban. From the same hand comes a complex of film studios of 1931–4 on Křížík Square (5/322).

To the S, formerly the village of Zbraslav, (bus Nos. 129, 241, 243, 245 or Anděl station, metro line B), is the complex of monastic buildings just S of where the Rivers Vltava and Berounka meet. Here the Přemyslid king Otakar II founded a hunting lodge which was adapted in 1292 to serve as a Cistercian monastery providing the burial place of the last Czech Přemyslids. Rebuilt by J. B. Santini-Aichl at the beginning of the 18C and then completed by Kaňka in 1732, it is an unusual building with a slightly oriental feel. It now belongs to the National Gallery, housing their superb collection of 19 and early 20C sculpture, including some fine Cubist work. Much remains of the original interior decoration with the stucco up to Soldati's high standard, and frescos by V. V. Reiner and F. X. Balko. This is a visit that is highly recommended.

Adjacent to the monastery is the Church of St James the Major, formerly Gothic and remodelled from 1650–4 with rich Baroque decoration in the interior. The altar paintings include work by Karel Škréta and Petr Brandl, with statues by J. J. Bendl. The High Altar carved in the Platzer workshop surrounds an Assumption by G. B. Piazetti of 1743–4.

Still in the village of Zbraslav are two important examples of modern architecture. The first is the villa of the publisher Otto by O. Novotný of 1908 in Žitavská, and the second is the villa of the writer Vančura of 1923, at 7/261 V. Vančura Street, by Jaromír Krejčár. The latter is a work influenced by Le Corbusier.

Prague 6

(The NE district)

This is a large area bordering the Hradčany and the Malá Strana and stretching to the airport. It is worth exploring, both for its fine examples of Renaissance and Baroque buildings, and for those of the early 20C. The modern centres are in Dejvice and Střešovice, but the nucleus of the earlier settlements are in Břevnov, Liboc and Bubeneč.

Taking a No. 22 tram from the centre of Prague in the direction of the airport, stop at Markétská Street to visit the remarkable Monastery of Břevnov (1/28), one of the most important buildings in Bohemia and an example of Czech 'Radical Baroque'. In 993, the Benedictines were asked to build the first monastery on Bohemian soil, at the request of Duke Boleslav II and under the protection of the great bishop of Prague and patron saint, Adalbert. From 1954, when the Communists took over, expelling the monks and imprisoning the abbots, the monastery was split up so that each part belonged to a different authority, a sort of divide and rule. The police took over the main monastic buildings for their archives, the State Library took another part; the fine Romanesque crypt under the present choir belongs to the Department of Ancient Monuments and the Church of St Margaret became the parish church. Even the cemetery was split. Now, after an absence of nearly forty years, the Benedictines are returning to this important shrine – a truly fine way to celebrate the coming millennium.

Arriving at the gates it is easy to forget the ugly motorway and high-rise flats around. The gateway is by K. I. Dientzenhofer and is topped by a statue of St Benedict by K. J. Hiernle. Architect and sculptor had worked together before at St Nicholas' in the Malá Strana. Many of the monastic buildings are now being restored for the millennium celebrations, but despite this, it is one of the few places in Prague where it is possible to sense the all-embracing aspects of monastic life.

First look at the exterior of the monastery and church. The present building was begun in 1708 by P. I. Bayer. He was dismissed in 1709 by Abbot Zinke who then started his long patronage of the Dientzenhofers by commissioning Kryštof Dientzenhofer to complete the monastery and redesign the church. The Church of St Margaret and the monastic buildings were more or less complete by 1722 and bear witness to the design skills of Kryštof Dientzenhofer. From 1716 it appears that Kilián Ignác Dientzenhofer was in charge of the construction of Břevnov and that after 1720 it was he who carried out most of the work. He, like his father, was taken on as official architect by the Benedictines and paid an annual fee.

Ignoring the church for a moment, keep to the path past the W end, go through the gates which were moved here out of the path of the motorway, and walk into the garden. On your left you will see a beautiful summer house which, up until the 1950s, displayed a carved wooden group depicting the scene of the founding of the monastery. The house was designed by Kilián Ignác and built between 1724 and 1738. The story goes that Duke Boleslav II had a dream in which he was told he had to found a monastery on the site of a freshwater spring in a wood. He and his confessor, Bishop Adalbert, went into the countryside and found just the spot that was required, thus fulfilling the dream. The summer house – now in poor repair – is said to have been built on the Adalberta Spring. Beyond, in ruins, rise four terraces with the vestiges of a vast hothouse, pavilions, curving steps and the outline of formal circular fountains, all by Kilián Ignác Dientzenhofer. The avenue to the left leads to the graveyard where many of the monks were buried, even during the years of exile of the Benedictines. Here too, is a charming, centrally planned cemetery chapel. As garden and monastic complex were designed by a father-and-son team, there is a great sense of unity. Look down on the monastery and church and enjoy the vistas which merge architecture and garden.

Before entering the church, walk around it to the right. Its form follows the Romanesque style of 1030–40, but in the hands of Kryštof Dientzenhofer, it became one of the most important Baroque churches in Bohemia. Note how he uses giant Ionic columns on high bases, a favourite motif. Note too the statues on the cornice by M. V. Jäckel of 1712. In the wall, half-way down the S side, there is a Romanesque tomb of the hermit Vintíř with an 18C *trompe-l'oeil* of the medieval church – an ecclesiastical architectural joke. This has relevance to the chapel on the other side of the wall, as you will see. Beyond the E end is a modern door leading into the beautiful Romanesque crypt, and beyond that are the fine monastic buildings by the Dientzenhofers, decorated inside with stucco by B. Spinetti and with frescos of 1727 by the great Bavarian C. D. Asam. Asam charged one thousand guilders for his work, the subject matter being the Miracle of the Hermit Günther who managed to bring back to life a roast pheasant at the table of King Stephen of Hungary.

The church is open from 07.30 to 18.00. The interior has recently been restored but it is all of the 1720s never having been touched by a later period. Its relative simplicity adds dignity to the breadth of the nave. The vaulting is painted with subjects from the Benedictine hierarchy, in the nave are the emperors who were their patrons, and nearer the High Altar, the Benedictine popes – all the work of J. J. Stevens of Steinfels. The altar paintings are marvellous examples of Petr Brandl's work, surrounded by *trompe-l'œil* frames. Brandl's paintings show, on the right, Bishop Otmar and, to the left, St Wenceslas. There follows a Crucifixion scene, then St Adalbert with Duke Boleslav II on the left, before the chancel. On the right is the story of the founding of the monastery and Boleslav's dream. No expense was spared by the cabinet-makers and the statuary is of high order by M. V. Jäckel, K. J. Hiernle and R. Prachner. The High Altar is dedicated to St Margaret, the patron saint of agriculture. Note the splendid silver-gilt candelabra and the rather good organ. The final altar is dedicated to the death of the Czech saint Vintíř, a member of this community who lived as a hermit. He was so holy that when he asked for the last rites from the priest, the king came too. His Romanesque tomb is outside, on the other side of the wall. Notice that above the painting of his death is another one depicting St Procopius. Vintíř was not an official saint while Procopius was.

Returning towards the centre of Prague, along Pionýrů Street, is the Cajetan House at Břevnov (Kajetanka), which belonged originally to the Counts of Matinice and was changed into a small Theatine monastery in 1666. In 1670 it became the Order's summer house and is now being restored. In a period of annual epidemics, nearly all the monastic orders had summer houses in the countryside. The gardens were linked to a curious neo-Romanesque tower farther up the road which was also built by the Theatines. This is all that remains of an enormous project, for which it was proposed that the influential Italian architect Guarino Guarini would be responsible. Up behind the summer house with its small lake, in the orchard, are some charming garden buildings, now split into houses. On the other side of the road are tall blocks of flats of deadening monotony, built in 1930 to house those on low incomes and with social problems.

In the opposite direction, going away from Břevnov is the Hvězda Summer Pavilion – the beautiful hunting lodge-cum-*maison de plaisaunce* built for the Governor of Prague, Archduke Ferdinand of Tyrol in 1555 within the Royal Park of Liboc (see p. 8). Ferdinand was the first to build this type of country villa, not for defence, but only perhaps to put others in awe and to give himself pleasure. Walk up the long, tree-lined avenue to it. As you arrive you will experience a sense of delight as its unique star form becomes clear. It was originally higher and it has lost its cupola. The whole was conceived as an intellectual game by the archduke, this most erudite of men, and was built by J. Maria del Pambio, H. Tirol, G. Lucchese and B. Wohlmut.

The interior of Hvězda was damaged by fire in the Second World War but has been well restored. The iconography of the interior is complex and was carried out in the most exquisite stucco, fine and sharp, which has been compared to that found in Rome of the first and second century. Note how greater depth is added by inscribing the background of the plaster-work. On the ground floor, in the star-shaped centre, the surfaces are decorated with scenes representing the Mirror of Virtues, while the adjoining vaulting develops the classical theme. Bacchantes, satyrs and other lighthearted classical figures throng the vaulting of the radiating passages and the rhomboidal-shaped rooms in between. The stucco work is thought to have been done by G. Campione and Ulrico Aostalli. There is a fine, wide marble staircase up to the first floor: see the curiously Bohemian vaulting of the ceilings. Here the main display of the museum is dedicated to the painter Mikoláš Aleš and the writer Alois Jirásek. The display includes some of the archaeological collection of Aleš which he used as props for his historical paintings. From the windows of the first floor you can enjoy the view over the formal avenues of trees.

The cellars are also worth visiting. They, presumably, were for servicing the parties of hunters. Here, texts displayed on the walls describe the second Defenestration of Prague and the Battle of the White Mountain which took place very close to the Hvězda (see p. 11). The Hvězda is open every day except Monday, 10.00–17.00.

Take a No. 22 tram to its terminus at the small pilgrimage Church of Bílá Hora, otherwise known as the Church of Our Lady Victorious. Soon after the Battle of the White Mountain, a small chapel was built on the battlefield along with a Servite monastery. Not large enough to hold all the pilgrims, the chapel was absorbed into the Church of Our Lady Victorious, built to a Greek cross plan with a dome between 1704 and 1730. Side chapels sprouted between 1717 and 1729. The whole is surrounded by a covered cloister with corner shrines and it has very much the feeling of a S Bohemian monastery, rather than a place of pilgrimage near the capital.

The church was erected by the Holy Brotherhood at the instigation of one of its number, the painter, Kristián Luna: J. B. Santini-Aichl and Kilián Ignác Dientzenhofer were involved with the building. On the entrance gate by K. I. Dientzenhofer, the 1729 statues are by J. O. Mayer. The interior of the church is small and of a curious shape: all the space is taken up by the High Altar with a very beautiful lunette above. From the short nave it is impossible to see the two later E altars on either side. The ceiling in the S chapel was decorated by V. V. Reiner, J. A. Schöpf painted that to the N and the dome was by C. D. Asam in 1728. The cloisters are by J. A. Schöpf. The church is open at 10.00 on Saturdays and Sundays but closes between 11.00 and 12.00 for Mass.

You will notice nearby as you return to Prague, a large white building on the left of the road. This was another monastery, but is now the excellent Pampa restaurant, a favourite watering-hole of journalists.

Those who are keen on aerodromes can take the bus from the terminal in the town centre to visit the old airport of Prague, built in 1932–6 by A. Benš.

In the other part of Prague 6, by the river in Bubeneč, is found the Královská Obora, the largest of Prague's public parks. Take a tram No. 18 to its terminus. Nearby, many of the attractive large villas have been turned into embassies. The best examples of neo-Renaissance and Art Nouveau can be found in Slavíčkova Street: see especially a villa by Kotěra (248/) from 1908 and two examples at Nos. 151 and 152 by J. E. Koula from 1896.

The Střešovice district is dominated by the Ořechovka villa quarter. This colony was built in 1920–3 after the example of the English garden city. It was planned by J. Vondrák and contained 29 different types of building designed by a variety of architects. It was considered such a success that the concept was enlarged in 1923–30 to include work by P. Janák, A. Loos, A. Dryák, B. Paul, B. Kozák, B. Hypšman, F. Roith and others. The upper-middle class housing of the colony was lent a luxurious park-like character. The best examples are perhaps three villas by P. Janák erected for Bohemian artists in 1924 at 41/484 Na Ořechovce, 10–12/486 Lomená and 24/489 Cukrovarnická. They show the influence of both the English Queen Anne Revival and Dutch style, with brick as the main building material. See also on the corner of Střešovická and Nad hradním vodojemem the so-called Villa Loos. This good example of Loos's work was built for a Dr Müller in 1930 with the collaboration of Karel Lhota. There are plans to turn the villa into a museum of the architect's work.

The main centre of Prague 6 is Dejvice, a post-First World War development on former farmland and private gardens. The planning was done by Antín Engel who proposed a town catering for civil servants and officials built round a circular space called Vítězné (metro line A). Around this square are several important buildings including 23/620 Roosevelt Street, which is the Military Geographic Institution by B. Feurstein, dating from 1925. There is also the famous Glass Palace, an avant-garde Constructivist tenement house designed by R. F. Podzemný in 1937 at 1/728 náměští Svobody. Away from the square are the buildings of the Czech Technical University. Note especially the interesting Constructivist gymnasium at 1/1784 Bílá Street, built in 1930–3 after a plan by Jan Gillar who worked closely with the Bauhaus group. The International Hotel of 1952–7 in Družba Square is a rare example of the building type known as SO-RE-LA, shorthand for 'Socialist realism following the example of Stalinist Russia'.

For an immediate change of mood, take a No. 123 bus to U Mateje station where you can stroll among the 30 small houses built in 1930–42 in the Constructivist style. This area, known as Baba, is demarcated by the streets Nad Paťankou, Průhledová, Matějská and Jarní. The idea of such an exclusive colony on the hills above Prague was based on ideas of the 1928 Stuttgart Siedlung exhibition of modern living. Pavel Janák, Professor of the School of Applied Arts was responsible in 1928 for setting out the project. Individuals – in the main artists and intellectuals – then commissioned different architects, for example Janák, Gočár, L. Žák, J. Grus, O. Starý, E. Linhart and the Dutch architect M. Stamm to build for them. Each house is in harmony with the next, the whole illustrating a decade when there can have been few capitals in Europe that could boast such a wealth of talent.

Just behind the Baba there is a further villa quarter – the so-called Hanspaulka. This is a garden area of villas and family houses built between 1925 and 1930 by many leading architects. Of note is 6/677 Neherovská which is a good example of Functionalism by L. Žák.

On the edge of Prague 6 there is a slice of the Hradčany near the metro station Hradčanská on line A. On the other side of the road to the castle, especially around the street Na Baště, are several houses built *c.*1910. Prime among them must be the exceptional house at 1/233 Mickiewiczova Street, built by the sculptor František Bílek for himself in 1912. It is built in brick in the form of a segment of a circle, and is decorated with Egyptian-style columns. But it is the detailing that is so remarkable – the stone, the wood and the metalwork in the best tradition of the Arts and Crafts Movement but surpassing it in sophistication and quality. The house is now a museum to this great Symbolist sculptor and a visit is a relevation. His brother-in-law built the eccentric house next door.

Anyone who is interested can take bus No. 235 from here to the Sports Arena in Strahov. This was built in 1926 by A. Dryák.

Prague 7

Prague 7 was one of the earliest developments outside the Prague city walls and includes Holešovice, Bubny, Troja and

Bubeneč. From the architectural point of view, this is one of the most important Prague districts, embracing both ancient and modern architecture. It has Prague's largest park at Letná, the once-Royal Enclosure at Stromovka, the exhibition halls and the important Troja Palace.

Holešovice – Bubny

Under the Hill of Letná, where the ancient ford crossed the River Vltava, was the hamlet of Bubny in an area of fishing villages, villas and country houses. Bubny is first mentioned in 1088 and later the land was owned by some of the most important families in Prague such as the Wallensteins, Martinic, Sternbergs and Nostics. In the 19c it came into the hands of the businessmen Jakub Wimmer and Josef Richter then, in 1859, Bubny with Holešovice were proclaimed a town and finaliy, in 1884, were joined to Prague. By the end of the 19c its character was changing with the building of the gasworks in 1887, the new trade port in 1892 and the city slaughterhouse in 1893.

The area built in the meander of the Vltava, originally laid out by the engineer Kořínek from 1884, is still an industrial zone and estate. Its centre is the Strossmayer Square, reached by trams 1, 8, 12, 17, or Vltavská station on metro line C. On the square is the Church of St Antonius, of neo-Gothic design dating from 1908–11 after a plan by F. Mikš, a pupil of J. Mocker. The church still retains its contemporary furnishings.

At the beginning of the main street, at 1/1477 Bubenská, near the embankment, is the Constructivist City Electric Corporation building by Adolf Benš and Josef Kříž, dating from 1927–35. The Hlávka Bridge which leads down from this was built by P. Janák in 1909–12 and is decorated with two groups of sculpture by Jan Štursa depicting Humanity and Work from 1911–13. The medallions of lord mayors of Prague are of 1908–10 by J. Mařatka and O. Gutfreund. The bridge connects this district with Štvanice (Chase Island). On the island is the first winter sports stadium in Czechoslovakia, built in 1930–2 by Josef Fuchs. Here too are the city tennis courts. There is a hydro-electric power station built in the 1920s at the head of the island by A. Dlabač, and upstream is the railway bridge of 1846 by A. Negrelli. The other large building on the embankment at 7/1000 is the State Planning Committee, formerly belonging to a security company, by Jaroslav Rössler.

With your back to the bridge turn left up Dukelských hrdinů Street and then left into Kostelní Street into the small park in front of St Clement Church. This was formerly the village church in the 13c but it was rebuilt between 1659 and 1677 by Maximilián Martinic and decorated with some good stucco. Continue up Kostelní to the Hill of Letná where there is the park bought by the city of Prague and laid out by J. Brauerl after a design by B. Wünscher in 1858.

Near the entrance to the park is the Praha Expo '58 Restaurant, built as part of the Czech exhibition created for Expo '58 in Brussels after a design by F. Cubr, J. Hrubý and Z. Pokorný. From here there is a superb view across central Prague. There are other restaurants here including the Letná Park Restaurant in neo-Renaissance disguise by J. Ullmann from 1863, and the Hanava Pavilion cast in iron for the Jubilee Exhibition in 1891 after a design by Z. Fiala.

At 42/1320 Kostelní Street are two modern buildings in the Constructivist style from 1938–41 by Milan Babuška. They now house the Technical Museum, founded in 1908 and moved here from the Schwarzenberg Palace in the Hradčany. Its model was the Parisian Musée des Découvertes, one of the largest museums of its kind then in Europe. Even if you are not technologically-minded, this museum is worth a visit. Here you will see something of the inquiring minds, invention and craftsmanship typical of the court of Rudolf II in the astrolabes and sextants of Tycho de Brahe, made in Prague by Erasmus Habermel. Other items on view show something of the industrial development of Czechoslovakia in the 19c and the machines brought back from his travels by Vojta Náprstek (see p. 135) are also here. Best known, however, is the public transport collection. There is also a scaled-down replica of a coalmine and an exhibition tracing the history of photography, film, radio and television.

Take either of the streets at the side of the museum into Letohradská where, at 60/760 is a Functionalist building of 1939 by Josef Havlíček. Walk to the end towards the square, turn right up Nad štolou then left in Obránců míru and, at 85/1498, is a white building with applied ceramics which is the Ministry of Internal Affairs erected in 1935–9 by J. Krejčár. The addition on the S was built in 1989.

Letná Plain which unfolds before you is a popular place for a variety of public demonstrations. Crowds gathered here both during the November revolution of 1989 and during the Pope's visit to Prague in the summer of 1990. The plain is dominated by a vast wall of tenement blocks (72–96/845–862) in Obránců míru, built in 1937–9 by J. Havlíček. At the time, the flats were the showpiece of advanced living standards and to illustrate the point, many Communist Party officials after 1945 chose an apartment here. Beneath lies the football stadium, built in the sixties for the most celebrated Czech team, Sparta.

From the stadium, turn right to Korunovační Street crossing it into the Bubeneč area once more. You are now in a well-planned housing estate of 1910. Situated in the neighbourhood of the Academy of Fine Arts, it is an area full of artists' studios – the Montmartre of Prague. The Academy is reached by following Nad Královskou oborou then turning right and first left into U akademie (4/127). This is the earliest Czech art school, founded in 1799 although it is now housed in a building of 1898–1903 built by Václav Roštlapil who trained in Vienna. The small pavilion of the School of Architecture nearby was built, fittingly, by Jan Kotěra and Josef Gočár in 1923.

From U akademie turn down any street to the right into Veletržní and walk until you reach 45/530. It is difficult to miss as it is the Trade Fair Palace. This vast building was put up between 1924–8 after plans by two young architects, Oldřich

Tyl and Josef Fuchs. This is one of the first examples of Constructivist architecture in Prague and is frankly ugly, as large areas of this type of architecture can be. It is interesting for its early date and for the fact that it shows how Czech planners were increasingly prepared to commission architecture from a pool of young designers. The building was much admired at the time by Le Corbusier. Damaged by fire in 1974, rebuilding is underway for a display of 20C art, both international and Czech, which will include applied arts and architecture. It is a vast space and it is taking its cue from the Centre Pompidou in Paris. The architects are M. Masák and partners from Stavoprojekt Liberec.

Continue down Veletržní Street, around the Park Hotel and across the railway to the old exhibition ground – the Park of Culture and Rest (Park Kultury a Oddechu). This area, previously a royal park, was the site of major exhibitions of industry and culture which were most influential from the end of the 19C and were one of the main means by which ideas were exchanged. The Ethnographical Exhibition of 1895 was held here and several of the exhibits still exist, stranded in Prague (see p. 86). The Jubilee Exhibition in 1891 was followed by the Architectural Exhibition of 1898. After 1918 the Prague trade fairs were held here and, from 1954, all the Congresses of the Czech Communist Party.

The exhibition of 1891 left behind it the two neo-Renaissance pavilions by the entrance. In the pavilion on the right (rebuilt in 1907) are the important collections of the Lapidarium of the National Museum. These contain a collection of sculpture from the 11 to the 19C from Prague itself, including some of the original works from Charles Bridge.

The Congress Palace represents a fine example of industrial architecture of 1891; the architect was B. Münzberger. Close to the Congress Palace or Iron Hall is Marold's Panorama. This is housed in a circular building and depicts the last battle of the Hussites in 1434 at Lipany, painted by Luděk Marold in 1898. Leaving the panorama, turn right then first left across the Royal Park of Stromovka which was founded in the first half of the 14C as the hunting ground of the Bohemian kings. At No. 56 is the Gothic Summer Pavilion. This medieval structure was enlarged during the late Gothic and Renaissance periods and was finally transformed into Romantic Gothic by Jiří Fischer *c.*1805 in emulation of the English Romantics.

During the reign of Emperor Rudolf II a lake was built within the enclosed boundary of the Royal Park and from 1584 it was fed with water from the River Vltava. The aqueduct carrying the water, called the Rudolf Adit, is an outstanding monument to the Rudolfine age and is still in use today. The Imperial Mill (22) was the gift to the Czech Estates from the emperor and was reconstructed as a complex garden with colonnade and artificial grotto some time after 1594 by G. Gargiolli and G. M. Filippi. During the 17C the famous lapidary for cutting precious stones and glass of the great Miseroni family from Milan was established here. The first of the family to arrive, around 1588, was Ottavio Miseroni who died in 1624. He was followed by his son Antonio Abondio who also worked in wax, and his son was Alessandro Abondio who also carried on the trade. The Miseronis together with the Castrucci were among the most important of the Italian craftsmen to bring fresh ideas and high standards of craftsmanship to the workshops of the capital. At the beginning of the 19C the mill saw the birth of the first machine-made paper.

It was under Count Chotek that the royal hunting ground was made into the first public garden in Prague. Nowadays, many of the attractive large neo-Renaissance and Art Nouveau villas in the park have been turned into embassies.

Troja

Turn north across the river and, crossing Trojsky Island, take the bridge to the Palace of Trója. If you do not wish to walk, take a No. 153 bus from Holešovice station on metro line B.

Trója is a stunning early Baroque château. The English terms 'country house' or 'castle' are not really adequate as a description. It was built in the style of a classical villa for Count Václav Vojtech of Sternberg between 1679 and 1685 by Giovanni Domenico Orsi and Silvestro Carlone, based on an idea by J. B. Mathey. The building has the exterior simplicity of an Italian villa and everywhere the star of the *nouveaux riches* Sternbergs shines.

Before visiting the house, turn towards the long low stable building. The luxury in which the horses were kept vies with anything similar in England. Trója's famous vineyards rise up around it and there is also a café. On the garden side of the house, the magnificent Baroque staircase will delight, with sculpture by G. and P. Heermann from 1685–1703, representing the Struggle of the Gods and Titans and with stone busts of 1707 from the workshop of J. Brokof. Beneath lies the first French Baroque garden in Bohemia, complete with broad terracing and beautiful terracotta vases. The original plans are on display in the house but they do not seem to have been taken too seriously.

The palace has taken years to restore but unfortunately has a deadening municipal feel about it, with much of the restoration work being regarded as controversial. However, that said, this is still one of the most important Baroque interiors in Prague. The ceilings and some walls were frescoed by the Netherlandish painter A. Godin; in the hall is his vast Apotheosis of the Habsburgs. The chapel too is glorious; this and the other rooms were painted by G. and G. F. Marchetti, with typical Baroque themes extolling the virtues of the Sternbergs.

In front of the palace beneath the vineyards with the tiny chapel of St Chiara is the main entrance to the Zoo. This was founded in 1931 by Professor J. Janda and was designed by J. Fuchs. Most famous among the rare species are the herd of Prezewalski horses. Nearby a new Botanical Garden has been opened.

Prague 8

(Including the early suburbs of Karlín, Libeň, Ďáblice and Kobylisy, the modern suburbs of Ďáblice and Prosek, and the villages of Čimice and Dolní Chabry)

Karlín (Florenc station on metro lines B and C, near the central bus station) is the oldest Prague suburb, founded in 1816 within an area of large hospitals and convalescent homes and gardens. The name derived from Carolina Augusta who was the wife of Francis I. Here, in part, the street grid-plan rules supreme. Several Empire and neo-Classical houses were built here, the best examples dating from 1830–50, mainly in Sokolovská Street which leads off Švermovy Sady. Note in particular Nos. 5, 21, 81, 91, 110 and 128. Such grandeur all in one street is due to the fact that Sokolovská was originally the main road through the suburb. There are also two houses of note at 140 and 144 Prvního pluku, which runs at right-angles to Sokolovská. Farther along, in Karlinské Square, is the Church of SS Cyril and Method, the two Slav patron saints. This is a neo-Romanesque building of 1854–63, planned by two architects, Karl Roesner from Vienna and Josef Ullmann from Prague. Such collaboration beween artists from the two capitals was most beneficial to the arts in many ways. Some of the foremost Czech artists worked on the interior, including Josef Manés and Václav Levý.

Karlín was a typical industrial zone from the beginning of the industrial revolution. Here, the first Prague factories and houses for rent were created. They are more a mecca for the industrial archaeologist than for the art historian. In 1846 the railway arrived and the first commercial port in Prague found a home here in the same year. Gasworks and textile factories followed, founded by an Englishman, E. Thomas. In 1903 Karlín was proclaimed a separate town. After this, new building around the Lyčkovo náměstí (at the E end of Křižíkova), designed by Josef Sakař from about 1905 is important as an example of Art Nouveau. Some good individual houses are the

School and the National House at 10/14 Lyčkovo náměstí, and at 550 Kubova, in the SE corner of the square. From the square walk north up Uxova Street into Sokolovská once more, and at 24/136 is the Invalidovna or Military Hospital. This large building of 1731–7 by K. I. Dientzenhofer was intended for war veterans, along the lines of Les Invalides in Paris or Wren's Chelsea Hospital. It now houses the Military Archive and some of the deposit of the Technical Museum.

Libeň

Many of the Prague nobility lived around the area of Libeň including the Wallenstein and the Nostic families. From the 19C, machine-making factories destroyed the area's gentility. One such interloper was Rushton's, a factory making prefabricated bridges, founded in 1832 by an Englishman John Andrews. The largest factory here was begun in 1871, the Kolben and Daněk electrical and engineering firm, now the ČKD. In 1891 Prague's largest port was established here and was further enlarged in 1926–9.

The centre of the area is around Rudé armády Street (tram No. 12). At 1/35 is a small castle adapted from earlier foundations by J. Prachner in 1769. Nearby is an interesting gym hall and St Adalbert's Church of 1904–5 just off U libeňského zámku. This was designed by Matěj Blecha. Walking round the area you will find a strange mix of 19C grand living and tenement buildings.

Ďáblice and Bohnice

For those interested in modern architecture, a visit to Ďáblice would be of interest. Here there is a housing development by V. Tuček of 1968 and a Cubist cemetery of 1912–14 off the main road Ďáblická, by Vlastislav Hofman. It can be reached by tram Nos. 10, 17 and 24. In Bohnice there are housing estates from 1972 by V. Havránek and also the remains of the original village from about 1800. Also a psychiatric sanatorium by V. Roštlapil of 1906–16, with a good church and convalescent home of 1973–5 by J. Línek and V. Milunič in Čimická Street. To reach Bohnice take a No. 102 bus from the metro station Holešovice, line B.

Prague 9

This a vast, intensely industrial area to the NE of Prague and is probably of most interest to industrial archaeologists and ecologists. It is made up of large industrial developments such as Vysočany, Hloubětín and Prosek, and smaller developments around the former villages of Běchovice, Čakovice, Počernice, Kyje, Kbely, Vinoř and others.

Some of these villages date from the 13C and in a few, Romanesque churches can be sought out, as in Prosek (St Wenceslas off Na Proseku) and in Kyje (St Bartolomeo in Krčínovo náměstí). In 1896, Kolben's factory for electrical engineering and locomotives was founded and then the floodgates opened with some of the largest factories in Prague being built here together with the attendant collective housing for the workers as in Prosek and Černý Most. The patchwork of villages added to Prague 9 since 1974 will, once more, become separate entities. There are examples of Baroque castles in Vinoř and Koloděje (bus Nos. 251 and 259) from about 1720 attributed to F. M. Kaňka. In Kbely there is the airfield designed by O. Novotný, with a good museum of aviation and cosmonautics. The Prosek Housing Estate is part of the North Town, built between 1964 and 1974 by J. Růžička. It can only be described as 9,500 housing units.

Prague 10

This is to the E of Prague, and is a bit of a job lot composed of part of the Vinohrady district (see p. 172), the 19C develop-

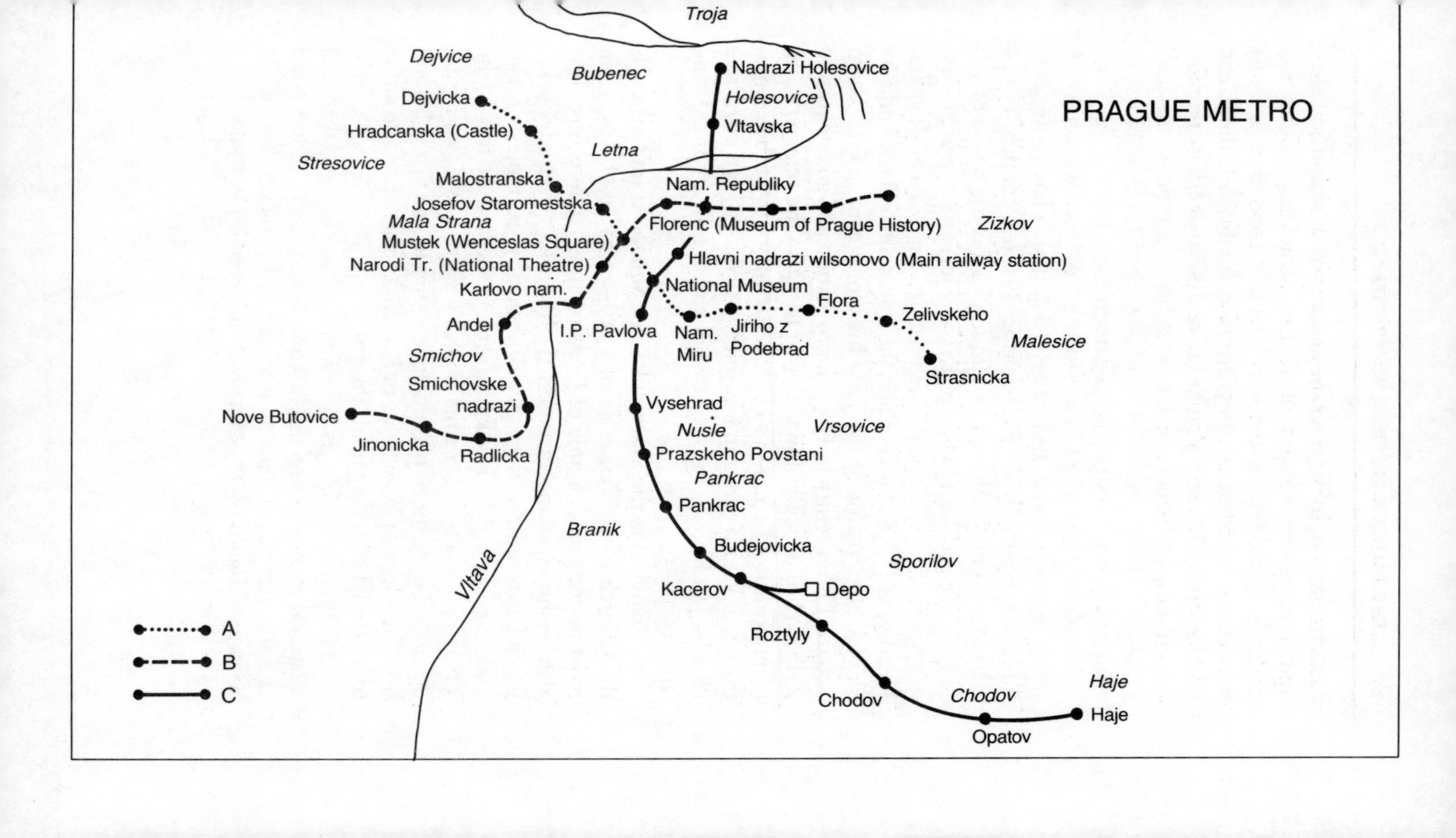
PRAGUE METRO
Troja
Dejvice
Bubenec
Nadrazi Holesovice
Holesovice
Vltavska
Dejvicka
Hradcanska (Castle)
Letna
Stresovice
Malostranska
Nam. Republiky
Josefov Staromestska
Mala Strana
Florenc (Museum of Prague History)
Zizkov
Mustek (Wenceslas Square)
Hlavni nadrazi wilsonovo (Main railway station)
Narodi Tr. (National Theatre)
National Museum
Karlovo nam.
Flora
Zelivskeho
Andel
I.P. Pavlova
Nam.
Miru
Jiriho z
Podebrad
Malesice
Smichov
Strasnicka
Smichovske
nadrazi
Nove Butovice
Vysehrad
Nusle
Vrsovice
Jinonicka
Radlicka
Prazskeho Povstani
Pankrac
Pankrac
Branik
Budejovicka
Sporilov
Vltava
Kacerov
Depo
Roztyly
A
B
C
Chodov
Chodov
Haje
Haje
Opatov

ments at Vršovice, Strašnice, Malešice, Hostivař and Spořilov, and the former villages of Dubeč, Kolovraty, Královice, Uhříněves, Petrovice and others. Out of all this there are only two areas worth exploring for the quality of their 20C architecture. They are Vinohrady and Vršovice. The remainder are a fog of 19 and 20C factories, housing estates and small villas, the latter mainly in Strašnice, Spořilov and Hostivař which have been designated as garden cities.

Vinohrady is reached by metro line A to Flora station. Walk south down Jičínská, to Hradešínská, which has some good buildings, especially the Evangelistic Hussite Church of 1932–5 by Pavel Janák. At 6/1542 Hradešínská is the house of Jan Kotěra, the architect, who created here in 1908 one of the first examples of Modernist architecture in Czechoslovakia. Nearby, at 2/1566 Slovenská is the studio and villa of Ladislav Šaloun, the creator of the Jan Hus monument in Old Town Square. Either return to Flora metro station and go one stop to Želivského, or walk down Vinohradská to the cemetery and crematorium of 1929–32 by A. Mezera. South of the crematorium is Vilová Street in Strašnice. At No. 91 is an attractive villa by Jan Kotěra, inspired by Bohemian folk art and dating from 1902–3.

In Vršovice on the Svatopluk Čech Square (tram No. 22) is the Church of St Wenceslas of 1929–30 by Josef Gočár – a most interesting example of Constructivist architecture. It is also within walking distance of Slovenská or Hradešínská. Round this square there are noteworthy examples of 19C buildings as in Moskevská Street. At the end of this is the Vršovicé náměstí where the bank at 8/67 is by Josef Fanta, decorated by some of his contemporaries in 1911–12. Behind the Church of St Wenceslas in Kodaňská there are also some interesting houses, again of the 19C.

In the outlying villages in Královice (bus No. 264) there is a medieval manor house and its church which was modernized in 1562 during the Renaissance, and in Uhříněves there is the Baroque Church of All Saints of 1740–3 by T. V. Budil.

APPENDIX I

The main rulers of Czechoslovakia

The Přemyslids

Wenceslas of Bohemia murdered by his brother Boleslav I (although tradition pointed to 929)	935
Boleslav II, Duke of Bohemia	967–999
Břatislav I, Duke of Bohemia	1034–1055 (Bohemia submits to Emperor Henry III, 1041)
Vratislav I, King of Bohemia	1085–1092
Vladislav II	1140–1197
Otakar I	1197–1230
Wenceslas I	1230–1253
Otakar II	1253–1278
Wenceslas II	1278–1305
Wenceslas III	1305–1306

The Luxemburgs

John of Luxemburg	1310–1346
Charles IV of Luxemburg	1346–1378 (crowned emperor in Rome, 1355)
Wenceslas IV	1378–1419
Sigismund	1419–1437 (period of Hussite Wars)
Ladislav Posthumus	1440–1458
George Poděbrady	1452–1471 (regent, then king in 1458)

The Jagiellos

Vladislav Jagiello	1471–1516
Ludvík II	1516–1526

The Habsburgs

Ferdinand I	1526–1564
Maximilian II	1564–1576
Rudolf II	1576–1611 (abdicated)
Matthias	1612–1619
Frederick V	1619–1620 (the Winter King)
Ferdinand II	1619–1637
Ferdinand III	1637–1657
(Ferdinand IV	1646–1654)
Leopold I	1657–1705
Josef I	1705–1711
Charles VI	1711–1740
Maria Theresa	1740–1780 (co-regent with her son from 1765)
Josef II	1765–1790
Leopold II	1790–1792
Francis II (František)	1792–1835
Ferdinand V	1835–December 1848 (abdicated)
Franz Josef	1848–1916
Charles (Karel)	1916–30 October 1918 (Czech State proclaimed in Prague)

APPENDIX 2

Brief biographies of major figures

Architects

Alliprandi, Giovanni Battista (1665–1720) Pupil of Fischer von Erlach. One of the more prolific architects within Prague, with important patrons.

Chochol, Josef (1880–1956) Leading representative of Czech Cubism. Early influence came from Wagner, built important houses below Vyšehrad (1911–13), some very pure in a style pre-empting post-war Functionalism. In 1920s influenced by Soviet Constructivism, an influence manifest in his unrealized design for the Liberated Theatre in Prague (1927).

Dientzenhofer, Kryštof (1655–1722) Came from a family of builders from Upper Bavaria, and was the most celebrated of five brothers trained as masons. Was one of the most important architects working in Prague at the turn of the 18C, introducing a plasticity in his bold architectural forms and a marvellous sense of internal space which was further developed by his son Kilián Ignác.

Dientzenhofer, Kilián Ignác (1686–1751) The last of the generation of great European Baroque architects influenced by the late Italian Baroque and Hildebrandt. He was involved with the most important of the Prague commissions including St Nicholas' in the Malá Strana and the Monastery of Břevnov, in both of which he continued his father's work. Working closely with sculptors, painters, cabinet-makers and goldsmiths, he created buildings of dynamism and unity.

von Erlach, Fischer, J. B. (1656–1723) A giant among Austrian Baroque architects working with all the main building types and borrowing his ideas from the late Baroque of Bernini and Borromini. His father was a sculptor and his work has a strong sculptural quality. In 1670/1 or 1674 he went to Rome, but by 1687 is known to have been in Vienna. He travelled to Naples, England, Berlin and

Venice. His best-known buildings are the Schönbrunn Palace and the Karlskirche in Vienna. His style of domestic architecture may be seen in the Clam-Gallas Palace in the Staré Město.

Frágner, Jaroslav (1898–1967) In 1945 Professor of Architecture at the Academy of Fine Arts in Prague. After the Second World War he concentrated on the restoration of historical monuments, among the most important of which were the Carolinum and Prague Castle.

Gočár, Josef (1880–1945) Avant-garde Cubist and follower of Jan Kotěra. From 1923 until his death he taught in the Academy of Fine Arts in Prague. With Pavel Janák and Otakar Novotný, he laid the foundations for Czech Functionalism between the wars.

Havlíček, Josef (1899–1961) Most outstanding of the avant-garde architects, a follower of Le Corbusier. His best-known building is the General Pension Institute (1932–4) in the Žižkov district of Prague which uses a uniform modular system based on cubes, cruciform blocks and pyramids. In an unrealized plan for the rebuilding of the New Town of Prague (1950), he proposed a system of pyramidal skyscrapers.

Hildebrandt, J. L. von (1668–1745) Born in Genoa and by 1696 was working in Vienna as the main rival to Fischer von Erlach. Was the court architect in Vienna and enjoyed the patronage of Prince Eugène of Savoy, the Harrachs and the Schönborns. His design of St Lawrence at Gabel in Bohemia (1699–1711) was most influential for Kilián Ignác Dientzenhofer.

Janák, Pavel (1882–1956) With Gočár and Chochol, a leading theoretician and exponent of Cubism. See his Riunione Adriatica di Sicurità building in the New Town. Later, under the influence of Dutch brickwork, he became more Functionalist. Succeeded Plečnik as chief architect of the castle (1936) and played an important part in the restoration of the Ball Game Pavilion, the Riding School and the Belvedere within the castle.

Kaňka, Franz Maximilián (1664–1766) He lived long and was therefore influenced by the major architects of his day including Santini-Aichl and Dientzenhofer. Some of the buildings originally ascribed to his hand, such as the Clementinum, have now been given to others, but he did a lot of work in Prague for the nobility, including palaces and gardens. As a friend of Braun he designed the bases for Braun's statues on Charles Bridge.

Kotěra, Jan (1871–1923) Born in Brno and in his early work (1898–1905) was influenced by the Vienna Secession, folk art and

English architecture. In 1903 travelled to the USA and was influenced by F. Lloyd Wright. Holland and England followed and the journey is evidenced by his subsequent use of brick and space. Designed everything from furniture to trams, and taught both Gočár and Novotní and the Functionalist Krejčár. He brought Czech architecture to the forefront of the European avant-garde.
Krejčár, Jaromír (1895–1949) One of the foremost architects of the avant-garde movement between the wars and main instigator with Karel Teige, of the Devětsil Group. Editor of the magazine *Život II* promoting the ideas of Constructivism and Purism for the first time in Czechoslovakia. Worked in Moscow 1933–6, then was Professor of Architecture in Brno. He later went to London to teach at the Architectural Association, and it was in London that he died.
Loos, Adolf (1870–1933) Born in Brno, son of a stonemason. One of the most influential architects of the Modern Movement. Studied in Bohemia and Dresden. Visited the USA in 1893 where he was influenced by industrial design. He attacked Art Nouveau for its use of ornament although he did use some decoration in his complex interiors which are hidden by aggressively simple exteriors. Awarded a life pension by Masaryk.
Lurago. What may only be described as a mafia clan of architects and builders working in Prague in the 17 and 18C. There were about 20 men of that name, some of the same family, some from the same area of N Italy, all at work in the capital. The best-known is Carlo (1615–1684) who worked mainly for the Jesuits.
Mathey, Jean-Baptiste (1630–1696) Born in Dijon. Trained as a painter at the French Academy in Rome and arrived in Prague with Archbishop Wallenstein (1675–95). Not being a citizen of Prague, he could not practise as an architect, but instead made the draughts of many buildings which others then executed. He died in Paris.
Mocker, Josef (1835–1899) The most important neo-Gothic architect and restorer working in Prague, known as the Czech Viollet-le-Duc. He trained in Vienna and worked for the Thun family, 1869–72. From 1871 he was at work on the nave of St Vitus' Cathedral.
Novotný, Otakar (1880–1959) Developed from 'Secession' or 'Modern' to Cubism and Functionalism. Under Dutch influence he turned to the use of brick (1909–14): see his Jan Štenc Publishing House in the Old Town.
Parler family. Their roots lay in Swabia but under the patronage of

the Luxemburg family, the Parler influence spread through architecture, sculpture and the decorative arts from Basle to Prague.

Parler, Peter (1330/5–1399) Apprenticed to his father and called to Prague *c.*1350, joining the lodge of St Vitus whose architect, Matthieu d'Arras died in 1352. Parler was master of works at St Vitus' (1356–8), completing the upper choir and two adjacent W bays with the triforium and clerestory (1386). Designed the choir stalls (now destroyed), the busts of patrons, builders and saints and St Wenceslas' Chapel. He introduced a highly decorated form of architecture. He constructed Charles Bridge with statues from his workshop upon its gates. He had five sons of whom Wenceslas and John followed him in St Vitus'.

Plečnik, Jože (1872–1957) Born in Ljubljana in Yugoslavia where much of his work is to be seen. He eschewed the international Functionalism of his generation and borrowed from Classicism and medieval forms. He was a deeply pious and ascetic man. Attended a school of craftsmen in Yugoslavia followed by the study of furniture in Vienna where Otto Wagner offered him a place in his atelier (1898–9). Studies in Italy and France followed after winning the Prix de Rome. Returned to Vienna where he pioneered the use of reinforced concrete in monumental architecture. At the invitation of Kotěra was offered the Chair of Applied Arts in Prague (1911). In 1921 returned to Ljubljana to teach. Major patron was Tomáš Masaryk for whom he transformed Prague Castle (1920–30).

Ried, Benedikt (c.*1454–1534*) Born in Upper Austria and died in Prague. The leading personality of the late Gothic working for the court of Vladislav Jagiello. He may have been sent to Prague as architect for the fortifications. His was the creation of the complex and eccentric vaulting system which singles Bohemia out in its original contribution to late Gothic art.

Santini-Aichl, Jan Blažej (1677–1723) One of the most important of the Bohemian architects in the 18C. Born in Prague, son of Antonín Aichl, of a family that had originated around Como in Italy. Trained as a painter and may have travelled in Austria and Italy. On his return, worked at Zbraslav for the Cistercians who, with the Benedictines, the Premonstratensians and major figures among the nobility were his main patrons. His ground plans are complex and exciting and he revived the Gothic vocabulary of the Jagellionian period in a Baroque Gothic Revival which finds echoes in England with Hawksmoor and Wren.

Teige, Karel (1900–1951) Art critic, theorist, painter, typographic artist and collagist; theoretician of Surrealism and leading figure of the avant-garde Devětsil group between the wars. He much admired Soviet Constructivism and the Soviet system, but died in obscurity.
Vredeman de Vries, Jan (1526/7–1606) Painter, decorator, architect and theoretician. Worked as a painter in Amsterdam and was well known in Antwerp. As a Protestant was forced to flee under the Spaniards and worked in Prague. Influenced by Serlio and was most important as a disseminator throughout northern Europe of Mannerist ideas.
Wagner, Otto (1841–1918) Pupil of Josef Maria Olbrich who worked on the principal that 'the only possible departure for artistic creation is modern life and nothing that is not practical can be beautiful'. Important as a pioneer of modern urbanism and for his influence on his pupils while teaching at the Academy of Fine Arts in Vienna. He wrote *Modern Architecture* (1895), attacking historicism.
Zítek, Josef (1832–1909) Trained in Vienna under Siccardsburg but was most influenced by Semper's rationalism. In 1868 won the competition for the building of the National Theatre, the most important commission in Prague. This was destroyed by fire. He refused to change his plans for the rebuilding and never entered the building again. Schulz took over from him. He built the Rudolfinum.

Artists

von Aachen, Hans (1552–1615) Born in Cologne where he was admitted to the guild of painters. Travelled to Venice and Rome where he painted for the Gesù. Perhaps while working for the Duke of Bavaria, he came to Prague where he worked for the court *c.*1592, as *Kammermaler*, but he also travelled frequently, buying for Rudolf's collections. He later worked for Emperor Matthias.
Aleš, Mikoláš (1852–1913) The leading painter in Czechoslovakia after the death of Mánes and Purkyně. After the 1880s he gave up painting in oils and concentrated on drawing. Almost all his paintings have a nationalistic and historic theme.
Archimboldo, Giuseppe (1527–1593) A Milanese painter of

fantastic heads composed of fragments of landscapes, vegetables, flowers, books, etc. He was court painter at Prague (1562–87) where he worked on theatrical costume and scenery. Rudolf II made him a Count Palatine.

Asam, Cosmas Damian (1686–1739) Architect and painter best known for his outstanding work with his brother Egid Quirin, sculptor and architect in Munich. Entered Bohemia through work at Kladruby Abbey (1712–27). Worked in the refectory of Břevnov, at Bílá Hora and St Nicholas' in the Staré Město.

Bys, Jan Rudolf (1660–1738) Swiss. Best known for his exquisite still-lifes but also worked in the Sternberg Palace decorating the intimate cabinet there with antique and chinoiserie themes. He also worked at Troja. An influence on the work of Brandl and for the development of the still-life in Czechoslovakia.

Grund, Norbert (1717–1767) Rococo painter who worked on small panels and used pale colours and loose brushstrokes. Rather similar in style to Guardi or Watteau.

Heintz, Josef (c.1564–1609) Important in the School of Prague under the patronage of Rudolf II (he was made *Kammermaler* in 1591). After travelling through Italy, he was later charged with the documentation and acquisition of objects for his master's collections.

Hoefnagel, Joris (1542–1600) Born in Antwerp and travelled to France, Spain, England and Italy. He illustrated townscapes and painted in miniature, working from 1582 for the great patron, Ferdinand of Tyrol. He arrived in Prague about 1590 and was employed at court until 1600. See, too, the miniatures of his son Jakub (1575–1630) who became a citizen of the Malá Strana in 1614 but who, because of his support of Frederick the Winter King, was forced to flee after the Battle of the White Mountain.

Hollar, Wenceslaus (1607–1677) Born in Prague but was the most important illustrator and topographer working in England. Travelled in Germany in 1627 and was taken into the service of the Earl of Arundel in Cologne in 1636. Captured by the Parliamentarians at the siege of Basing House in 1645 and went to Antwerp. Returned to England in 1652, and after the Restoration worked for King Charles II.

Kupecký, Jan (1667–1740) Entered a workshop in Vienna (1684–6) and later went to Italy. Established a workshop of his own in 1700. In 1729 returned to Vienna at the invitation of Prince Adam von Lichtenstein. Has been declared to have 'the power of Rubens, the delicacy and the spirituality of Van Dyck and the . . . magic of Rembrandt'. His portraits are powerful.

Kupka, František (1871–1957) Worked mainly in Paris and was influential for Czech artists coming to the French capital, however the whole time, he was also Professor of Fine Art in Prague. Beginning to work in the Art Nouveau as a contemporary of Mucha, he turned early to abstract painting and his first canvases date from 1908/9.

Liška, Jan Kryštof (1650–1712) Born in Silesia, the son-in-law of Willmann who was also his teacher. Travelled to Italy then Prague, was influenced by Rubens and pioneered fresco painting in Bohemia. His important altarpieces are in the churches of SS Simon and Jude and St Ursula.

Mánes, Josef (1820–1871) Patriot influenced by Czech peasant life, costumes, architecture and legends which he depicted in a realistic style. He was well known for his book illustrations and lithographs which hold an important place in Czech national art. He attended Prague Academy in 1835–44 and visited Munich and Dresden. His most important work was the scenes of the months for the clockface for the Staré Město Town Hall (1865–6), now in the Museum of Czech History.

Master Theodoric. One of the major court painters at the Caroline court. In 1367, in Prague, he was styled in the course of an Imperial grant 'beloved master . . . our painter and familiaris'. Working on the Karlštejn frescos and from 1360 using a variety of styles culled from all over Europe, he was responsible for the emergence of a 'Bohemian' style. Stong colour and a disrespect for spatial values are his hallmark.

Master of Třeboň. A central figure in 14c European painting. From his work derives the roots of the 'Soft Style', which began around 1400 as a characteristic Czech branch of the International Gothic style, taking much from the Franco-Flemish school of the 1370s and 1380s.

Master of the Vyšší Brod altarpiece. One of the great figures of 14c Bohemian painting working for the Rosembergs and the Imperial court. A love of colour and nature and the inspiration of Italian art is clearly seen in his work and that of his workshop.

Maulpertsch, Franz Anton (1724–1796) Born at Lake Constance, went to Vienna in 1739 where he was refused a post as professor in the Viennese Academy as being 'too daring'. He was a follower of C. D. Asam.

Mucha, Alfons (1860–1939) Czech painter, designer and decorator and leading exponent of Art Nouveau. Designed many posters especially for Sarah Bernhardt. Studied in Prague and Munich before moving to Paris in 1887, where he worked with Laurens and at the Académie Julien. In 1904–13 visited the USA, but Prague became his main base from 1910.

Navrátil, Josef (1798–1865) Fresco painter, decorator and painter of landscapes, basing the latter on the work of Norbert Grund. His still-lifes are fine and examples of his work may be seen in the Postal Museum.

Purkyně, Karel (1834–1868) Son of physiologist Jan E. Purkyně. Went to France and studied Courbet in the 1850s. He introduced French influence to his realist painting and produced some masterly portraits and still-lifes. He was important for the development of 19C painting in Czechoslovakia.

Reiner, Václav Vavřinec (1689–1743) Fresco painter who worked closely with the architects K. I. Dientzenhofer and F. M. Kaňka, giving superb unity to the internal space of such churches as St John Nepomuk (a good example of the partnership between Reiner and Dientzenhofer). His painting gained new strength in the interior of St Thomas', and he painted a lovely airy bacchanale in the summer house of Dientzenhofer. He also worked in the Church of St Bartholomew. His later work shows an increasing monumentality, for example in St Katherine's.

Savery, Roelant (1590–1639) Still-life and landscape painter. In Amsterdam in 1591 and in Prague by 1603, working for the emperor (1604) who sent him to paint the Alps (1606/7). He was landscape painter to Emperor Matthias but returned to the Low Countries in 1613.

Škréta, Karel (1610–1674) One of the greatest of the early Baroque classical painters in Bohemia, he trained in Rome. In 1628, as a Protestant, he fled to Freiburg and then continued to Venice, Bologna, Florence and Rome. He became a Roman Catholic before settling in Prague. He followed Caravaggio in his interest in realism, although the Classicism of Poussin, whom he had met in Rome, also played an important part in his work. See his altar in the Týn Church.

Spranger, Bartholomeus (1546–1611) Was originally a painter from Antwerp who worked in Rome for Alexander Farnese and then

Pope Pius V. Called to Vienna by Emperor Maximilian II in 1575. He later worked for Rudolf II from 1580 and died in Prague. He also worked as a sculptor and looked after the royal collections. He is a Mannerist, influenced by Correggio and Parmigianino.
Willmann, Michal Leopold (1630–1706) Early Baroque painter born in East Prussia. Studied Netherlandish art and was strongly influenced by Rembrandt, especially in his brushwork and *chiaroscuro*. He was in Prague *c.*1670–90, then returned to Silesia.

Decorative arts

Castrucci, Cosimo and from 1595, *Giovanni*, whose work is better known. They brought with them from Florence the technique of mosaic in hard stone (*commesso in pietra dura*). They developed the technique using the rare hard stones of Bohemia to decorate furniture with exquisite scenes of landscapes, etc.
Dobner, Johann and *Josef* of the Malá Strana. These worked to the designs of K. I. Dientzenhofer, bringing furniture-making to a highly complex art and making it an integral part of the Baroque interior, whether for secular or ecclesiastical use.
Miseroni family. The finest cutters of semi-precious and precious stones were to be found in Milan and it was from here that Emperor Rudolf II commissioned all his work. He managed to attract the Miseroni, one of the foremost families in this art, from Milan to Prague. Ottavio was in Prague 1588–1624, and Dionysio (*c.*1603–1661) worked in semi-precious stones and rock crystal. The Miseroni were the hereditary keepers of the Imperial treasury during the 17C and were close to the court. From stone-cutting they turned to the cutting of glass and were joined in Prague by Lehmann who came in 1603 as a friend of Aachen and van Vianen of the court of Rudolf II. Lehmann received a privilege for glass-cutting in 1609, and this monopoly was passed to his pupil George Schwanhardt and his family, so laying the foundations for the Bohemian cut-glass industry.

Musicians

Dvořák, Antonín (1841–1904) Alongside Smetana and Janáček, one of the greatest composers of this period and of vital importance for the nationalist movement in Czechoslovakia. Trained in the Prague Organ School and as a church musician, and worked under Smetana from 1866. His compositions began to be recognized from 1873 and his music was published by Starý in Prague. Performances of his work were given in Birmingham and Leeds in 1886. Travelled to Russia where he met Tchaikovsky (1890), and received honorary degrees from Prague and Cambridge universities (1891). Travelled to America to teach at the National Conservatory in New York (1892–5) and wrote *From the New World Symphony* (1893). *Rusalka* was first performed in Prague in 1901 in the National Theatre. It has been said about Dvořák and Smetana, 'In regard to the originality of the national music, they had few equals'.

Janáček, Leoš (1854–1928) Born in Moravia, and lived mainly in Brno. Received his basic musical training in the Abbey of St Augustine in Brno, studied the organ in Prague (1874–5), then at the Leipzig and Viennese conservatoires. Founded an organ school in Brno in 1882 which became the conservatoire (1919). From 1888, he formed a collection of Moravian folk music and turned increasingly towards composing. *Jenůfa*, his first performed opera, was premièred in Prague in 1916. The majority of his later operas were premièred in Brno.

Martinů, Bohuslav (1890–1959) Son of a shoemaker who studied at the Prague Conservatoire (1906) until his expulsion for 'incorrigible negligence' (1910). Joined the Czech Philharmonic (1920) then left for France (1923) to concentrate on composition. Went to the USA 1941 and lived in New York until 1953. At the end of the war he accepted a Chair at the Prague Conservatoire, but he never returned to Bohemia.

Smetana, Bedřich (1824–1884) Arrived in Prague in 1838 as a piano tutor to the Thun family. Helped defend the barricades in 1848 and learnt Czech. Went to Sweden (1856) and returned to help set up the Czech National Opera with encouragement from Count Harrach. Found it difficult to get accepted as a composer as he was already known as a teacher and pianist. Première of *The Bartered Bride* in the National Theatre in 1866. Premières in Prague of *Dalibor* (1868), *Dvě Vdovy* (1874), *Hubička* (1876) and *Tajemství* (1878). For the grand opening of the new Prague National Theatre he wrote *Libuše* in 1881 as a glorification of the Czech nation.

Politicians

Beneš, Dr Eduard (1884–1948) Studied philosophy under Masaryk, was a prominent member of the Czech National Liberation Movement and served as first foreign minister in the Czech government of 1918–35. In foreign policy he favoured France and supported the League of Nations seeking to establish the balance of power in eastern Europe. He succeeded Masaryk as president of Czechoslovakia, 1935–8. He resigned and went into exile after Munich and became president of the Czech government in exile in London. Returning to Prague in 1945, he was president until the Communist takeover in 1948.

Dubček, Alexander (1921–) Active in the underground in Slovakia in the Second World War and joined the Communist Party. Head of the Slovak Communist Party from 1963. Led the opposition to Antonín Novotný whom he succeeded as national party chief in January 1968. Forced to renege on key reforms after the Prague Spring. Replaced by Husák in 1969.

Frank, Karl Hermann (1898–1946) Nazi, assistant to the Reichsprotektor, and leading German political representative in Bohemia and Moravia after March 1939. Executed in Prague in 1946.

Gottwald, Klement (1896–1953) Founder of the Czech Communist Party in 1921 and general secretary from 1927; on the executive committee of Comintern (1928–43) and a member of the Czech parliament (1928–38). Went to Moscow for the duration of the Second World War. Deputy premier (1945–6) and premier (1946–8). He succeeded Beneš as president until his death in 1953. He was responsible for creating a Stalinist state in Czechoslovakia, sending many to imprisonment and labour camps and conducting the infamous Slansky trials at which many of his colleagues – all Jews – were condemned to death.

Havel, Václav (1936–) Czech playwright and president of Czechoslovakia. Finding work at the Divadlo Na zábradlí (The Theatre on the Balustrade) in 1960, he rose from stagehand to playwright in eight years and is now regarded as the leading Czech playwright of his generation. He wrote *The Garden Party* (1964), *The Memorandum* (1965) and *The Increased Difficulty of Concentration* (1968). After 1968 his works were banned and had to be published abroad. During this period he wrote *The Interview* (1975), *A Private View* (1975) and *The Protest* (1978). In 1977 he was one of three spokesmen for Charter 77, charging the Czech government with the violation of human rights according to the 1975 Helsinki Agreement. Convicted of subversion in 1979, he spent four years in prison. After further imprisonment, he became leader of Civic Forum and president of Czechoslovakia in December 1989.

Husák, Gustav (1913–) Activist in the Slovak Communist Party from 1933. Trained as a lawyer and was a leader of the anti-Nazi Slovak uprising in 1944. Victim of the Stalinist purges, imprisoned 1951–60, and rehabilitated in 1963. Deputy premier 1968. Replaced Dubček as party secretary in 1969, harshly suppressing the liberal developments of 1968. Czech president, 1975–89.

Masaryk, Jan (1886–1948) Diplomat. Son of T. G. Masaryk and chargé d'affaires to the United States (1919), minister to Great Britain (1925–38). He was foreign minister to the Czech government in exile during the Second World War. Much rumour and speculation surrounds his death by falling from a window in the Černín Palace.

Masaryk, Tomáš Garrigue (1850–1937) Intellectual and Professor of Philosophy at Charles University (1882) before becoming the first president of the Czech Republic (CSR) in 1918, a position he held until 1935. Wrote one of the earliest critiques of Communism. Studied in the US and married an American, but took little part in international politics during the 20s and 30s.

Saints

St Adalbert (Vojta) (956–997) Ordained bishop of Prague in 983 but made no headway and went to Rome where he became a Benedictine. He returned to Prague and founded the Břevnov monastery. Opposed by the nobility, he deserted Prague two more times. He preached in Poland, Prussia, Hungary and in Russia. He was murdered by the Prussians near Danzig.

St Agnes (1200–1282) Born in Prague, daughter of King Otakar I and educated by the Cistercian nuns of Trebnitz. In spite of being twice betrothed, she refused to marry and with the help of Pope Gregory IX she became a Poor Clare in her own foundation in Prague (now St Agnes') to which St Clare sent five nuns from Assisi. She remained here until her death. Was canonized at the end of 1989.

St Ludmila (d.*921)* Duchess of Bohemia entrusted with the educa-

tion of Prince Wenceslas, whom she converted to Christianity. Fell victim to the jealousy of her daughter-in-law and was strangled.
St John Nepomuk (flourished c.1390) The patron saint of the Habsburgs was canonized in 1729 and was one of the most important saints of the Counter-Reformation. He was promoted by the Catholic party to counterbalance his contemporary the religious reformer Jan Hus. He was confessor to the queen of Wenceslas IV and refused to divulge the secrets of the confessional, especially when Wenceslas wished to prove his queen unfaithful. This row in fact masked a tussle between Church and State. He was martyred by being thrown from Charles Bridge.
St Procopius (980–1053) Patron saint of the Slavs. Born in Bohemia and studied in Prague where he was ordained and became canon and later a hermit. Canonized in 1804.
St Sigismund. A Hungarian king and patron saint of the Luxemburg dynasty.
St Vitus. Venerated from early times. He was an impoverished Sicilian who, against his father's wishes, became a Christian and was twice persecuted for his faith, eventually being martyred in the time of Diocletian. His links with Bohemia are obscure but Charles IV collected his relics and they rest in the main altar of St Vitus' Cathedral.
St Wenceslas (907–935) Duke of Bohemia, received a Christian upbringing and governed from 922 at a time of severe pagan reaction. Murdered by his brother Boleslav in 935 at the door of the Church of Alt-Bunzlau. Disinterred and reburied in St Vitus' Cathedral. The patron saint of Bohemia and the subject of a well-known Christmas carol.

Sculptors

Bendl, Jan Jiří (1620–1680) A pioneer of early Baroque in Prague with a strong leaning towards realism. His sculpture may be seen as parallel to Škréta's paintings. Examples of his work are to be found in St Salvator.
Bílek, František (1872–1941) Born in Tábor and then studied at the Prague Academy of Arts as a painter until he discovered he was colour-blind. In 1891, under the patronage of the industrialist Lanna, he travelled to Paris. He is one of the foremost members of

the Arts and Crafts Movement in Czechoslovakia, working in all branches of the arts. His religion as a Czech Brother was important to him and this is evident in much of his work.

Braun, Matthias Bernhard (1684–1738) Greatest Bohemian sculptor of the Baroque. Born in Muhlau near Getz in the northern Tyrol, but received his training in Italy. In 1709–10 he arrived in Prague under the patronage of Count Franz Sporck, the man who introduced the French horn and harboured Antonio Denzio's *Orlando Furioso* under his roof. Braun's first masterpiece was created in 1710, he was given the freedom of Nové Město in 1711. His style is almost painterly and finds echoes in the work of contemporaries such as Brandl.

Brokof, Ferdinand Maximilián (1688–1731) With Braun, the finest of the Bohemian Baroque sculptors. After training in Vienna he returned to Prague where he was further influenced by the work of his fellow-Czechs.

Jan Brokof or *Brokoff (1652–1718)* Born in Slovakia and began his career as a woodcarver. Arrived in Prague as a journeyman in 1675. Jan was responsible for the St John of Nepomuk on Charles Bridge in 1682. The Brokofs moved to Prague in 1692. Two of Jan's sons were sculptors: the elder son was Michal Jan Josef (1686–1721), while Ferdinand Maximilián (see above) (1688–1731) was the most gifted of the family.

Gutfreund, Otto (1889–1929) Professor of Applied Arts at the Academy in Prague. In 1911 he worked with Cubism and was in France during the First World War as a prisoner. He was very much influenced by Bourdelle. In the early 1920s he was producing the most original and striking polychrome terracottas, examples of which are well worth visiting Zbraslav to see. He mysteriously disappeared in 1927.

Jäckel, Matěj Václav (1655–1738) From the north of Bohemia, one of the pioneer Baroque sculptors working at least ten years before Braun in this style in Prague, creating the first Baroque sculptures on Charles Bridge. He prepared the way for Brokof and Braun and his work should be seen as akin to that of Liška in painting.

Myslbek, Josef Václav (1848–1929) The most important figure in late 19C sculpture in Czechoslovakia. Trained in Germany but later influenced by Rodin and, like him, worked in a style both impressionistic and expressionistic. He was influential in being the first

professor of sculpture at the Academy of Fine Arts in Prague (1890).
Platzer, Ignác (1757–1826) One of the last sculptors to work in the Baroque style and, as so often in Prague, an artist who worked in numerous styles, turning his hand also to Rococo and the neo-Classical. At the end of his life he produced some fine headstones in the Empire style.
Štursa, Jan (1888–1935) Trained at the Academy of Arts in Prague and was a pupil of Myslbek. His early work was Cubist in style but later he came under French influence. He was an important founder of Czech modern sculpture.
Vredeman de Vries, Adrian (1545–1626) Sculptor working for some of the greatest patrons of his time including Rudolf II and Albrecht Wallenstein. He was important in founding a school of bronze-casting in Prague, encouraging other artists from the Low Countries.

Writers and poets

Hašek, Jaroslav (1883–1923) Czech novelist, journalist and editor of a pre-First World War anarchist journal. Served in the Austrian army in the Czech Legion, was taken prisoner on the eastern front and spent several years in Russian prison camps. On his return he began to write *The Good Soldier Švejk* (1920–3) which, although unfinished at his death, made a major impact on Czechoslovakia with its strong use of satire.
Kafka, Franz (1883–1924) Member of the German-speaking Jewish community in Prague. Gained a doctorate in law (1906) and then worked in a government insurance office (1908–22). His writings have had a major influence on post-war literature: *The Trial* (1925), *The Castle* (1926) and *Amerika* (1927) amongst others. Little recognized in his lifetime.
Němcová, Božena (1820–1862) Czech romantic writer, the so-called Czech George Sand. Collector and editor of sagas and fairy tales. She is attributed with writing in 1855 the first truly Czech novel, the famous *Babička* or 'Grandmother', an important work for the Czech nationalist movement. Promoted by Vojta Náprstek.
Neruda, Jan (1834–1891) Writer, poet and journalist. His best-known work is the *Mala Strana Tales*.
Seifert, Jaroslav (1901–86) Czech poet who was introduced to

Surrealism in Paris in 1923. This was influential in his work, much of which concerned Prague. From 1950–60 he was a critic of the Communist government, then chairman of the Union of Czech Writers (1968–70) and a signatory of Charter 77. Was the first Czech to win the Nobel prize for Literature (1984). Wrote *The Plague Monument* (1980), *The Casting of Bells* (1983) and *An Umbrella from Piccadilly* (1985).

Others

Balbin, Bohuslaus (1621–1688) Jesuit priest and most distinguished historian of Bohemian Baroque. Wrote *Epitomie Historica Rerum Bohemicarum.* This was suppressed and Balbin went into exile where he wrote his *Apology for the Slavic and especially the Bohemian Tongue.* He died canon of Prešina.

de Brahe, Tycho (1546–1601) Danish astrologer who travelled to Germany and Switzerland. He was only in Prague a short time (1598–1601) having been lured by the offer of a pension and the castle of Benátky by Rudolf II. Was most influential as a bridge between the Carolinum and the court. Wrote *De Nova Stella* (1573) and *Astronomiae Instauratae Progymnasmata* (1602/3) which was finished after his death by Kepler. He gave his name to the Tychonic system – the earth in the centre of the cosmos with the moon and sun revolving around it. He died in 1601.

Hus, Jan (c.*1369–1415*) Cleric and academic. Began his studies at Charles University around 1390, and became dean of the Faculty of Arts in 1401. Preached in Czech in the Bethlehem Chapel in Prague in 1402, became rector of the university in 1409 and was excommunicated in 1410. Was one of the great religious reformers of the late Middle Ages. He absorbed ideas already current at Charles University and from John Wycliff, the English reformer. Through his preaching against the power and corruption of the clergy and Pope, he laid down the basis for later Protestantism and indeed nationalism in Bohemia. His followers also promoted the idea that the laity should receive communion under the forms of both bread and wine, *sub utraque specie* (utraquism). After his death at the stake at the Council of Constance in 1415 (to which he had been promised free passage), Hussitism became a social and political force. The movement became more extreme under the leadership of Žižka who, for a time, was successful against the Habsburgs and the Pope. The more extreme of the Hussites set up a commune in the town of Tábor, organizing a communistic community there. This fell apart through internal faction and they were defeated at the Battle of Lipany in 1434. The arts suffered during this time of religious wars, but religious tracts flourished.

Jungmann, Josef (1773–1847) Translator of Milton, Pope, Goethe and Chateaubriand and author of a history of Bohemian literature. Most important in the rise of Czech nationalism.

Kepler, Johannes (1571–1630) Mathematician, physicist and astronomer, famous for his laws of planetary motion. Was forced to flee Gräz as a Protestant under Archduke Ferdinand and joined Tycho de Brahe in Prague (1600). Appointed Imperial Mathematician on the death of de Brahe in 1601. He moved to Linz where he lived from 1612–26. His best work was done in Prague on optics and refraction.

Purkyně, Jan (1787–1869) Pioneer physiologist who was educated by Piarist monks and went to Prague to study philosophy, then medicine. He graduated in 1813 with a thesis on the subjective aspects of vision. A friend of Goethe, he explained the main characteristics of the cell theory in 1837 and was the first to use the term protoplasm in the scientific sense. He was voted foreign member of the Royal Society in London in 1850.

Sternberg, Count Caspar (1761–1838) A younger son of this important family, he trained to be a priest and became a canon in Regensburg. He later became a scientist and amateur botanist and decided to leave the Church and return to Bohemia. He was one of the founders of the National Museum, giving the nation his own collections and library in 1818. The museum was founded in 1822. A kinsman, František Sternberg, founded the National Gallery of Art.

Strada, Jacopo (1515–1588) A celebrated antiquary who, with his son Ottavio (1550–1578), was art advisor to Rudolf II. Jacopo's daughter was Rudolf II's mistress.

APPENDIX 3

Culture in Prague

Museums in Prague are generally closed on Mondays. Exceptions to the rule are mentioned in the text.

Each month a small booklet is published listing all the concerts, theatres, operas and ballet performances. The Prague Spring Festival takes place each year from 12 May to 1 June. To book performances at any time of the year, contact the following:

Černá Růže, Prague 1, Panská 4 (passage). Open 10.00–18.00 (Monday to Friday) Tel: 26 51 24 and 22 12 06

Alfa, Prague 1, Václavské náměstí (Wenceslas Square) 28 (passage). Open 10.00–18.00 (Monday to Friday). Tel: 26 16 02 and 26 06 93

Melantrich, Prague 1, Václavské náměstí (Wenceslas Square) 36 (passage). Open 10.00–18.00 (Monday to Friday). Tel: 22 87 14

APPENDIX 4

Eating in Prague

At the time of writing prices are rising fast in Prague but visitors should still be able to eat moderately well for reasonable prices. The actual choice of menu is limited, with duck and pork predominant. Fresh vegetables can be hard to come by. Prague is not yet the place for gastronomes. Most of the larger hotels, restaurants and central *vinárny* take credit cards.

Most restaurants mentioned here are in the centre and therefore fill up quickly. It is best to eat lunch between 12.00 and 13.30; if you arrive after that you may not get served. As yet, few of the restaurants are prepared to serve food after 20.00 and like to see the back of you by 22.00. Perhaps with the influx of tourists, this timetable will become less rigid. To be honest, the food is very similar in most restaurants but as you will notice the standard of service and the prices differ.

Try some of the excellent beer halls for lunch, many of which prepare simple, typical food and have the most jovial atmospheres. They serve excellent beers although now there are only one or two brands, where once each pub used to brew its own. For food, try eating Tlačenka, pork offal and herbs cooked rather like a haggis, Špekáčky sausages and mustard, Utopenec, 'drowned sausage', pickled in onion and vinegar, or Pivní Sýr, smoked cream cheese with mustard and onion – mix this with beer, paprika or chili and spread it on bread.

The *vinárny* are wine bars, the majority serving the excellent Moravian wines. But the wine-growing regions of central and eastern Europe are all represented in Prague. Many of the *vinárny* serve simple food too. Most are open from 17.00 until 23.00 or 24.00 but if you wish to have a full meal, it is advisable to arrive about 20.00 as most serve meals only until 22.00. During the tourist season it is wise to book. Alcohol is not served to those under 18. The *vinárny* are closed on Mondays and a few close on Sundays.

It can be difficult to find places to eat in the suburbs and frankfurter stalls are still the only 'fast food' outlets in Prague. By far the best cooking in Prague is to be found in private houses if you are lucky enough to have Czech friends.

* Especially recommended

Wenceslas Square and surroundings. (The so-called 'Golden Cross', that is the crossing of Národní and Na příkopě with Wenceslas Square)

The Jalta Hotel, Václavské nám. (Wenceslas Square) 45. Tel: 26 55 41. As well as a restaurant, this has a bar overlooking Wenceslas Square.

The Palace Hotel, Panská 12. Tel: 26 83 41 or 26 84 78. Very expensive, non-smokers only and clients will be mainly tourists.

The Ambassador Hotel, Václavské nám. (Wenceslas Square) 5. Tel: 22 13 51. The restaurant here serves game.

Zlatá Husa Hotel, Václavské nám. (Wenceslas Square) 7. Tel: 214 31 20. This hotel has the Staročeská rychta Restaurant and the Znojemská *vinárna*.

The Alcron Hotel in Štěpánská Street 40. Tel: 235 92 16.

ČKD House at Můstek over the metro. There is a café on the ground floor with quick service and moderately good food. There is also a simple restaurant on the first floor and on the top floor, with a view over the city, is the terrace café and a night club.

Pelikán at Na Příkopě 7. Tel: 22 07 82. This serves international food.

Moskva, Na Příkopě 29. Tel: 22 54 70, or 26 58 21. Buffet restaurant on the first floor serving Russian food.

Obecní dům, Náměstí Republiky. Tel: 231 06 16 or 231 00 68. Simple restaurant in splendid Art Nouveau surroundings. Usually there is a seat. There is also a café in the Viennese style.

U Palivce. Tel: 29 03 73. Brand new and privately owned, on the corner of Sokolovská (Vitězného února) and Fügnerovo náměstí.

The Old Town (Staré Město)

U Zelené žáby, U radnice 8 (near the Malé náměstí). Tel: 26 28 15. Evenings only and with a *vinárna* serving just cold dishes.

U sedmi andělů, Jilská Street 20. Tel: 26 63 55. Evenings only, offering an international cuisine with Moravian wines.

Uzlaté konvice, Melantrichova 20. Tel: 26 21 28.

U Zlaté studně, Karlova Street on the corner with Seminářská Street. Tel: 26 33 02. A *vinárna* serving simple food and Moravian wines.

U zlatého hada, on the corner of Karlova and Anenská Street. Tel: 235 87 78. More of a café with a good atmosphere, serving food and wine.

Tři gracie, Novotného lávka next to the Smetana Museum. Tel: 26 87 46, Ext. 273. Offering an international cuisine with Moravian wines from Valtice.

Bellevue, Smetanovo nábřeží. This was the seat of the Union of Czechoslovak-Soviet Friendship and has suffered a sea-change having now become the home of the Society of Friends of the USA. The old restaurant and café have been reopened and serve food from 11.00 to 23.00.

* Opera Grill, Karolíny Světlé 35. Tel: 26 55 08. At present closed for modernization, but was one of the best restaurants in Prague.

* U Plebána, Betlémské Square. Tel: 26 52 23. An attractive *vinárna* serving Moravian food and wine.

Divadelní, the restaurant and café of the National Theatre. Tel: 21 44 208. There is a café on the ground floor which spreads into the garden in the summer months. On the first floor it is usually easy to find a seat from 11.00 to 24.00.

The Paris Hotel, U Obecního domu. Tel: 231 58 93. The restaurant in this Art Nouveau hotel has been recently reopened, but the management tends to make leaving noises at about 22.00. There is quite a wide choice of food including Czech national dishes. There is a café and a late-night bar.

* U pavouka, Celetná 17. Tel: 231 87 14. Includes a bar, restaurant serving both international and Czech food, and a *vinárna* serving Moravian wines. There is music in the evenings.

* U Zlatého jelena, Celetná 11. Tel: 26 85 95. Restaurant and *vinárna*.

* U Sixtů, Celetná 2. Tel: 236 79 80. Newly-opened *vinárna* serving international food. On the ground floor there is an attractive café.

Berjozka, Rytířská 31. Tel: 22 38 22. This is a Russian restaurant serving national food and wines.

U Golema, Maislova Street. Tel: 26 18 98. A Jewish restaurant in the former Prague ghetto. Open for lunch and dinner. Closed on Saturdays and Sundays.

Košer Restaurant, Maislova Street near the Old-New Synagogue. Tel: 231 09 09. A good, cheap and simple Jewish restaurant open for lunch during weekdays.

U Anežky, in St Agnes Convent. Tel: 231 42 51, Ext. 35. A simple but good bar-café, open until 21.00. Closed Mondays. In summer you can sit on an attractive balcony under the trees in the garden.

* U Červeného kola, Anežská 2. Tel: 231 89 41. Open daily, serving food from 11.00 to 20.00. Comprising three rooms plus the garden in the summer.

The Intercontinental Hotel, nám. Curieových 5. Tel: 32 10 51 and 33 91 11. Brasserie with a good buffet restaurant. More expensive restaurant in the basement with a pianist and violin. On the top floor is the Golden Prague Restaurant with a view of the city which, as a friend points out, is a 'quite expensive view'.

Šumická vinárna, Mikulandská Street/Národní třída 16. Tel: 29 52 08. *Vinárna* serving Moravian wines. There is gypsy music in the evenings.

Vysočina Restaurant, Národní Street 28. Tel: 22 57 73. Serves international food.

Slovenská jizba, Purkyňova Street and the Národní metro. Restaurant and *vinárna* serving Slovak food and wines. There is Slovak folk music in the evenings.

Malá Strana

Strangely enough, this beautiful area has very few attractive places to eat. Here it is vital to book ahead.

* U tří pštrosů (The Three Ostriches), Dražického náměstí. Tel: 53 60 07. One of the best hotels and restaurants and most popular with tourists.

U Patrona, Dražického náměstí. Tel: 53 16 61. This small *vinárna* is situated opposite the above hotel.

* U Malířů, Maltezské náměstí 11. Tel: 53 38 83. This popular restaurant is at present being redesigned to become one of the first privately-owned restaurants in Prague.

* U Mecenáše, Malostranské náměstí 10. Tel: 53 38 81. A restaurant with one of the best wine cellars in Prague, serving international

food. It is small however, and it is necessary to book one week in advance.

* Valdštejnská hospoda, Valdštejnské náměstí. Tel: 53 61 95. A restaurant serving good international and Czech food at lunch and dinner, Moravian wines and beer.

* Nebozízek, Na Nebozízku in the middle of the Petřín Hill by the funicular station from Karmelitská Street. Tel: 53 79 05. The situation is lovely, overlooking the city. International cuisine with wine and beer, but tends to be very popular with tourist groups unless you eat after 20.00.

Hradčany and Prague Castle

Na Vikárce, by the side of the Cathedral of St Vitus in the third castle courtyard, Vikářská Street 6. Tel: 53 64 97. This is the most practical place to eat during a visit to the castle. There is a good wine-cellar which serves food too. The only problem is that this restaurant tends to cater for tourist groups.

* U labutí, Hradčanské náměstí 11. Tel: 53 94 76. A snack-bar and the so-called Konírna Restaurant which is quite expensive.

* U zlaté hrušky, Nový Svět 3. Tel: 53 11 33. Its location, intimate atmosphere and rather good food make it an attractive place to eat.

U Lorety, beside the Loretto monastery in Loretánská 8. Tel: 53 13 95 and 53 60 25. Simple, cheap food with quick service for a midday meal during sightseeing.

U Ševce Matouše, opposite the Černín Palace in Loretánská. Convenient and open until 21.00.

Beyond the historical centre

U Pastýřky, Bělehradská, Prague 4. Tel: 43 40 93. This specializes in Slovak food, grilled meats and wine. Housed in a wooden pavilion – very 'folk'.

Bruselský Pavilion, Prague 7. Tel: 37 73 37. This is the former Czech pavilion from the 1958 Brussels World Exhibition. With a terrace café and good restaurant.

Hanavský Pavilion, Letenské sady, Prague 7. Tel: 32 57 92. This was the pavilion built in 1891 for the Jubilee Exhibition. Here is a small restaurant with a café and a late-night bar.

The International Hotel, Prague 6, Dejvice. Tel: 33 19 111. Built in the fifties and a typical example of Socialist Realism architecture. It offers a French restaurant and international cuisine. A café, late-night bar and disco are on the top floor in the winter-garden.

Trója Castle Restaurant. Tel: 84 27 06. This belongs to the great castle of the Sternbergs, newly-opened to the public. There are two differently priced restaurants serving international cuisine.

Outside Prague (car essential)

Konopiště Castle. Tel: 0301 30 17. One of the most beautiful and exciting 19th-century castles with splendid and interesting contents, once belonging to Archduke Franz Ferdinand. Here you will find the Myslivna Restaurant specializing in venison. There is also a restaurant nearby in Motel Konopiště. Tel: 0301 27 48.

Mělník. Tel: 0206 20 96. Situated in the courtyard of Mělník Castle, this restaurant offers the famous wines from the vineyards of the Lobkovic family, including the celebrated Ludmila wine. An international cuisine is served all day until 21.00.

Roztoky. Tel: 39 65 09. A restaurant housed in a small medieval castle to the north of Prague, rebuilt during the Renaissance and overlooking the Vltava.

INDEX

Entries in bold type indicate places and buildings

Aachen, Hans von, 207, 211
Academy of Applied Arts, 120
Academy of Fine Arts, 17, 110, 192
Academy of Sciences, 18, 107, 143, 167
Achterman, T., 43
Adalbert (Vojta), St, Bishop of Prague, 37, 40, 44, 79, 182–3, 214
Adam's Apotheke, 148
Adria Palace, 145
Agnes, St (Agnes of Bohemia), 3, 127, 214
Aichbauer, J. G., 64, 90
Albrecht, Duke of Austria, 6
Aleš, Mikoláš, 84, 113, 116, 142, 149, 154, 186; grave, 171; biography, 207
Alfa Palace, 149
Allio, A., 63
Alliprandi, Giovanni Battista, 58, 72, 74, 76, 80, 82–3, 96, 130, 153, 203
All Saints' Chapel, 54
Ambrozzi, V. B., 87, 152
Anabaptists (Bohemian Brethren), 8–9
Anne, wife of Emperor Ferdinand, 7, 36, 46
Anne of Bohemia, Queen of Richard I of England, 5
Aostalli, Ulrico, 36, 50, 56, 186
Archbishop's Palace, 56, 58, 60
Archimboldo, Giuseppe, 34, 207–8
Asam, Cosmas Damian, 119, 184, 187, 208, 209
Augustinian nuns, 164
Ausperg Palace, 96
Austro-Hungarian Empire, 19, 20, 30
Automobile Club of Czechoslovakia, 159

Baba estate, 20, 188–9
Balbin, Bohuslaus, 218
Balko, Frans Xavier, 32, 75, 78, 93, 181
Ball Game Hall (castle), 36, 204
Balšánek, Antonín, 139, 154, 176
Barnabite Order, 61
Barrandov villa quarter, 181
Barvitius, A., 171, 174
Basle, council of, 162
Bassano, F. and J., 35
Baťa shoe store, 148
Baum, A., 115, 126, 130
Bayer, P. I., 134, 163, 167, 183
Beata Electa Chapel, 97–8
Bechteler, Kaspar, 43, 45–6
Beethoven, Ludwig van, 91
Benda, Franz and Georg, 15
Bendl, Jan Jiří, 47, 105–6, 115, 117, 147, 149, 160, 181, 215
Benedictine Order, 167, 180, 182–4
Beneš, Eduard, 21, 24, 25, 213
Beneš of Weitmil, 132
Berka, Count František Antonín, of Dubá, 87
Bernini, Lorenzo, 12, 62
Bertramka (summer house), 179
Bethlehem Chapel, 135
Bianco, B., 95–6
Bílá Hora, 72
Bílek, František, 19, 40, 46, 123, 168, 171, 189, 215–16
Black Madonna, House of, 131
Black Rose, House at the, 152

Black Tower, 55
Blecha, Matěj, 148–9, 151–2, 162, 197
Bohemia: union with Moravia (1918), 2, 20; under John, 3; dominance in Middle Ages, 4; civil war (1419), 5; Renaissance art in, 8; declared hereditary Habsburg land, 11, 13; post-war parliament, 24–5
Bohemian Confession (religious), 9
Boleslav I, King of Bohemia, 215
Boleslav II, Duke, *later* King of Bohemia, 51, 169, 182–3
Borromini, Francesco, 12, 77
Bossi, Campion de, 91
Bossi, Domenico de, 73
Bossi, Santini de, 73, 170
Brahe, Tycho de, 62, 117, 191, 218, 219
Brandl, Petr, 13, 35, 45, 53, 64, 84–5, 92, 108, 129, 144, 181, 184, 208
Braník (district), 177
Brauerl, J., 191
Braul, J., 66, 86
Braun, Matthew Bernhard, 13, 42–3, 53, 74–5, 82–3, 102–4, 108, 153, 164, 204; school of, 97; workshop, 107, 111, 130–1; death, 163; biography, 216
Bretfeld Palace, 72
Breughel, Pieter, 34
Břevnov (district), 182–5
Břevnov Monastery, 13, 182–4
Brocca, Giovanni Antonio, 31
Brokof, Ferdinand Maximilián, 13, 87, 91, 94, 102–4, 129; followers, 126; workshop, 130, 160; biography, 216
Brokof, Jan (the Elder), 100, 167, 195, 216
Brokof, Michal Jan Josef, 55, 60, 61, 72, 76, 93, 103, 216
Bubeneč (district), 182, 187, 190, 192
Bubny, 189–91
Buquoy, Count Karel, 130
Buquoy Palace (*now* French Embassy), 88, 90, 130
Buquoy (Portheim) Summer House, 178
Burgrave's House, 55
Bylandt-Rheidtovsky Palace, 81
Bys, Jan Rudolf, 35, 53, 58, 126, 144, 208

Cajetan House at Břevnov (Kajetanka), 185
Čakovice (*formerly* village), 198
Calvinism, 8
Campione, G., 186
Canevale, Marco Antonio, 143
Canevalle, J. D., 118
Capauli, Giovanni da, 170
Čapek, J., 20, 161
Čapek, Karel, 171
Capuchin Order, 62
Caratti, Francesco, 48, 54, 62, 85, 87, 96
Carlone, C., 111
Carlone, Silvestro, 195
Carmelites, 84–5
Carolina Augusta, wife of Francis I, 196
Carolinum (Charles University), 4, 67, 82, 104, 114, 130, 132
Castle Gardens, 55
Castrucci family, 34, 194
Castrucci, Cosimo and Giovanni, 121, 211
Čedok (national tourist office), 153
Central Bohemian Gallery, 111
Central Trade Union Council (*formerly* General Pension Institute), 176, 204
Černín family, 45, 81
Černín Palace, 58, 62, 64
Černín Palace, Little, 97
Černín, Count Humprecht, 62
Chapel of Holy Mary of Einsiedel, 55
Chapel of the Holy Rood (Prague castle), 31–2
Charles IV (Václav), Emperor and King of Bohemia, 4–5, 32, 37–8, 42, 46, 48, 66, 68, 91, 104, 114, 118, 124, 128, 132, 138, 146–7, 155, 162, 164, 166–7, 169, 215
Charles V, Emperor, 7
Charles VI, Emperor, 13, 35
Charles University, *see* Carolinum
Charter 77, 27
Chochol, Josef, 20, 22, 168, 203
Chopin, Frédéric, 156
Chotek, Count Karel, 17, 66, 120, 170, 194

Christian of Anhalt, 11
CHURCHES
All Saints (Uhříněves), 200
Assumption of Our Lady, 165
Bíla Hora (Our Lady Victorious), 186–7
Evangelistic Hussite, 200
Holy Ghost, 126
Holy Rood, 153
Holy Trinity (Nové Město), 162
Holy Trinity (Prague 5), 179
Loretto (of the Nativity), 63–4
Maltese (Our Lady Under the Chain), 90–1
Most Sacred Heart of Our Lord, 175
Order of the Knights of the Cross of the Red Star, 105
Our Lady Before Týn, 52, 114, 116–17, 129
Our Lady of the Snows, 146
Our Lady of Unceasing Succour at the Theatines, 75
Our Lady Under the Chain, *see* Maltese, *above*
St Adalbert, 197
St Antonius, 190
St Apolinaire, 166
St Barbara, 127
St Bartolomeo, 198
St Catherine, 13, 164
St Charles Borromeo, 23, 73
St Clement, 106–8
St Clement (Bubny), 191
Saints Cyril and Method, 167, 196
St Francis, 15, 127
St Gastulus, 126
St George, 53–4
St Giles (St Jiljí), 112
St Havel, 134
St Henry, 160
St Ignatius, 163
St James, 15, 128–9
St James the Major, 181
St John Nepomuk, 61
St John on the Rock, 166
St John the Beheaded, 170
St Joseph, 92, 97
St Joseph of the Capucines, 155
St Lawrence, 56, 67, 171
St Ludmila, 173
St Margaret, 182–3
St Martin's in the Wall, 134
St Mary, 66
St Mary Magdalene of the Domenican nuns, 85
St Michael, 113
St Nicholas (Malá Strana), 13, 76–81, 83
St Nicholas (Staré Město), 114, 119
St Peter, 156–7
Saints Peter and Paul, 171
St Procopius, 176
St Saviour (Na Františku), 127
Saint Saviour in Salvátorská, 118, 126
St Salvator, 106–7
Saints Simon and Jude, 126
St Thomas, 59, 92–4
St Ursula, 143
St Wenceslas (Malá Strana), 77
St Wenceslas (Nové Město), 167–8
St Wenceslas (Prosek), 198
St Wenceslas (Smíchov), 178
St Wenceslas (Vršovice), 200
Santa Maria della Vittoria, 63, 84–5
Týn church, *see* Our Lady Before Týn, *above*
Utraquist, 130
Cibulka, 180
ČKD engineering works, 152, 197
Clam Gallas Gardens, 180
Clam-Gallas Palace, 110, 204
Clam Martinic Palace, 58
Clementinum (Jesuit College), 106–10, 112, 114, 204
Collin, Alexander, 46
Colloredo-Mansfeld Palace, 107
Column of the Holy Trinity, 76
Columna Cellata, 72
Congress Palace (Iron Hall), 193
Constance, Council of (1415), 5, 218
Corpus Christi Chapel, 162
Cubr, František, 51, 191
Cukrovarnická (villa), 188
Czech Brothers, 126, 134–5
Czech Confession, 83
Czech Industrial Museum, 135
Czech language, 15–16, 133
Czech Radio Building, 174
Czech State Savings Bank, 149
Czech Technical University, 188
Czech Television (*formerly* Stock Exchange), 160, 177

Czechoslovakia: history, 1–3; three estates, 3; position in Holy Roman Empire, 4; religious movements, 5–10; language revival, 15–16, 133; industrial development, 17, 97; republic formed (1918), 21, 30, 115; and Munich agreement, 23; in World War II, 23–4; Communism in, 23–5, 36; 1989 'Velvet Revolution', 27, 190

Ďáblice (suburb), 197–8
Daliborka (tower), 54
Danube Palace, 144
Decorative Arts Museum, 17–18, 53, 120–1
Dee, John, 33
Dejvice (district), 182, 188–9
Desfours Palace, 145
Destinová, Emma, 83, 109, 171
Dětský or Jews' Island, 88
Devětsil Group, 21–3, 145, 148, 205, 207
Diamant (house), 162
Dientzenhofer, Kryštof, 13, 77–9, 85–6, 98, 113, 164, 183–4, 203
Dientzenhofer, Kilián Ignác, 13, 61, 63, 77–8, 82, 85–6, 88, 92, 94, 97, 108, 110, 119, 121, 152, 161, 164, 166, 178, 183, 187, 197, 203, 210, 211
Diettrichstein family, 90
Dittman, Christian, 50
Dlabač, A., 148, 191
Dobrovský, Josef, 16, 87, 89
Domenican nuns, 85
Domenican Order, 112
Dryák, A., 147, 151, 173, 188–9
Dubček, Alexander, 26, 213, 214
Dürer, Albrecht, 34, 59
Dušek, František and Josefina, 179–80
Dvořák, Antonín, 19, 105, 164, 171, 211–12
Dvořák, Karel, 38, 41, 103, 145–6, 160

Eiffel Tower replica, 66–7
Elizabeth (Stuart) of Bohemia, Queen of Frederick ('The Winter Queen'), 11, 100
Elizabethine Monastery (*now* State Hospital), 166
Emblem of the Holy Trinity, 73
Engel, Anton, 177, 188
Erlach, Fischer von, 44, 58, 64, 74, 111, 129, 203
Escompt Bank, 154

Faculty of Law building, 121–2
Fanta, Josef, 149, 159, 200
Faust House, 167
Federal Assembly, 150
Fénix Palace, 149
Ferdinand, Emperor, 7–8
Ferdinand I, King of Bohemia, 35–6, 46, 122, 129
Ferdinand I, Emperor of Austria, 17
Ferdinand II (of Styria), King of Bohemia, 10–11, 35, 50, 95, 107
Ferdinand III, King of Bohemia, 35
Ferdinand of Tyrol, Archduke, 8, 185–6, 219
Ferdinand V (the Gracious), Emperor and King of Bohemia, 32
Filippi, Giovanni Maria, 30, 82, 194
Filla, E., 20
Fischer, Jiří, 18, 155
Foehr, A., 144, 153, 162
Foerster, V., 146, 151
Fontana, Carlo, 58, 61
Frágner, Jaroslav, 22, 31, 132, 135, 181, 204
Francis I, Emperor, 136
Franciscan Order, 128, 146
Frank, Karl Hermann, 62, 213
Franz Ferdinand, Archduke of Austria, 20, 59
Franz Josef, Emperor of Austro-Hungary, 17, 32, 103, 144
Frederick Barbarossa, Emperor, 2
Frederick III, Emperor, 6
Frederick II (the Great), King of Prussia, 13
Frederick V, Elector Palatine, 11, 43, 45, 208
French Crown, House at the, 107
Fuchs, Josef, 191, 193, 195
funicular railway, 67, 86
Fürstenberg, Prince Karl Egon von, 16, 96–7

Gallas, Johann Wenzel, 111
Galli, Domenico, 55, 88, 106
Gargiolli, Giovanni, 33, 50, 194

General Pension Institute, 176, 204
Georg and Martin of Cluj, 47
George Poděbrady, King of Bohemia, 6, 46, 100, 112, 117
German Knights, Order of, 157
Glass Palace, 188
Gočár, Josef, 20, 130–1, 149, 156, 160, 173, 181, 189, 192, 200, 204, 205
Golden Deer of St Hubert, House of the, 94
Golden Goose Hotel, 151
Golden Lily, House of, 113
Golden Snake, House of the, 107
Golden Swan, House of the, 81
Golden Unicorn, House at the, 91, 116
Golden Well, House at the, 107
Goltz-Kinský Palace, 118
Gottwald, Klement, 24, 118, 213
Grand Prior's Palace, 90
Graphic Arts Group (Tÿrdošíjní), 20, 21, 168
Green Tree, House at the, 113
Grund, Norbert, 53, 208
Guarini, Guarino, 12, 77, 185
Gutfreund, Otto, 20, 145, 156, 173, 190, 216

Habsburg dynasty, 7–8, 15, 19, 73
Haffenecker, Antonín, 87, 91, 133, 156
Haffenecker, Thomas, 91
Hager, Joseph, 78, 126, 153
Hall of Mirrors, 67, 110
Hanava Pavilion, 191
Hanspaulka estate, 189
Haringa, J. J., 106
Harrach, Count, 212
Harrach Palace, 160
Hartig family, 80
Hartig, Karl, 174
Hašek, Jaroslav, 217; *The Good Soldier Svejk*, 61, 164, 175
Hauf, L., 144
Hausknecht, J., 134, 145, 153
Havel, V. (Václav's grandfather), 149, 168
Havel, Václav, 24, 27, 30, 49, 123, 136, 145, 149, 213–14
Havelské Město (Gall Town), 114
Havlíček, Josef, 145, 176–7, 192, 204
Havlíčkovy Sady, *see* Riegrovy sady
Haydn, Josef, 126
Heintz, Josef, 34, 53, 73, 94, 106, 208
Henry VII, Count of Luxembourg, *later* Emperor, 3
Hergessel, F., 154–5
Heydrich, Reinhard, 23, 62
Hibernians (Franciscan Order), 155
Hiebel, Jan, 108–10
Hiernle, K. J., 183, 185
Hilbert, Kamil, 38, 41, 44, 134
Hildebrandt, J. L. von, 204
Hlávka, Josef, 18, 120, 143, 166
Hloubětín (district), 198
Hlupočepy, 181
Hodkovická, 177
Hoefnagel, Joris, 53
Hofman, Vlastislav, 20, 147, 197
Holešovice, 189–91
Hollar, Wenceslaus, 208
Holy Cross rotunda, 136
Holy Roman Empire, 2–4
Honzík, K., 22, 176–7
Horse Gate, place of the, 149
House of Czech Children for the Pioneers, 55
Hrzán Palace, 130
Huerta, Balthasar, 84
Hunger Wall, 66–7
Hus, Jan, 5, 51, 113, 132, 135, 174, 215, 218; statue, 115
Husák, Gustav, 27, 36, 213, 214
Hussites, 5–6, 37–8, 90, 119, 139, 146, 162, 174, 176, 218–19
Hut Theatre, 147
Hvězda Summer Pavilion, 9, 185–6
Hynais, V., 142, 150
Hypotecs Bank, 145
Hypšman, B., 144, 151, 168, 188

Ignatius Loyola, St, 77
Imperial Mill, 194
Institute of Gentlewomen, 54
International Gothic (style), 4, 37, 47, 51–2
International Slav Congress (1848), 16
Invalidovna (Military Hospital), 197
I. P., Master, 52, 117
Italian Orphanage, 73
Italian quarter (Malá Strana), 69, 72–3
I.W. (monogram), 42

Jäckel, Matěj Václav, 64, 75, 92, 103–5, 118, 157, 162–3, 184–5, 216
Jägr, Josef, 82, 91
Jamnitzer family, 34
Janáček, Leoš, 21, 212
Janák, Pavel, 62, 145–6, 149, 173, 188, 189–90, 204
Jesuit College, *see* Clementinum
Jesuit Gymnasium, 82
Jesuits, 9–10, 14–15, 77–9, 81, 83, 89, 106, 109–10, 114, 135, 163, 178
Jewish Town Hall, 123, 125
Jews, 122–5, 159
Jihlava, 43
John of Luxemburg, Emperor, 3, 37, 118, 128
John Lennon Wall, 90
John Nepomuk, St, *see* Nepomuk, St John
Josef II, Emperor, 14–15, 33, 59, 65–6, 75, 85, 110, 127, 139, 155
Jubilee Exhibition (1891), 191, 193
Jubilee Synagogue, 159
Julius II, Pope, 34, 59
Judith Bridge (destroyed), 99, 114
June Uprising, 1848, 16–17
Jungmann, Josef, 16, 146, 219

Kafka, Bohumil, 65, 142, 145, 171, 173, 176
Kafka, Franz, 21, 54, 74, 116, 118–19, 130, 151, 176, 217
Kaiser- Stejn Palace, 83
Kaňka, Franz Maximilian, 42, 45, 62–3, 80–1, 83, 107, 144, 153, 165, 181, 198, 204, 210
Kaňka, V., 131
Karlín (suburb), 196–7
Karlov monastery (*now* Police Museum), 164–6
Karlštejn Castle, 4, 52
Kaunic family, 91
Kaunic, Jan Adam, 91
Kaunic Palace, 153
Kbely (*formerly* village), 198
Keck, Peter, 129
Kelley, Edward, 33, 167
Kepler, Johannes, 107, 219
Kern, Antonín, 53
Khrushchev, Nikita S., 25, 61
Kinský family, 97, 118
Kinský, Count F. J., 16, 109
Kinský Summer Palace and Gardens (*now* Museum of Costume), 86, 135, 180
Klausen Synagogue, 124
Klement Gottwald Museum, 133
Klouček, C., 147, 151–4
Knights of Malta, Convent of (*now* Institute of Oriental Studies), 91
Knights of the Cross with the Red Star, 157
Koch, Heinrich, 86, 180
Kohl, Hieronym, 31, 143
Kohl-Severa, J. B., 63, 77, 92, 102
Kokoschka, Oskar, 88
Kolben and Danek (factory), 197–8
Kolowrat family of Liebstein, 74–5, 77–8
Kolowrat, F., 103
Kolowrat Palace, 97, 133
Konopiště (castle), 59
Koširé, 86
Kotěra, Jan, 110, 120, 122, 146, 148, 161, 168, 173, 175–7, 187, 192, 200, 204
Koula, J. E., 121, 149, 187
Kovář, Karle, 93, 166
Kozák, B., 151, 178, 188
Kracker, Jan Lukáš, 78–9, 166
Králíček, J., 148–9, 151, 162
Královice (village), 200
Královská Obora (park), 187
Kramolín, Josef, 66, 79, 108
Kranner, Josef, 19, 38, 46, 136, 156
Kranner, Ondrej, 73
Krč (district), 177
Krejčar, Jaromír, 22, 145, 148, 182, 192, 205
Kučera Palace, 64
Kundera, Milan, 26
Kunštát and Poděbrady, Palace of the Lords of, 112
Kupecký, Jan, 35, 53, 208
Kupka, František, 208–9
Kutná Hora, 4, 43, 138
Kyje (*formerly* village), 198
Kysela, František, 40, 47
Kysela, L., 148–9, 153

Ladislav Posthumus, 6, 46
Langweil Model (of Prague), 158

Lanna House, 156
Lanna, Vojté, 17, 120, 156, 215
Lapidarium, *see* National Museum
Laterna magika Theatre, 145
Law Courts, 163
Lažanský Palace (*formerly* Wallenstein Palace; *now* Academy of Music, Film and Theatre), 81, 142–3
Ledebour Palace, 96
Legio Bank, 156
Leitmeritz, Master of, 41
Lenin Museum, 156
Leopold, Emperor, 100
Leopold II, King of Bohemia, 15, 92, 133
Leslie, Walter, Count, 81, 95
Letka, 151
Letná Hill and park, 190–1
Letná Plain, 192
Letter of Majesty, 9–10, 84
Levý, Václav, 44, 171, 196
Lhota, Antonín, 43
Lhota, Karel, 188
Libeň (suburb), 197
Liboc (district), 182, 185
Libra, F. A., 160, 177, 181
Libuše, Queen, 2, 48, 169
Lichtenstein Palace (*now* Academy of Music), 76, 89
Lidiče (village), 24
Lindt's House, 148
Linhart, E., 22, 189
Lion Court (castle), 36
Lipany, Battle of (1434), 219
Liška, Jan Kryštof, 45, 105, 144, 209, 216
Liszt, Franz, 145, 154
Lobkovic family, 42, 60, 63, 74, 93
Lobkovic Palace (*now* German Embassy), 55–6, 74, 92
Lobkovic, Benigna Katerina, 63–4
Loew ben Bezalel, Judah, 123–4
Lomená (villa), 188
Loos, Adolf, 180, 188, 205
Loretto Monastery, 13, 85
Losy Palace, 156
Lucerna Palace, 149, 161
Ludmila, St, 32, 40, 79, 214–15
Ludvik II, King of Bohemia, 7, 41
Luna, Kristián, 72, 187
Lurago, Anselmo, 31, 54, 110, 130, 152
Lurago, Carlo, 55, 74, 90, 106, 108–9, 112, 156, 163, 170, 172, 205
Lutheranism, 8
Luxemburg family and dynasty, 3–5, 45, 52

Machoň, L., 110, 122, 151
Mac Neven Palace, 161
Maisl Synagogue (Museum of Jewish Silver), 125
Malostranský hrbitov (Lesser Town Cemetery), 86, 179
Maltese garden, 90
Mander, Karel van, 34
Manés, Antonín ('Bohemus'), 127–8
Manés, Josef, 115, 143, 158, 196, 209
Mansfeld-Fondi, Prince Vinzenz Paul, 107
Mardochee (Jewish printer), 125
Maria Theresa, Empress, 13–14, 28, 50
Martinic family, 43
Martinic, Maximilián, 191
Martinic Palace, 60–1
Martinů, Bohuslav, 89, 212
Mary, Queen of Ludvik II, 7
Masaryk, Alice, 48
Masaryk, Jan, 62, 214
Masaryk, Tomáš Garrigue, 21, 30–1, 80, 205, 206, 213, 214
Mašek, K. V., 154, 161
Master Theodoric, 52, 209
Master of Třeboň, 209
Mathematical Hall (Clementinum), 109
Mathey, Jean-Baptiste, 35, 56, 61, 75, 92, 103, 105, 176, 195, 205
Matthias Corvinus, King of Hungary, 6, 51
Matthias, Emperor, 9–11, 30, 80, 210
Matthias Gate (castle), 30–1
Matthieu d'Arras, 4, 37, 43, 138, 206
Maulpertsch, Franz Anton, 65, 162, 209
Max, Emanuel, 18–19, 32, 40, 100, 103–4, 136
Max, Josef, 18–19, 100, 103, 136
Maximilian I, Emperor, 7, 34, 59, 115

Maximilian II, Emperor, 8–9, 46, 122, 210
Mayer, J. O., 75, 102–3, 107, 146, 187
Mayer, Matthias, 40, 76
Mayer, Václav, 65–6
Medigo de Candia, Josef Salomo ben Elias del ('The Wandering Jew'), 125
Meizl, Mordecai, 122–4
Melantrich House, 149
Mettychů z Čečova Palace, 90
Michna, Jan, 164
Michna Palace (*now* Museum of Sport), 13, 86, 88
Michna Summer Palace, *see* Villa Amerika
Mikuláš of Kadaň, 115
Milíč, John, 38
Military Museum, 176
Millesimovský, Count Jan Caretto, 130
Ministry of Finance, 98
Ministry of Internal Affairs, 192
Ministry of Machine Industries, 160
Ministry of Science and Technical Progress, 20, 173
Ministry of Transport, 158
Minute, House at the, 115
Miseroni family, 10, 34, 53, 121, 194, 211
Miseroni, Alessandro Abondio, 194
Miseroni, Antonio Abondio, 194
Miseroni, Dionysio, 211
Miseroni, Lehmann, 211
Miseroni, Ottavio, 121, 194, 211
Mitrowitz, Count, 129
Mocker, Josef, 19, 38, 42, 44, 51, 124, 132, 157, 160, 166, 171, 173, 176, 205
Modřany (district), 177
Móhacs, Battle of (1526), 7
Molitor, P., 91, 131, 157
Montague, Lady Mary Wortley, 12
Moravia, 2, 3, 11, 20, 24–5
Morzin Palace, 76
Mosto, Ottaviano, 61, 83, 128
Mozart, Wolfgang Amadeus, 15, 66, 72, 78, 81, 91, 126, 133, 173, 179
Mozarteum, 146
Mucha, Alfons, 19, 40, 46, 61, 155, 157, 171, 210
Munich Agreement (1938), 23
Municipal Library, 111
Muscon (house), 91
Museum of Arms and Armour, 60
Museum of Bohemian History (Lobkovic Palace), 55
Museum of Musical Instruments (Buquoy Palace), 90
Museum of Prague History and Art, 158
Museum of the City of Prague, *see* Prague City Museum
Myslbek, Josef Václav, 19, 44–5, 142–3, 147, 171–3, 216–17

Na Slovanech (or Emmaus) Monastery, 167
Náprstek Museum (of Australasian, African and American Cultures), 135
Náprstek, Vojta, 135–6, 152, 191, 217
National Cemetery, 170–1
National Gallery of Czechoslovakia, 58–61, 82, 111
National Monument, Vitkov Hill, 176
National Museum, 18, 149–50; Lapidarium, 100, 193
National Technical Museum, Letná, 135
National Theatre, 19, 139, 142
Navrátil, Josef, 128, 157–8, 210
Němcová, Božena, 152, 171, 217
Nepomuk, St John, Archbishop of Prague, 32, 40, 43, 51, 54, 64, 72, 75, 78, 97, 100, 103, 116, 131, 143, 146, 160, 162, 167, 215
Neruda, Jan, 72, 171, 217
Neuburg Palace, 153
New Castle Staircase, 55, 80
New Deanery, 51
New Jewish Cemetery, 125, 176
New Stage Scene (theatre), 142
New Town College (Jesuit), 163
New Town Hall (Staré Město), 110, 113, 115–16
New Town Hall (Nové Město), 163
New World (Nový Svét), 62
Nostic family, 45, 87, 89, 153, 197
Nostic, Count Francis, 15
Nostic, Count Jan Hartvik, 87

Nostic Gardens, 88
Nostic Palace (*now* Dutch Embassy), 87
Nostic Theatre, 133
Novák House, 161
Novotný, Otto, 20, 122, 126, 168, 182, 198, 204, 205
Nusle (district), 177

Obecní dům (Representatives' House), 20, 154–5
Observatory, 66–7
Ohmann, Friedrich, 131, 144, 156
Old Deanery, 47
Old Jewish Cemetery, 125
Old Market Hall, 173
Old-New Synagogue (Staré Město), 3, 123, 159
Old Shul, 126
Olšany Cemetery, 175
Opatovice (district), 138
Orsi, Domenico, 63, 65, 80, 82
Orsi, G. D., 108–9, 133, 163, 195
Otakar I, King of Bohemia, 44
Otakar II, King of Bohemia, 44, 68, 181

Pacassi, Nicolo, 14–15, 28, 30–2, 47
Pachta Palace, 131
Palace Chicago, 145
Palace of Culture, 166, 172, 177
Palach, Jan, 26, 147
Palacký, František, 16, 75, 161, 168
Palffy Palace, 96
Palliardi, I. J., 66, 74, 81, 96–7, 133, 144–5, 156, 160–1
Pankrác (district), 177
Park of Culture and Rest (Park Kultury a Oddechu), 193
Parler family, 205–6
Parler, Henry, 42
Parler, John, 37, 206
Parler, Peter, 37–8, 41–6, 48, 50, 60, 94, 104, 116, 129, 150, 206
Parler, Wenceslas, 37, 206
Pauline Monastery, 118
Pernštejn family, 45, 55
Peršteýn house, 134
Petřín Hill, 66, 69, 86, 162, 180
Piccolomini family, 73, 152
Piccolomini, Jan Testa, 73, 95
Pinkas Synagogue, 123, 125
Platey's House, 134, 145
Platzer family, 78, 118
Platzer, I. M., 180
Platzer, Ignác F., 30, 32, 44, 47, 51, 55, 64, 78, 92, 97, 129, 131, 136, 143, 152, 156, 217
Plečnik, Jože, 20, 30–1, 35, 47–8, 55, 175, 204, 206
Počernice (*formerly* village), 198
Poděbrad Palace, 112
Poděbrady, George, *see* George Poděbrady, King of Bohemia
Podolí (district), 177
Podskalí quarter, 168
Podzemný, R. F., 177, 188
Pokorný, Karel, 40–1, 133
Polívka, O., 111, 118, 143–4, 145, 149, 151, 153–4, 161
Ponc, Mirslav, 23
Poor Clares (order), 127
Popp, A., 120, 150, 173
Poříčí (district), 138, 156–7
Portheim (or Buquoy) Summer House, 178
Postal Museum, 128, 157, 180
Powder Tower, 130, 154
Pozzo, Andrea del, 108–9
Práce publishing house, 151
Prachner, Petr, 50, 79, 85, 113
Prachner, Richard, 79, 105, 163, 185
Prague: importance in 12th century, 3; as early capital, 4, 37; First Defenestration of (1419), 6, 163; as capital of Holy Roman Empire, 9, 123; Second Defenestration of (1618), 10, 82, 107, 186; in War of Austrian Succession, 13; Jews expelled from (1748), 14; theatre in, 15; music in, 15; Germans occupy (1939), 23; 1944 uprising, 24; German population, 24; 1968 'Spring', 26; street lighting, 60; Model of, 158
Prague Bank, 152
Prague, Battle of (1757), 14
Prague City Museum, 109, 113
Prague Music Festival (Spring), 154, 172
Prague Polytechnique, 18
Praha Palace, 151
Preisler, J., 153, 155, 161
Preiss, František, 41, 44, 117, 143

Přemysl, Prince, 2
Přemyslid dukes, 3, 169, 181
Procopius, St, 79, 185, 215
Promenade Garden, 48
Prosek (district), 198
Purkyně, Jan E., 145, 162, 172, 210, 219
Purkyně, Karel, 210

Quitainer, J. A., 44, 63, 66, 93, 105, 113, 163

Raab, Ignác, 66, 78–9, 108
Rechter House, 113
Red Cross Building, 80
Regensburg, Diet of (1158), 2
Reiner, Václav Vavřinec, 50, 53–4, 62, 64, 83, 93, 96, 105, 110, 112, 126, 129, 134, 146, 157, 160, 164, 178, 181, 187, 210
Rejsek, Matěj, 7, 116, 117, 132
Riding School (castle), 35
Ried, Benedikt, 7, 35, 40, 43, 49–50, 163, 206
Riegrovy or Havlíčkovy Sady, 173–4
Rilke, Rainer Maria, 160
Riunione Adriatica di Sicurità building, 204
Rodin, Auguste, 9
Rohan Palace, 85
Roith, F., 98, 111, 158, 168, 188
Roland of Bruncvík, 100
Rosemberg family, 54, 80, 209
Roškot, Kamil, 43
Rössler, Jaroslav, 150, 191
Roštlapil, Václav, 192, 198
Rottmayer, Otto, 31, 35, 50
Royal Gardens (castle), 35–6
Royal Palace, 48–51, 54
Royal Park of Stromovka, 193–4
Rudolf I, Duke of Saxony, 91
Rudolf II, King of Bohemia and Emperor, 9–10, 30–1, 33–4, 36, 45, 49, 59, 69, 87, 121, 123–4, 208, 210, 217, 219; court, 191
Rudolf of Habsburg, Prince, 120
Rudolf Adit (aqueduct), 194
Rudolf Picture Gallery (castle), 31, 33
Rudolfinum, 58, 120
Ruthenia, 21
Rybníček (district), 138

Sady Svatopluk Čecha Park, 173
St Agnes Convent (*now* National Gallery of Nineteenth Century Painting), 3, 18, 114, 124, 127, 142, 214
St Francis Monastery, 127
St Gall district, 133, 138
St George's Convent, 51
St George's Gallery, 33, 35, 51
St James, Monastery of, 114
St Martin's rotunda, 170, 172
St Matthew Chapel, 63
St Roch, Chapel of, 176
St Vitus' Cathedral, 4, 15, 19, 36–48
St Wenceslas' Chapel, 4
Sakař, Josef, 149, 151, 196
Salm Palace, 58
Šaloun, Ladislav, 115, 142–3, 155, 200
Santa Casa (House of Mary), 63
Santini, Francesco, 72–6, 81
Santini, J., 165, 172
Santini-Aichl, Jan Bležej, 181, 187, 204, 206
Savery, Roelant, 34, 53, 210
Savings Bank of Prague, 143
Schirding Palace, 144
Schlansowsky, J. J., 165–6
Schnirch, B., 120, 142, 150–1, 154, 162, 174
Schönborn Palace (*now* US Embassy), 56, 74
Schönherr, M., 64, 113
School of Prague (artistic), 33
Schorr, Johann Ferdinand, 67, 85, 164
Schulz, Josef, 60, 90, 120, 142, 150, 174
Schützen Palace, 130–1
Schwarzenberg family, 47, 60, 88
Schwarzenberg Palace, 144, 191
Schwarzenberg, Cardinal Friedrich Josef, Archbishop of Prague, 45
Sebregondi, Nicolo, 94, 96
Security Company building, 162
Seifert, Jaroslav, 26, 54, 217–18
Sequens, František, 43, 46, 178
Sevastopol Palace, 154
Shod Carmelites, Order of, 134
Sigismund, St, King of Hungary, 37, 45, 79, 215
Sigismund of Luxemburg, King of Bohemia, 6, 176

Silesia, 4, 13
Šíma, Josef, 22
Šimek, Ludvik, 46, 100, 146, 157
Singing Fountain (castle), 36
Škréta, Karel, 13, 53, 79, 90, 93–4, 117–18, 130, 134, 160, 181, 210
Slansky trials, 213
Slavata Palace, 80
Šlik, General Field Marshal, 42
Slovak Culture, House of, 145
Slovakia, 2, 21, 24–5
Smetana, Bedřich, 19, 116, 143, 212; Museum, 88, 136–7; grave, 171–2; *Libuše*, 170; *Má Vlast*, 154
Smetana Theatre (*formerly* Deutscher Opera), 151
Smíchov (district), 178–80
Socialist Realism (SO-RE-LA), 26, 188
Society for Bohemian Industry, 16
Society for the Study of Bohemian Culture, 16
Society of the Patriotic Friends of the Arts, 16, 58, 82
Sokol (international body), 88
Soldati, Tommaso, 74, 143, 163, 181
Sovovy mill, 88–9
Špaček, F., 112
Špála Gallery, 145
Španiel, O., 38, 171
Spanish Hall (castle), 31
Spanish Synagogue, 126
Spazio, Giovanni, 35–6
Spezza, Andrea, 94–6
Špička Gate, 172
Spiess, Hans, 7, 43, 49
Spinetti, B., 54, 119, 184
Sporck, Count Franz von, 15, 216
Sporck Palace, 73
Spranger, Bartholomeus, 34, 46, 53, 73, 80, 94, 210
Stádník, Karel, 47, 106, 108
Stahlberg Palace, 153
Stalin, Josef V., 121
Stamp Museum, 61, 157
State Bank (*formerly* Wiener Bankverein), 152
State Bank (*former*), 153
State Commercial Bank, 156
State Library, 109, 182
Štenc Publishing House, 126, 205
Stephen, King of Hungary, 184
Sternberg family, 44, 58, 82, 107, 195
Sternberg, Count Caspar, 16, 58, 82, 120, 149, 219
Sternberg, František, 219
Sternberg, Václav Vojtěch, 58, 195
Sternberg Palace, 58, 208
Sternigovsky family, 81
Stevens, J. J., of Steinfels, 74, 143, 184
Štipl, Karel, 41, 47
Stockar, R., 151, 181
Stone Bell, House at the, 118
Stone Ram, House at the, 116
Storch's House, 116
Strada, Jacopo and Ottavio, 34, 219
Strahov Monastery (and Library), 56, 59, 64–5, 69
Střešovice district, 182, 187–8
Stromovka, 190, 193–4
Štursa, Jan, 72, 142, 146, 173, 190, 217
Sucharda, S., 159, 168
Sucharda, Vojtěch, 38, 149, 151, 154
Sudetenland, 21, 23, 24
Summer Pavilion, Stromovka, 194
Švabinský, Max, 40–1, 46, 154–5
Svoboda, General Ludwig, 26
Svolinský, Karel, 40, 47–8
Swedish Embassy, 64
Sweert-Sporck Palace, 156
Sylva-Taroucca Palace, 152

Tábor Gate, 172
Táborites (movement), 5
Technical Museum, 191
Teige, Karel, 22, 205, 207
Theatine Monastery, 55
Theatine Order, 75, 185
Thirty Years' War, 10–13, 74
Thomayer, Josef, 86, 162
Three Magi, At the (coffee house), 130
Thun family, 81, 212
Thun, Michael, 61
Thun-Hohenstein, Leopold, Bishop of Passau, 179–80
Thun-Hohenstein Palace (*now* Italian Embassy), 75
Thurn, Count, 10–11
Thurn-Taxis family, 91

Tilly, Count von, 11
Tintoretto, 35
Toscana Palace (*formerly* Thun-Hohenstein Palace), 61
Town Hall (Hradčany), 61, 72
Town Hall (Malá Strana), 82–3
Toyen, Marie Čermínová, 22
Trade Fair Palace, 192
Trojá, 189, 194–6, 208
Trojá Palace, 58, 121, 190, 194–5
Turba Palace (*now* Japanese Embassy), 91
Two Bears, The (beer hall), 134
Two Golden Bears, House at the, 113
Tyl, Oldrich, 192–3
Týn Presbytery, 130
Týn School, 116

Uhříněves (village), 200
Ullmann, Ignác, 143, 145, 153, 161–2
Ullmann, Josef, 191, 196
Ullmann, V. I., 136, 155
Ungelt (Customs House), 114, 129
Union of Artists building, 168
Union of Soviet Socialist Republics (USSR), 24–6
Ursuline convent (Hradčany), 61
Ursuline nuns, 144
Utraquists, 6, 8–9, 117, 218

Valdštejn (Wallenstein) Palace, 12, 80, 94–5
Valdštejn Riding School, 97
Valter Palace, 144
Vávra Mill, 157
Velkopřevorský mill, 89
Vernier Palace, 154
Veronese, Paolo, 35
Versailles, Treaty of (1919), 21
Villa Amerika or Michna Summer House, 13, 164
Villa Loos, 188
Viňohrady quarter, 172–4, 198, 200
Vinoř (*formerly* village), 198
Virgin Mary, House of, 102
Vítězne, 188
Vítkov Hill, 174, 176
Vitus, St, 38, 79, 215
Vladislav II, King of Bohemia, 2, 65, 99
Vladislav Jagiello (Ladislav), King of Bohemia and Hungary, 6–7, 41, 43, 48, 131–2, 154, 206
Vladislav Hall, 7
Vlašim family, 44
Vojanovy Sady, 97
Vosmík, Čeněk, 41, 56, 159, 162
Vries, Adrian Vredeman de, 12, 32, 34, 52, 90, 96, 217
Vries, Jan Vredeman de, 35–6, 45, 50, 52–3, 207
Vršovice district, 200
Vrtba, Count, 83
Vrtba Gardens, 83–4
Vysočany (district), 198

Wagner, A., 142, 150
Wagner, Otto, 98, 144, 148, 175, 206, 207
Waldhauser, Konrad, 38, 134
Wallenstein family, 43, 93, 97, 197
Wallenstein, Albrecht von, 77, 81, 94–6, 217
Wallenstein, Count Ernst, 16
Wallenstein garden, 53
Wallenstein, Archbishop Jan Bědrich, 56, 205
Wallenstein Palace, *see* Valdštejn Palace
Weiss, F. I., 45, 50, 113, 164
Wenceslas, St, 2, 37, 40–1, 42, 47, 56, 79, 96, 100–1, 147–9, 215
Wenceslas I, King of Bohemia, 3, 127–8, 133
Wenceslas II, King of Bohemia, 92
Wenceslas III, King of Bohemia, 3
Wenceslas IV (Luxemburg), King of Bohemia, 5–6, 38, 46, 51, 104, 215
White Mountain, Battle of the (1620), 11, 45, 68, 77, 84–5, 107, 114–16, 186
White Tower, 36
Wiehl, Antonín, 136, 149, 171, 174
Wiehl House, 149
Willmann, Michal Leopold, 53, 105, 209, 211
Wimmer, Jakub, 173, 190
Windischgrätz, Prince, 17, 76, 100; wife killed, 131
Wirch, Jan Josef, 58, 72, 97, 131, 136
Wohlmut, Bonifac, 36, 46, 48, 50, 165, 186

Writers' Union, 26
Wycliff, John, 5, 110, 218

Žák, L., 177, 189
Zasche, Josef, 145, 152, 160, 168, 176
Zbraslav (district), 181–2
Zbraslav Castle, 128
Želivský, Jan, 146, 163
Ženíšek, František, 142, 150, 155
Zimprecht, Matthew, 85, 93
Zitek, Josef, 120, 142, 207
Živnobanka, 153
Zižka, General Jan, 174, 176, 218
Žižkov quarter, 125, 174–6
Zlute lazne swimming stadium, 177